# NEW TESTAMENT WOMEN

# The Storyteller's Companion to the Bible™

Dennis E. Smith and
Michael E. Williams, editors

## VOLUME THIRTEEN

# NEW TESTAMENT
# WOMEN

Abingdon Press
Nashville

NEW TESTAMENT WOMEN

*Copyright © 1999 by Abingdon Press*

*This book is printed on recycled, acid-free paper.*

**Library of Congress Cataloging-in-Publication Data**

The Storyteller's companion to the Bible.
   Includes indexes.
   Contents: v. 1. Genesis—v. 2. Exodus-Joshua—[etc.]—v. 6. The Prophets—v. 13. New
Testament Women.

   1. Bible—Paraphrases, English. 2. Bible—Criticism, interpretation, etc. I. Williams,
Michael E. (Michael Edward), 1950-
BS550.2.S764    1991                    220.9'505                    90-26289
**ISBN 0-687-39670-0 (v. 1 : alk. paper)**
**ISBN 0-687-39671-9 (v. 2 : alk. paper)**
**ISBN 0-687-39672-7 (v. 3 : alk. paper)**
**ISBN 0-687-39674-3 (v. 4 : alk. paper)**
**ISBN 0-687-39675-1 (v. 5 : alk. paper)**
**ISBN 0-687-00838-7 (v. 6 : alk. paper)**
**ISBN 0-687-00120-X (v. 7: alk. paper)**
**ISBN 0-687-05585-7 (v. 10: alk. paper)**
**ISBN 0-687-08249-8 (v. 12: alk. paper)**
**ISBN 0-687-08272-2 (v. 13: alk. paper)**

Unless otherwise noted, scripture quotations are from *The Revised English Bible.* © Oxford
University and Cambridge University Press 1989. Used by permission.

Scripture quotations noted NRSV are from the New Revised Standard Version Bible, copyright 1989 by the Division of Christian Education of the National Council of the Churches
of Christ in the United States of America.

Scripture quotations noted KJV are from the King James Version of the Bible.

Scripture quotations noted AT are the author's translation.

99 00 01 02 03 04 05 06 07 08 — 10 9 8 7 6 5 4 3 2 1

To
Feisty and Forgotten Women
Past and Present

# Contributors

**Elaine Mary Wainwright** lectures in biblical studies and feminist theology in the Brisbane College of Theology, Brisbane, Australia. Previous publications include a study of the women of the Matthean Gospel, *Toward a Feminist Critical Reading of the Gospel According to Matthew,* and a number of articles and reviews.

**Elizabeth Ellis** is a professional storyteller who lives in Dallas, Texas, and performs in schools and at storytelling festivals around the nation. She was recently selected as a member of the prestigious Circle of Excellence of the National Storytelling Association.

**Phyllis Williams Kumorowski** is an ordained elder in The United Methodist Church and is pastor of the Rose Hill United Methodist Church in Rose Hill, Kansas. She also was a storyteller for The Storyteller's Companion to the Bible, Volume Ten: *John.*

**Barbara McBride-Smith** is a librarian, seminary instructor, and professional storyteller who lives in Stillwater, Oklahoma. She performs in storytelling festivals around the nation and is a former member of the board of the National Storytelling Association. She was also a storyteller and contributing editor for The Storyteller's Companion to the Bible, Volume Ten: *John.*

**Dennis E. Smith** is Professor of New Testament at Phillips Theological Seminary in Tulsa, Oklahoma. He is also the commentator and editor for The Storyteller's Companion to the Bible, Volume Ten: *John,* and editor for The Storyteller's Companion to the Bible, Volume Twelve: *Acts of the Apostles.*

# Contents

# A Storyteller's Companion

## Dennis E. Smith

We have always known that the Bible was full of stories. But we have not always known how to handle those stories most effectively. These days scholars apply narrative analysis to Bible stories, and thereby attempt to understand how they function as stories. This approach has revolutionized modern biblical study since the late 1970s. At the same time, narrative preaching has also begun to receive greater prominence as a form of proclamation. Add to this the resurgence of the art and practice of storytelling during this same period and you have the ingredients that have gone into this series. It is an opportune time to reexamine the riches of the biblical stories.

Women's stories can be identified as a separate category of biblical narrative. They are scattered throughout the New Testament documents in forms ranging from brief anecdotes to longer narratives. But because the culture in which they originated was overwhelmingly patriarchal, women are often pictured as minor characters. Nevertheless, when we read beneath the surface of the stories, we find significant data about the important roles women played in Christian origins. Indeed, many of these stories may have originally been told by women storytellers themselves. A modern retelling of these stories, therefore, can restore to life these forgotten voices from the Christian past.

### The Stories

The starting point for our study is the biblical story itself. Any interpretation of the text should start with a fresh rereading. These stories have survived for so long because of their power as stories. That power still comes across to us as we read them today. And each close reading of the text can bring new insights into its meaning. It is especially helpful to try to come to the text afresh, listening to it as if for the first time.

This collection draws together a wide range of women's stories from throughout the New Testament. Some, like the story of the Samaritan woman, are composed in lengthy narrative segments. Others, like the reference to Tryphaena and Tryphosa, are given but a mere mention, masking whatever larger story may have caused their names to surface in the text. When collected together, these stories give us a wide range of women's voices and roles, from widows to queens to businesswomen to prostitutes, from mothers and daughters to wives and sisters, from apostles and prophetesses to householders and benefactors of the church, women whose importance to the overall Christian story can no longer be overlooked.

The translation used in this book is *The Revised English Bible,* chosen because its contemporary style can make the stories more accessible to us. You are encouraged to utilize a variety of modern translations as well to give you a perspective on the range of possibilities for translation that the original language of the text presents.

## Comments on the Stories

The commentator for this volume is Elaine Mary Wainwright, a scholar in New Testament studies and feminist theology who teaches at the Brisbane College of Theology in Australia. She is a specialist in the narrative analysis of the Gospels who is able not only to explain how these stories work but also how we can find meaning in them for today. Her comments provide invaluable insights for contemporary retellings of the biblical story.

## Retelling the Stories

To help you in developing your own stories, we have provided a sample story with each biblical text. These are intended to serve as models for how a retelling can be done, but they are not expected to exhaust the possibilities in each story.

Various approaches have been used in the retellings. Sometimes the retelling will take the point of view of a character in the original story and develop it further. The retelling may follow the original plotline of the biblical story, it may expand on one detail of the plot, or it may explore the aftereffects of the original story. Retellings may utilize the first-century setting as their starting point, or they may be placed in modern settings. In some cases, a folktale or family story or even a historical narrative may be found to offer a parallel to the biblical story. The possibilities are many, and you are encouraged to develop your own retellings according to a format and style that works for you.

Three storytellers have contributed stories for this volume. Each wrote ten original stories just for this collection.

Elizabeth Ellis provided the stories for chapters 1–10. Her style is to find parallels to the biblical stories in historical narratives about famous women in American history. The parallels she finds are insightful and touching and cause us to understand the biblical stories in new ways.

Phyllis Williams Kumorowski provided the stories for chapters 11–20. She draws on her experience as a pastor and pulpit storyteller to reconstruct powerful new retellings of the biblical stories.

Barbara McBride-Smith provided the stories for chapters 21–30. With her trademark sharp wit and clever style, she draws pictures of biblical characters that capture both the humor and pathos of real life in our contemporary world.

## Parallel Stories

None of the biblical stories developed in a vacuum. They came out of a rich storytelling culture. The parallel stories are provided to bring to our attention the storytelling milieu out of which these stories came. They present a wide variety of storytelling data that forms the background for the ancient telling and retelling of these stores. The purpose is to acquaint us with the ancient world of storytelling so that we can better understand how these stories were heard by their original audience.

The parallel stories in the New Testament volumes take the place of the midrashim in the Old Testament volumes of the Storyteller's Companion to the Bible. The midrashim are traditional Jewish interpretations of biblical texts in story form. There are no such traditions for New Testament texts.

## How to Use This Book

Bible stories share many characteristics with traditional stories. As every storyteller knows, there is no one way to tell a story, but a storyteller cannot tell a story any way he or she wants.

On the one hand, it is often difficult for people of faith to think that Bible stories can be retold imaginatively. We tend to think of the Bible in rigid terms—as having one, clear, divine meaning. But the plurality of the Gospels, for example, in which stories about Jesus were told and retold in different ways, teaches us to think of Bible stories differently—as imaginative retellings that showcase the art of the storyteller.

On the other hand, the possibilities are not endless; it is possible to tell a story in a form that is inappropriate to the original. Successful storytelling involves a delicate balance between the meanings inherent in the original tradition, the parameters of understanding in the community within which the story is told, and the imagination of the storyteller. Bible stories have a range of meanings that are considered appropriate based on our sense for a balance between how they were understood then and how they can best be understood now. But we are remiss if we overlook the medium as a component part of the message, for the biblical narratives present stories that function as stories—they always have and always will. New Testament stories are created out of the tradition of the church, but retold in an imaginative form that is constructed to fit the needs of the storyteller's community.

This book is intended to be a resource to promote the telling of Bible stories.

But there is an important component that is not present within these pages. That is what you, the reader, bring to the text. Your experiences and understandings are vital to your own creation of viable retellings of the biblical stories. Only in this way can these ancient stories become real and pertinent to our lives today.

# A Narrative Introduction to Women's Stories in the Christian Testament

## Elaine Mary Wainwright

The first century of the common era in which the Christian Scriptures were written was a significant period for women in the Greco-Roman world. It was a time when some women inherited and managed property, some contributed as benefactors of cities and villages, others were leaders of synagogues, or priestesses in religious festivals and householders. Women were engaged in a number of occupations in both the public and private arena. They experienced the range of socioeconomic contexts that existed within the empire, participated in the varieties of religions that characterized this era, and were shaped by the diverse cultures across the empire.

The many changes that characterized the lives of women at this time were not sufficient, however, to shift the dominant cultural pattern that placed some propertied or privileged men in power over the lives of women, children, and other men. This dominant pattern found expression in social structures like households, in cultural codes like kinship and public/private divisions, and particularly in all forms of storytelling and literature of the period.

In examining the stories of and references to women within the Christian Scriptures, it will not be surprising to find these different worlds in conflict within the same story. At times, the reader may catch glimpses of women's storytelling that talks about their sisters in the reign-of-God movement from the perspective of their own lives and some of the changes mentioned above that they were experiencing. At other times, the glimpse may reveal some of the restraints that characterized the lives of some women or attempts to place further restraints on women's lives through the very storytelling itself. There are many voices in the stories examined in this volume and readers are invited to hear the different voices.

Attention will be given to the way in which women are portrayed in the texts examined. Their characterization in the narrative—what the women say, what others, including the narrator, say about them, and what they do—will be a primary focus. The sociocultural codes that are inscribed either within the particular story or its broader literary context, or both, also influence the way a story was both told and received. At times these will be highlighted. The different ways listeners might have heard the story, especially female listeners, because of their differing circumstances or that of the communities to which they belonged, are also significant in seeking to understand how women were portrayed. It is hoped that what might emerge from a rereading and a retelling of the stories of women in the Christian Scriptures would be a heightened awareness of women's agency in the formation of first-century Judaism and early Christianity and their contribution to the storytelling and meaning-making in their synagogues and developing house-churches.

In concluding this introduction, it must be acknowledged that the task being undertaken in this volume is a limited one. First, it is limited to those texts chosen as canonical within emerging Christianity. Recent scholarship on women's lives in first-century Judaism and emerging Christianity has extended the boundaries of the canonical to include a wide variety of both religious and popular texts that enrich a perception of the portrayal of women in literary texts during that time frame. This breadth of study will, in its turn, inform this work whose focus is the canonical literature.

Second, it is limited to a consideration of those texts in which women function as significant characters in a range of narratives within the canonical literature or in which they are referents within other literary types. The women so portrayed may not, however, represent the variety of roles, tasks, and activities in which Jewish, Greco-Roman, and early Christian women were engaged. Our engagement, however, with the women named in early Christian literature, the women who participated in ministry and leadership within the early expansion of the reign-of-God movement, and the women whose lives are storied in narratives, offer at least a glimpse into some aspects of the lives of Jewish and Christian women in the first century of the common era.

Finally, there is the limitation resulting from choosing from a limited number of texts. These choices are taken from the wide variety of literature contained within the Christian Testament, but even so, a selection had to be made. At times, particular stories that were told in quite different ways in different Gospels could only be considered in one of their literary contexts. The reader may also experience the difficulty of shifting between different types of texts. This, however, can also work positively to provide a sampling of the richness of storytelling about the lives of women in early Christianity for those who have ears to hear.

# What Are New Testament Parallel Stories?

## Dennis E. Smith

If a story is told about a modern day president in which he eventually says, "I cannot tell a lie," we might think immediately of the first such story, the one about George Washington and the cherry tree. Stories are like that. They often draw on traditional formats or motifs or plots. It is the stock-in-trade of a good storyteller to utilize shared cultural data to make her stories come alive.

The stories in the New Testament work the same way. They are often adapted to standard plots from the culture. Stories about women, for example, draw on stereotypes about roles of women that are standard in the culture. Women tend to be identified according to their relation to men. They are either daughters, wives, widows, or mothers-in-law, or else they are prostitutes. They are found in traditional roles associated with the world of women, whether it be the household or the village well. Yet here and there stories emerge that break with the stereotype and remind us that women could also appear as strong individuals.

"Parallel stories" are provided here to help us trace some of the background and foreground of these stories about women. They are intended to give us a sense for the different ways these stories would have been heard by different Christian groups at different times in early church history. The parallel stories collected here offer a variety of types of information.

### Jewish Traditions

In some cases, similar stories are found in the Jewish tradition. In this way, we can see how the stories told about Christian women would be similar to stories told about women in the Jewish tradition. Such stories are especially found in the Old Testament and in the Old Testament apocrypha, which served as the Scriptures of the early Christians and provided a rich source for their story traditions.

### Christian Traditions

Early Christian literature continued to celebrate famous women saints. A significant collection of legends grew up about Mary Magdalene and other characters from the New Testament. Other heroines of the faith who were cele-brated in story were the women martyrs, Christian prophetesses, and women apostles and preachers. These examples from other early Christian literature illustrate to us how women's story traditions continued to grow in the early church.

## "Pagan" Traditions

The New Testament stories usually picture women in stereotypical roles in society. In order to understand what these roles were and how they were per-ceived, we have to consult pagan literary materials. For example, it is in pagan literature where we find most of our data about how women functioned at wed-dings and funerals, how the household was run, and the roles women played in non-Christian religious settings. This data about societal norms regarding women often functioned as the nuts and bolts that held a story together. It is the kind of information that the storyteller could assume the ancient audience knew as he or she wove the story. We also find standard story motifs related to women and their stories that were the stock-in-trade of ancient storytellers, including Christian storytellers.

The parallel stories remind us of the cultural norms and stereotypes about women that the New Testament stories are built on. It is hoped they will pro-vide a basis for understanding better how these stories functioned in early Christian storytelling, and thereby enable us to retell them more effectively to our communities today.

# Learning to Tell Bible Stories

## A Self-Directed Workshop

1. Read the story aloud at least twice. You may choose to read the translation included here or the one you are accustomed to reading. I recommend that you examine at least two translations as you prepare, so you can hear the differences in the way they sound when read aloud.

Do read them *aloud.* Yes, if you are not by yourself, people may give you funny looks, but this really is important. Your ear will hear things about the passage that your eye will miss. Besides, you can't skim when you read aloud. You are forced to take your time, and you might notice aspects of the story that you never saw (or heard) before.

As you read, pay special attention to *where* the story takes place, *when* the story takes place, *who* the characters are, *what* objects are important to the story, and the general *order of events* in the story.

2. Now close your eyes and imagine the story taking place. This is your chance to become a playwright/director or screenwriter/filmmaker because you will experience the story on the stage or screen in your imagination. Enjoy this part of the process. It takes only a few minutes, and the budget is within everybody's reach.

3. Look back at the story briefly to make sure you haven't left out any important people, places, things, or events.

4. Try telling the story. This works better if you have someone to listen (even the family pet will do). You can try speaking aloud to yourself or to an imaginary listener. Afterward ask your listener or yourself what questions arise as a result of this telling. Is the information you need about the people, places, things, or language in the story? Is it appropriate to the age, experiences, and interests of those who will be hearing it? Does the story capture your imagination? One more thing: You don't have to be able to explain the meaning of a story to tell it. In fact, those of the most enduring interest have an element of mystery about them.

5. Read the "Comments on the Story" provided for each passage. Are some of your questions answered there? You may wish also to look at a good Bible dictionary for place names, characters, professions, objects, or worlds that you need to learn more about. *The Interpreter's Dictionary of the Bible* (Nashville: Abingdon Press, 1962) and *The Anchor Bible Dictionary* (New York: Doubleday, 1992) are the most complete sources for storytellers.

6. Read the "Retelling the Story" section for the passage you are learning to tell. Does it give you any ideas about how you will tell the story? How would you tell it differently? Would you tell it from another character's point of view? How would that make it a different story? Would you transfer it to a modern setting? What places and characters will you choose to correspond to those in the biblical story? Remember, the retellings that are provided are not meant to be told exactly as they are written here. They are to serve as springboards for your imagination as you develop your telling.

7. Read the "parallel stories" that accompany each passage. These give you insights into how the story was heard or retold at various times in the early church. Do these variations on the story respond to any of your questions or relate to any of your life situations or those of your listeners? Do the alternative stories parallel cultural "stories" from today that you know of? Sometimes you may find that experiences and points of view from the past are mirrored fairly closely in the modern setting.

8. Once you have the elements of the story in mind and have chosen the approach you are going to take in retelling it, you need to practice, practice, practice. Tell the story aloud ten or twenty or fifty times over a period of several days or weeks. Listen as you tell your story. Revise your telling as you go along. Remember that you are not memorizing a text; you are preparing a living event. Each time you tell the story, it will be a little different, because you will be different (if for no other reason than that you have told the story before).

9. Then "taste and see" that even the stories of God are good—not all sweet, but good and good for us and for those who hunger to hear.

# Elizabeth

*Elizabeth, though old and childless, bears a child of promise, John.*

## The Story

IN the reign of Herod king of Judaea there was a priest named Zechariah, of the division of the priesthood called after Abijah. His wife, whose name was Elizabeth, was also of priestly descent. Both of them were upright and devout, blamelessly observing all the commandments and ordinances of the Lord. But they had no children, for Elizabeth was barren, and both were well on in years.

Once, when it was the turn of his division and he was there to take part in the temple service, he was chosen by lot, by priestly custom, to enter the sanctuary of the Lord and offer the incense; and at the hour of the offering the people were all assembled at prayer outside. There appeared to him an angel of the Lord, standing on the right of the altar of incense. At this sight, Zechariah was startled and overcome by fear. But the angel said to him, 'Do not be afraid, Zechariah; your prayer has been heard: your wife Elizabeth will bear you a son, and you are to name him John. His birth will fill you with joy and delight, and will bring gladness to many; for he will be great in the eyes of the Lord. He is never to touch wine or strong drink. From his very birth he will be filled with the Holy Spirit; and he will bring back many Israelites to the Lord their God. He will go before him as forerunner, possessed by the spirit and power

of Elijah, to reconcile father and child, to convert the rebellious to the ways of the righteous, to prepare a people that shall be fit for the Lord.'

Zechariah said to the angel, 'How can I be sure of this? I am an old man and my wife is well on in years.'

The angel replied, 'I am Gabriel; I stand in attendance on God, and I have been sent to speak to you and bring you this good news. But now, because you have not believed me, you will lose all power of speech and remain silent until the day when these things take place; at their proper time my words will be proved true.'

Meanwhile the people were waiting for Zechariah, surprised that he was staying so long inside the sanctuary. When he did come out he could not speak to them, and they realized that he had had a vision. He stood there making signs to them, and remained dumb.

When his period of duty was completed Zechariah returned home. His wife Elizabeth conceived, and for five months she lived in seclusion, thinking, 'This is the Lord's doing; now at last he has shown me favour and taken away from me the disgrace of childlessness.'

. . . . . . . . . . . . . . . . . . . . . . . . . . .

Soon afterwards Mary set out and hurried away to a town in the uplands

19

of Judah. She went into Zechariah's house and greeted Elizabeth. And when Elizabeth heard Mary's greeting, the baby stirred in her womb. Then Elizabeth was filled with the Holy Spirit and exclaimed in a loud voice, 'God's blessing is on you above all women, and his blessing is on the fruit of your womb. Who am I, that the mother of my Lord should visit me? I tell you, when your greeting sounded in my ears, the baby in my womb leapt for joy. Happy is she who has had faith that the Lord's promise to her would be fulfilled!'

. . . . . . . . . . . . . . . . . . . . . . . .

WHEN the time came for Elizabeth's child to be born, she gave birth to a son. Her neighbours and relatives heard what great kindness the Lord had shown her, and they shared her delight. On the eighth day they came to circumcise the child; and they were going to name him Zechariah after his father, but his mother spoke up: 'No!' she said. 'He is to be called John.' 'But', they said, 'there is nobody in your family who has that name.' They enquired of his father by signs what he would like him to be called. He asked for a writing tablet and to everybody's astonishment wrote, 'His name is John.' Immediately his lips and tongue were freed and he began to speak, praising God. All the neighbours were overcome with awe, and throughout the uplands of Judaea the whole story became common talk. All who heard it were deeply impressed and said, 'What will this child become?' For indeed the hand of the Lord was upon him.

## Comments on the Story

The reader of Luke's Gospel encounters Elizabeth as the second character introduced into the narrative, in the first scene in the Gospel story. She is introduced in conventional form for a first-century woman, as the "wife" of Zechariah, her husband (1:5). She is named and referred to by her name nine times within this first and subsequent narrative segments (1:5, 7, 13, 24, 36, 40, 41 [twice], 57) indicating her significance as a character. Other elements in the introductory scene situate her firmly within Israel's covenantal story. She belongs to the priestly line of Aaron and, like her husband Zechariah, is described as "upright and devout, blamelessly observing all the commandments and ordinances" (1:6), praise generally reserved for the male Israelite. Her female narrative ancestry is that line of women considered barren and hence unable to produce Israel's favored sons for the accomplishment of the divine purpose [Sarah, Rachel, and Hannah, to name a few]. The text continues the androcentric perspective that has characterized Israel's history, seeing the woman as the cause of childlessness. It states simply in a way that obscures the experience not only of Elizabeth but also of Zechariah that Elizabeth was barren (1:7).

As with Sarah, her Israelite foresister, Elizabeth's conceiving of a son in her old age is announced by a divine messenger to her husband (1:13; cf. Gen.

18:10). The reader learns from the angel that it is in answer to Zechariah's prayer that Elizabeth will bear a son, but it is a son to Zechariah and he is commissioned to name the child. The woman is constructed as passive agent of divine intervention. Indeed, the interpretation given to Elizabeth of the lack of children experienced by herself and Zechariah is that of the culture—she is responsible and hence has brought shame to the family by the "disgrace of childlessness" (1:25*b*). On the other hand, however, she is portrayed as prophet in that she interprets her conception of a child as an act of divine mediation—God's doing—and God has shown favour (1:25*a*).

Elizabeth is not visited by a divine messenger and yet there is a hint in the text of her prophetic interpretation of these new events in her life as divine visitation. Only later will Zechariah offer a similar interpretation in his prophetic song—God has turned to this people to set them free (1:68). Elizabeth is, however, visited by a human messenger, her kinswoman Mary. Immediately upon receiving the announcement of the birth of her son from the divine messenger, Mary visits Elizabeth. She comes into the house of Zechariah and greets Elizabeth just as the angel entered and greeted her (1:28, 40). As readers, we do not hear the words of Mary's greeting as we heard that of the angel. The absence of words, however, turns attention to the simple yet profound embrace of kinswomen of the flesh, each of whom knew the experience of conceiving a divinely favored child in her body. The embrace of these two pregnant women, the apparent silence of their greeting, becomes the narrated moment of divine visitation for Elizabeth—the child leaps in her womb and she is filled with the Holy Spirit as Mary was overshadowed by this same Spirit (1:35, 41).

It is at this point that Elizabeth's prophetic voice bursts forth. First, she proclaims blessed both her young kinswoman and the fruit of her womb. Her proclamation of blessing is extraordinary in that she blesses Mary among women recalling two of the female savior figures of Israel: Jael (Judg. 5:24) and Judith (Jdt. 13:18). In blessing the fruit of Mary's womb, Elizabeth acknowledges in the voice of a woman, woman's unique role in carrying and bringing forth a child. This differs from the patriarchal perspective of the angel who sees the woman simply as instrument for bringing forth the son to Zechariah or even son to the Most High (1:13, 35).

In the second place, Elizabeth's prophetic voice is directed toward her own situation. Initially, she proclaims her wonderment at the divine visitation she has experienced and then she interprets what was previously stated by the narrator. She now acknowledges the voice of Mary's greeting that the narrator has silenced and claims it as the stimulus not only for the child leaping in her womb but also leaping for joy. She interprets the divine visitation mediated through Mary as one of joy just as the angel will interpret the birth of Mary's child as good news of great joy (1:44; 2:10).

The final third-person address of Elizabeth—happy is she (1:45)—is enigmatic. It could be directed away from the moment of female encounter toward Mary's more universal role in God's saving work for humanity. It may also be directed toward the reader/hearer initially designated male—most excellent Theophilus (1:3)—and here designated female—she who has had faith (1:45). This may also be an indication that the story of female mediation of divine visitation told in Luke 1:39-45 had its origin in women's storytelling circles. It is here that the accounts of children leaping in the womb would be told and that the believer would be designated female.

The Lukan narrator has placed such a story at a key moment in the unfolding narrative. It brings together the threads of the two stories announcing the births of sons to Elizabeth and Mary and it leads out into the story of their actual births. For a brief moment, however, we hear the powerful and prophetic voices of the two women raised in blessing and praise of both a woman and of God [see also Mary's song of praise 1:46-55 in response to Elizabeth's blessing].

Following this scene, Elizabeth's exit from the narrative seems quiet. The narrator states very simply that she gave birth to a son (1:57) and that her neighbors and relatives shared her delight (1:58). It is, however, her powerful voice that we hear as a final note. In response to the suggestion that her son be called Zechariah after his father, she states emphatically: "No! . . . He is to be called John" (1:60). It is Elizabeth, therefore, and not Zechariah who fulfills the angel's command that the child be called John. Zechariah merely reiterates what Elizabeth has directed. The reader can, therefore, remember Elizabeth as a woman of prophetic voice recognizing and proclaiming the divine visitation, characterizing one human response to that visitation in the Lukan infancy narrative, a female response.

### Retelling the Story

> Then Elizabeth was filled with the Holy Spirit and exclaimed in a loud voice, . . . "Happy is she who has had faith that the Lord's promise to her would be fulfilled!" (Luke 1:41*b*, 45)

### Antoinette Brown (1825–1921)

Nettie listened to her father read from the Bible. This was her favorite time of day, when her family gathered for worship. It was so peaceful and loving. "God is in this room. A gentle and loving God. Not the angry, punishing God the preacher screams about in church," she thought to herself. "If people knew how much God loves them they would not be so afraid to live, or die." She longed to share this peace with everyone she knew.

Nettie had a happy childhood. She often heard her beloved father say, "The service of God is man's noblest calling." Everyone in the family was overjoyed when her brother William went to college to study for the ministry. Nettie played "church" in the barn. The children sat on pews made of hay bales. Nettie always led these services, but she had never seen a woman minister. No woman in America had ever been officially ordained.

At fifteen, Antoinette completed her schooling, and took a position as a teacher. One by one, her friends married. She knew if she married, further schooling would be out of the question. The idea of becoming a minister kept growing within her.

"Father, it is my dream to continue my education. Oberlin College in Ohio admits Negroes and women." It also had a theological school, but she did not mention that. She had never spoken to anyone about her desire for the ministry.

Elizabeth's story is intended to remind the hearers of other biblical stories of famous women who bore heroic offspring. Like Sarah, mother of Isaac (Genesis 17), Hannah, mother of Samuel (1 Samuel 1), and the mother of Samson (Judges 13), Elizabeth is old and barren. Like Elizabeth (through Zechariah), Sarah (through Abraham) and Samson's mother receive an angelic announcement indicating that a child will be born who will be destined for great things. Often the divine instructions also include the name the child is to be given (Gen. 17:19; see also the story of Hagar in Genesis 16). Under the circumstances, it is clear that the conception of the child is to be considered miraculous, though it takes place through normal human intercourse.

Her father's answer was firm. "I am far from being a wealthy man. I need all my money to send your brothers to college. Boys have much more use for higher education." His answer made her sad, but she was determined to go anyway. She taught three years, saving every penny. She wrote to Oberlin, telling them of her education, and she was accepted in the ladies' literary course.

In August of 1846 she made the ten-day trip from New York to Ohio by steamship. One evening on deck, she was joined by an elderly minister. The two began to talk about the beauty of the evening. The old man asked, "Are you traveling to visit relatives in Ohio?"

"I am on my way to Oberlin Collegiate Institute." Looking at his kind face, she decided for the first time to speak aloud the desire of her heart. "I hope one day to become a minister."

The old man's face turned red with rage. He began railing at her, "Do you not know the Scriptures? What you say is blasphemy! Have you not read the words of the apostle Paul? 'Let your women keep silence in the churches: for it is not permitted unto them to speak"? Tears wet Nettie's cheeks as she ran to the women's cabin.

Oberlin was a progressive school, but not all of the faculty were equally committed to the radical idea of coeducation. All, however, were concerned with abolition and temperance. Antoinette threw herself into the life of the student body, attending lectures and debates. She became close friends with women's rights activist Lucy Stone.

At the end of her senior year she wrote two letters. One asked for admittance to the theological school. The other was to her father. She told him for years she had cherished the idea of serving God as a minister, and hoped that he would approve. The money she had made from teaching was gone and she hoped he would help her financially.

The faculty denounced her request as "defiant of Christian precepts." But Oberlin's charter said the college was open to anyone regardless of their race, color, or sex. The faculty passed the problem to the board of trustees. The board came together to reason with "the blasphemous Miss Brown."

"You are trying to defy the teachings of the Bible," they said, quoting Paul.

She replied calmly, "I believe the teachings of Paul have been misinterpreted, and one day I intend to prove it."

They sent their wives to call on her. "If you persist in this willfulness you will never be able to have a husband and children. No man would marry you!" Antoinette wanted a family, but she would not be swayed. Finally a compromise was struck: she could attend classes, but she would not be registered as a student.

Origen (third century C.E.) extolled Elizabeth and Mary in these terms: "Elizabeth prophesies before John; before the birth of the Lord and Savior, Mary prophesies. Sin began from the woman and then spread to the man. In the same way, salvation had its first beginnings from women. Thus the rest of women can also lay aside the weakness of their sex and imitate as closely as possible the lives and conduct of these holy women whom the Gospel now describes." (*Homilies on Luke* 8)

The answer from her father was a heavier blow. "I am shocked by your audacity and lack of wisdom. I am doing you a kindness in refusing to help you carry out a plan that can bring you only unhappiness and disgrace." She determined to continue, taking a job as a housekeeper to pay her expenses.

Every night she worked on her project, translating the words of Paul from the original Greek, challenging the accepted translation. " 'Let your women keep silence . . . for it is not permitted unto them to speak.' *Lalein* means 'to chatter, to make the sound of monkeys,' " Antoinette said. "Paul was cautioning women to speak wisely and not to babble. If we

24

take his admonition literally, we should not even feel free to teach our own children.

"In Acts 2:17 and 18 the prophet Joel is quoted, 'And it shall come to pass in the last days, saith God, I will pour out of my Spirit upon all flesh: and your sons and your daughters shall prophesy, and your young men shall see visions' (KJV). In the eleventh chapter of First Corinthians we learn that females were accustomed to act as prophetesses in those days under the direct sanction of the apostles. We have no reason to think it was therefore unlawful for women of that time to speak in church." Her exegesis went on for thirty pages, filled with sound theological scholarship.

The president of Oberlin praised her work and had it printed in the *Oberlin Quarterly*. However, her application to the trustees for license to preach was denied. Since she was not a registered student, she would not be allowed to graduate with her class. She received no offers from churches.

A Women's Rights Convention was scheduled in Worcester, Massachusetts. Lucy Stone asked her to speak on the status of women as set forth in the Scriptures. She stood before the assembly nearly sick with fright. She began hesitantly, "In the book of Galatians we read, 'There is neither Jew nor Greek, there is neither bond nor free, there is neither male nor female: for ye are all one in Christ Jesus.' " She shared her fresh translation of the words of Paul. The women, who had often been denounced by the old interpretation of Paul's message, cheered her.

She was invited to make a lecture tour, speaking on abolition, the rights of women, and temperance. Often, after her lectures, she was invited to stay over and preach. In 1853, the Congregational Church in South Butler, New York, called her to fill their pulpit. She was ordained a minister of the gospel!

Antoinette was happy as the shepherd of her small congregation, yet she was often lonely. Watching the women of her flock with their husbands and children sometimes made her sad. She was thirty-one years old by now, long past the time when women of her day married. She began to think people had been right when they said no man would want to marry her.

One day a stranger came to call on her. He said he had business in the area and had come to pay his respects at the insistence of his sister, Elizabeth. It was not long before he and Nettie were married. She would have a happy home and children after all. Samuel Blackwell was always proud of his wife's vision and courage. He came from a family that admired strong women. His brother Henry would marry Lucy Stone, and his sister Elizabeth would be America's first woman doctor. *(Elizabeth Ellis)*

# Mary of Nazareth I

*Mary, though an unmarried virgin, bears a child of promise, Jesus.*

### The Story

IN the sixth month the angel Gabriel was sent by God to Nazareth, a town in Galilee, with a message for a girl betrothed to a man named Joseph, a descendant of David; the girl's name was Mary. The angel went in and said to her, Greetings, most favoured one! The Lord is with you.' But she was deeply troubled by what he said and wondered what this greeting could mean. Then the angel said to her, 'Do not be afraid, Mary, for God has been gracious to you; you will conceive and give birth to a son, and you are to give him the name Jesus. He will be great, and will be called Son of the Most High. The Lord God will give him the throne of his ancestor David, and he will be king over Israel for ever; his reign shall never end.' 'How can this be?' said Mary. 'I am still a virgin.' The angel answered, 'The Holy Spirit will come upon you, and the power of the Most High will overshadow you; for that reason the holy child to be born will be called Son of God. Moreover your kinswoman Elizabeth has herself conceived a son in her old age; and she who is reputed barren is now in her sixth month, for God's promises can never fail.' 'I am the Lord's servant,' said Mary; 'may it be as you have said.' Then the angel left her.

Soon afterwards Mary set out and hurried away to a town in the uplands of Judah. She went into Zechariah's house and greeted Elizabeth. And when Elizabeth heard Mary's greeting, the baby stirred in her womb. Then Elizabeth was filled with the Holy Spirit and exclaimed in a loud voice, 'God's blessing is on you above all women, and his blessing is on the fruit of your womb. Who am I, that the mother of my Lord should visit me? I tell you, when your greeting sounded in my ears, the baby in my womb leapt for joy. Happy is she who has had faith that the Lord's promise to her would be fulfilled!'

And Mary said:

'My soul tells out the greatness of
   the Lord,
my spirit has rejoiced in God my
   Saviour;
for he has looked with favour on his
   servant,
lowly as she is.
From this day forward
all generations will count me
   blessed,
for the Mighty God has done great
   things for me.
His name is holy,
his mercy sure from generation to
   generation
toward those who fear him.
He has shown the might of his arm,
he has routed the proud and all
   their schemes;
he has brought down monarchs
   from their thrones,

26

and raised on high the lowly.
He has filled the hungry with goods
  things,
and sent the rich away empty.
He has come to the help of Israel
  his servant,
as he promised to our forefathers;
he has not forgotten to show mercy
to Abraham and his children's children for ever.'

Mary stayed with Elizabeth about three months and then returned home.

. . . . . . . . . . . . . . . . . . . . . . . . . .

IN those days a decree was issued by the emperor Augustus for a census to be taken throughout the Roman world. This was the first registration of its kind; it took place when Quirinius was governor of Syria. Everyone made his way to his own town to be registered. Joseph went up to Judaea from the town of Nazareth in Galilee, to register in the city of David called Bethlehem, because he was of the house of David by descent; and with him went Mary, his betrothed, who was expecting her child. While they were there the time came for her to have her baby, and she gave birth to a son, her firstborn. She wrapped him in swaddling clothes, and laid him in a manger, because there was no room for them at the inn.

Now in this same district there were shepherds out in the fields, keeping watch through the night over their flock. Suddenly an angel of the Lord appeared to them, and the glory of the Lord shone round them. They were terrified, but the angel said, 'Do not be afraid; I bring you good news, news of great joy for the whole nation. Today there has been born to

you in the city of David a deliverer—
the Messiah, the Lord. This will be
the sign for you: you will find a baby
wrapped in swaddling clothes, and
lying in a manger.' All at once there
was with the angel a great company
of the heavenly host, singing praise to
God:

'Glory to God in highest heaven,
  and on earth peace to all in whom
    he delights.'

After the angels had left them and returned to heaven the shepherds said to one another, 'Come, let us go straight to Bethlehem and see this thing that has happened, which the Lord has made known to us.' They hurried off and found Mary and Joseph, and the baby lying in the manger. When they saw the child, they related what they had been told about him; and all who heard were astonished at what the shepherds said. But Mary treasured up all these things and pondered over them. The shepherds returned glorifying and praising God for what they had heard and seen; it had all happened as they had been told.

Eight days later the time came to circumcise him, and he was given the name Jesus, the name given by the angel before he was conceived.

Then, after the purification had been completed in accordance with the law of Moses, they brought him up to Jerusalem to present him to the Lord (as prescribed in the law of the Lord: 'Every firstborn male shall be deemed to belong to the Lord'), and also to make the offering as stated in the law: 'a pair of turtle-doves or two young pigeons'.

27

There was at that time in Jerusalem a man called Simeon. The man was upright and devout, one who watched and waited for the restoration of Israel, and the Holy Spirit was upon him. It had been revealed to him by the Holy Spirit that he would not see death until he had seen the Lord's Messiah. Guided by the Spirit he came into the temple; and when the parents brought in the child Jesus to do for him what the law required, he took him in his arms, praised God, and said:

'Now, Lord, you are releasing your
    servant in peace,
according to your promise.
For I have seen with my own eyes
the deliverance you have made
    ready in full view of all nations:
a light that will bring revelation to
    the Gentiles
and glory to your people Israel.'

The child's father and mother were full of wonder at what was being said about him. Simeon blessed them and said to Mary his mother, 'This child is destined to be a sign that will be rejected; and you too will be pierced to the heart. Many in Israel will stand or fall because of him; and so the secret thoughts of many will be laid bare.'

When they had done everything prescribed in the law of the Lord, they returned to Galilee to their own town of Nazareth.

. . . . . . . . . . . . . . . . . . . . . . . .

THIS is how the birth of Jesus Christ came about. His mother Mary was betrothed to Joseph; before their marriage she found she was going to have a child through the Holy Spirit. Being a man of principle, and at the same time wanting to save her from exposure, Joseph made up his mind to have the marriage contract quietly set aside. He had resolved on this, when an angel of the Lord appeared to him in a dream and said, 'Joseph, son of David, do not be afraid to take Mary home with you to be your wife. It is through the Holy Spirit that she has conceived. She will bear a son; and you shall give him the name Jesus, for he will save his people from their sins.' All this happened in order to fulfil what the Lord declared through the prophet: 'A virgin will conceive and bear a son, and he shall be called Emmanuel,' a name which means 'God is with us'. When he woke Joseph did as the angel of the Lord had directed him; he took Mary home to be his wife, but had no intercourse with her until her son was born. And he named the child Jesus.

## Comments on the Story

Only the shadow of Mary of Nazareth passes across the Matthean infancy narrative. She is continually referred to in the third person by the narrator and always in her role as either mother of Jesus or betrothed wife of Joseph or both (Matt. 1:18, 20, 24; 2:11, 13, 14, 19, 21). It is Joseph who receives the announcement of the birth of Jesus by way of a dream and who initiates the many actions in the narrative in which Mary is presented as passive participant only. The traces of women's remembering of Mary are all but lost in a male-centered world of patrilineage and political intrigue.

In the Lukan infancy narrative, on the other hand, Mary emerges as woman of word and deed. She enters the narrative without prestige or lineage. She is simply named young woman or virgin, and she is betrothed. Such a designation, however, opens for the readers the two perspectives on Mary that intersect in the opening chapters of the Lukan narrative. Reference to her betrothal embeds her firmly within the patriarchal marriage system in its initial phase. Her virginity, on the other hand, especially viewed from a female perspective, is a time of transition, of potential to life possibilities. Her name, Mary/Miriam, evokes her foremother-prophet and leader during Israel's most sacred memory of God's visitation of them as a people, the Exodus.

The announcement to Mary can be read in a number of ways. On the one hand, the context is presumably that of a house as the angel "went in" to Mary (1:28). Household imagery is reinforced by the designation of Joseph as descendant of David [literally of the "house of David"]. The child whose birth is announced is not to be called Mary's son but rather son of the "Most High" (1:32), the one whose power will overshadow her. Power, both human and divine and imaged in the narrative as male, surrounds Mary in this announcement of birth. Her words of acquiescence at the close of the scene sound frightening in such a context—"I am the Lord's servant" [Lord is used as the designation of the male head of the household as well as the title evoking the head of the divine household], "may it be as you have said" (1:38). This language of household would have been very familiar to first-century storytellers and their recipients, both women and men, as it was the foundation for their familial and political lives. Such a reading would have fixed the birth of Jesus within the parameters of the empire.

Alternative readings of this scene, however, deconstruct or come into tension with the above reading, opening up the possibility of an entirely different experience of receiving the story and encountering the character, Mary. Both the announcement of the angel and its effect take place in the body of this young woman. The one who is to be great, holy, born of the Most High God, the one in whom God visits Israel for their liberation, is to be conceived in the womb of the woman, Mary. Her body, her flesh, is the place of divine visitation. It is on this body that the spirit of holiness comes and over this flesh that the shadow of divine power falls. From this body comes the "yes" stating cooperation with the divine power that promises new and undreamt of possibilities for God's suffering people.

Mary carries this promise in her body as she resolutely arises and goes with haste to visit her kinswoman Elizabeth, who likewise has received the divine visitation in her body (1:36-37). Mary enters the space of the house of Zechariah but the male-designated household becomes a place of female encounter in which women mediate the divine to each other and to the child borne in each woman's body.

Although Mary's voice has been heard in the dialogue with the angel, it resounds forth now in praise of the God whom these two women have encountered in their bodies and in the meeting of those bodies. As prophetic interpreter of the divine visitation, Mary echoes the song of Hannah, the voices of the prophets, the lyrics of the psalmists. It is a song not only of an individual woman, such individuality being inconceivable within a first-century context. It is rather the voice of a people sounding through the words of this woman. God has regarded the humiliation of a suffering people and has come among them in this promised child. From the mouth of Mary comes forth a vision of a new humanity (1:46-55). From her womb comes forth the child (2:7) whose birth is good news of great joy for the whole nation (2:10).

Although Mary delivers the child of her womb, she still carries all that surrounds the child in her heart, in her body. Throughout the infancy narrative, the divine visitation and the making of meaning in relation to this visitation is carried in the body of Mary. This is particularly visible immediately following the brief account of the birth of Jesus. The announcement to the shepherds of good news of great joy for the whole nation echoes the proclamation of the birth of Augustus, the emperor (2:10). The imagery of new king born in the city of David evokes messianic hopes within an oppressed people. The liberation, however, in keeping with the strains of the Magnificat is proclaimed in a context of peace and not war (2:14). This vision of liberation and of peace on a grand scale is carried within the heart of Mary of Nazareth and focused in her helpless newborn son whom she has just wrapped in swaddling clothes and laid on animal straw "because there was no room for them at the inn" (2:7).

Mary leaves the narrative on this same note, carrying the attempts to give meaning to the life of her child in her body, in her heart (2:51). This second reference follows Jesus' action of remaining in the Temple among the teachers instead of returning with his parents and kinsfolk. This action is a sign that Jesus interprets to point away from his family and home in Nazareth and toward what was designated for him at his birth, the work of one divinely begotten. It is as if this final reference to Mary treasuring "all these things" in her heart characterizes not only this moment but also the rest of the narrative in which she will not appear as character, but will in fact be participant—the events of the life of Jesus and its meaning being written on her body as they were from his conception. The words of Simeon to her, that a sword would pierce through her very soul (2:35) could confirm such a reading.

Subsequent histories of reading beyond the first century have laid heavy burdens on the body of Mary, burdens of immaculate purity, of divinity, of perpetual virginity and many more. These, in their turn, have laid burdens upon the bodies of women in Christian history. A reading of Mary in the Lukan infancy narrative as the one in whose body the divine visitation took flesh may enable today's readers to reclaim embodiment for women and men as the place of today's divine visitation.

### Retelling the Story

And Mary said: 'My soul tells out the greatness of the Lord, my spirit has rejoiced in God my Saviour; for he has looked with favour on his servant, lowly as she is.' (Luke 1:46-48*a*)

### Sojourner Truth (1797?–1883)

"I was born Isabelle. All called me 'Belle.' I was a slave. We weren't given the last name. We were owned by old Dutch settlers in New York. Spoke only Dutch. My English still not so good as my Dutch. My mother, called 'Maumau Bett,' sang a lullaby to me that came from Africa. She taught me the Lord's Prayer in Dutch. And, she taught me about God. She teach me he love us and he help us if we turn to him. I turn to him many times in the thirty years I was a slave." And with a smile she added, "And always since then."

She was speaking to an abolitionist woman named Olive Gilbert who told her, "I want to print the story of your life in a book so people can see slavery was just as cruel in the North as the South. It may help people work to put an end to slavery."

Olive prompted her to continue by saying, "I know that you must have been freed on July 4, 1827, when New York abolished slavery."

"No!" came the quick reply. "I free myself before that. I was owned by Mr. Dumont by then. He broke a promise to me. God said walk away. Walk away from this man who do not keep his word. So, I walk away. I walk away from Mr. Dumont. I walk away from slavery." She gazed at Olive with her piercing black eyes. "I talk to God and he talk to me."

The first hearers of the story of Mary's conception of Jesus while betrothed to Joseph would picture her as a twelve-year-old girl, since that was the normal age in which betrothal, or engagement, took place in Jewish society. Betrothal resulted from a marriage contract between the families in which the young girl was legally transferred from the family of her father to the family of her husband-to-be. Actual consummation of the marriage, represented by the bride moving in with the husband, might not take place for several months. But betrothal was still the legal equivalent of marriage and could only be broken by a decree of divorce. (Davies and Allison, 1.199)

Many hearers of Mary's story would connect her with a long line of biblical heroines. According to Luke, she receives an announcement of a birth of a promised child who will do great things, much like Hagar, mother of Ishmael (Genesis 16), and the unnamed mother of Samson (Judges 13). According to Matthew, the birth announcement is given to Joseph, much like the announcement of Isaac that is given to Abraham (Genesis 17). Furthermore, Mary is a woman honored by God who must overcome the stigma of being shamed according to human standards, much like the women named in Matthew's genealogy (1:2-6), namely Tamar (a seductress, Gen. 38:14), Rahab (a harlot, Josh. 2:2), Ruth (a seductress, Ruth 3:7), and "the wife of Uriah" (Bathsheba, an adulteress, 2 Sam. 11:4). (from Schüssler Fiorenza, ed., *Searching the Scriptures*, 2.642-43)

Olive nodded and asked, "How did you become 'Sojourner Truth'?"

"Well, I'd had my freedom sixteen years," the woman answered. "Mostly I work for families for wages. All that time I get closer to God. I talk to him and he talk to me. One day he wants me to leave the city. So the next day I quit my job and walk east toward Long Island. As I walk he tells me my mission is to travel up and down the land, showing people their sins and being a sign to them. He said to take 'Sojourner' for my first name. A sojourner is a traveler. I never stay in one place for long. I took the name 'Truth' because it is what I tell. It is one of his names, too."

The book the two women worked on would be called *Narrative of Sojourner Truth, A Northern Slave*. It would influence many people to work to put an end to slavery.

Many runaway slaves made their way north to the states where slavery had been abolished. There they could be relatively safe and free. However, in 1850 the United States Congress passed the Fugitive Slave Law. It said that runaway slaves must be returned to their masters—even from states where slavery was now illegal. The law further stated that any person caught helping a runaway slave would have to pay heavy fines. They stepped up their efforts to end slavery by organizing more meetings and sending out more speakers.

Sojourner Truth would be the first African American woman to go on a lengthy lecture tour. She knew it would not be easy. Women had few legal rights. Their behavior was rigidly controlled by a strict code of conduct enforced by family, church, and community. She knew that any woman who dared to break those rules would be confronted with ridicule, perhaps even with violence.

Some people came to the lectures to taunt her; others threw eggs or stones. Many people refused to believe that any woman could present a public lecture.

Sojourner Truth was a tall, strong woman, fully six feet tall. When she spoke, her deep, throaty voice was powerful. In Indiana, a heckler refused to believe she was a woman at all. He demanded she allow a group of local women to examine her bosom to prove she was female. If he thought to silence her, he could not have been more mistaken. She responded, "Thirty years as a slave I spent. Thirty years. Often I was forced to nurse White children while my poor babes cried out from hunger." Then she ripped open her blouse, baring her aging breasts to the stunned audience. "See for yourselves," she sneered. "It is not my shame but yours that I do this."

Not everyone who came to hear her jeered. More and more people came to listen and found themselves moved by the power of her message. She could be witty as well as eloquent. When a man approached her saying, "Old woman, do you think your talk about slavery does any good? Do you suppose people care what you say? Why I don't care any more for your talk than I do for the bite of a flea."

"Perhaps not," responded Sojourner Truth, "but the Lord willing, I'll keep you scratching!"

In 1851 she attended the Ohio Women's Rights Convention as a delegate. Ohio was a free state, but most of its citizens held mixed feelings about slavery. Many of the women were surprised by the presence of a Black delegate. They did not want her to speak for fear she would alienate some of their supporters.

Sojourner sat quietly listening to speakers who supported equal education for women, the right of women to sue in court, and the right to keep their own property if they married. The most controversial subject was giving women the right to vote. This idea was too much for one of the clergymen who was present. He denounced the entire idea as nonsense, saying women were too fragile to deal with the demands of voting. He went on to say it was obvious women were never intended to be men's equals, because Christ wasn't a woman.

Sojourner Truth moved slowly and solemnly to the front. Many of the delegates made hissing noises, but her steady gaze was enough to quiet the room. She began, "That man over there says that women need to be helped into carriages, and lifted over ditches, and to have the best place everywhere. Nobody ever helps me into carriages, or over mud puddles, or gives me any best place! And ain't I a woman?

"Look at me!" She rolled up the sleeve of her plain gray dress. "Look at my arm! I have plowed and planted, and gathered into barns, and no man could head me! And ain't I a woman?

"I could work as much and eat as much as a man—when I could get it—and bear the lash as well! And ain't I a woman?"

Then her voice grew quiet. "I have borne me thirteen children, and seen

33

them most all sold off to slavery, and when I cried out with my mother's grief, none but Jesus heard me. And ain't I a woman?"

She stared at the minister who had just spoken. "Then that little man in black there, he says women can't have as much rights as men, 'cause Christ wasn't a woman! Where did your Christ come from? Where did your Christ come from? From God and a woman! Man had nothing to do with it!" *(Elizabeth Ellis)*

Pagan hearers of Mary's story would recognize parallels with Greek and Roman birth stories of heroic figures. To be sure, the normal pattern in the Greek and Roman stories was for the woman to be seduced or raped by a god. That pattern is not followed in Mary's story, since the language, "through the Holy Spirit that she has conceived" (Matt. 1:20) or "the Holy Spirit will come upon you, and the power of the Most High will overshadow you" (Luke 1:35), does not present an explicit picture of a god copulating with a human. Nevertheless the result is the same: the child is born of a human mother but a divine father; consequently he is destined to be a hero.

# Mary of Nazareth II

*Mary follows the career of Jesus from the background and plays a role in the birth of the church.*

### The Story

Then his mother and his brothers arrived; they stayed outside and sent in a message asking him to come out to them. A crowd was sitting round him when word was brought that his mother and brothers were outside asking for him. 'Who are my mother and my brothers?' he replied. And looking round at those who were sitting in the circle about him he said, 'Here are my mother and my brothers. Whoever does the will of God is my brother and sister and mother.'

. . . . . . . . . . . . . . . . . . . . . . . .

From there he went to his home town accompanied by his disciples. When the sabbath came he began to teach in the synagogue; and the large congregation who heard him asked in amazement, 'Where does he get it from? What is this wisdom he has been given? How does he perform such miracles? Is he not the carpenter, the son of Mary, the brother of James and Joses and Judas and Simon? Are not his sisters here with us?' So they turned against him.

. . . . . . . . . . . . . . . . . . . . . . . .

Meanwhile near the cross on which Jesus hung, his mother was standing with her sister, Mary wife of Clopas, and Mary of Magdala. Seeing his mother, with the disciple who he loved standing beside her, Jesus said to her, 'Mother, there is your son'; and to the disciple, 'There is your mother'; and from that moment the disciple took her into his home.

. . . . . . . . . . . . . . . . . . . . . . . .

After [Jesus] had said this, he was lifted up before their very eyes, and a cloud took him from their sight. They were gazing intently into the sky as he went, and all at once there stood beside them two men robed in white, who said, 'Men of Galilee, why stand there looking up into the sky? This Jesus who has been taken from you up to heaven will come in the same way as you have seen him go.' THEY then returned to Jerusalem from the hill called Olivet, which is near the city, no farther than a sabbath day's journey. On their arrival they went to the upstairs room where they were lodging: Peter and John and James and Andrew, Philip and Thomas, Bartholomew and Matthew, James son of Alphaeus, Simon the Zealot, and Judas son of James. All these with one accord were constantly at prayer, together with a group of women, and Mary the mother of Jesus, and his brothers.

. . . . . . . . . . . . . . . . . . . . . . . .

THE day of Pentecost had come, and they were all together in one place. Suddenly there came from the sky

35

what sounded like a strong, driving wind, a noise which filled the whole house where they were sitting. And there appeared to them flames like tongues of fire distributed among them and coming to rest on each one. They were all filled with the Holy Spirit and began to talk in other tongues, as the Spirit gave them power of utterance.

## Comments on the Story

Variety characterizes the traditions associated with Mary across the Gospel narratives. Outside the Matthean and Lukan infancy narratives, she appears as mother of Jesus in two Markan texts that seek to establish what belonging to the reign of God ["kingdom of God"] might mean (Mark 3:31-35; 6:3). She is named Mary and again identified as "mother of Jesus" in the opening verses of Acts (1:14); and she stands as mother of Jesus beneath the foot of the cross in the Johannine account of Jesus' death (19:25-27).

The brevity and the variety of these references may point to a number of possibilities historically. They may be the result of a sociocultural context in which men were considered the norm and the center and hence their stories dominated narratives. They may suggest that historical memories of Mary were not retained and that she, therefore, functioned symbolically in early Christian storytelling and meaning-making in relation to Jesus. Such traditions as have been retained may have arisen among men perhaps even more than women in that it is not the memory of the woman but her symbolic significance that is central. Women's traditions may be lost to us or retained only in aspects of the infancy narratives.

Each of the texts under consideration associates Mary with the inauguration of the new community of believers either narratively or symbolically. In the Markan story, Mary is associated with the "scandal" that Jesus' ministry and memory represents. He is "son of Mary" [perhaps an oblique reference to a charge of illegitimacy—Mark 6:3], a carpenter and resident of the village of Nazareth in the backwater of Galilee, and yet he is performing mighty works and displaying extraordinary wisdom (6:2). The challenge to accept Jesus' prophetic message is perhaps greatest among those who knew Jesus and those among whom he had dwelt for most of his life. They are challenged to accept that one of "their own" might be speaking and acting prophetically and calling them to believe in and live according to God's vision for humanity imaged as "reign of God" or "kingdom of God" (Mark 1:15). Jesus uses familial imagery to shift the boundaries of people's imagination in relation to this vision of God. It will not be confined by known kinship ties and structures but these will be shifted to include all those doing the "will of God" (Mark 3:35). A new kinship will pertain in the new community known as the "reign of God."

The opening verses of Acts establish the group that gathered together in Jerusalem following the departure of Jesus, the group on whom the Spirit would come at Pentecost (Acts 2:1), the group who had constituted Jesus' companions, Jesus' disciples, and who would continue the "reign-of-God" movement beyond Jerusalem and Galilee to the ends of the earth (Acts 1:8). Among this group is Mary, the mother of Jesus, together with "his brothers," "a group of women" and the eleven named disciples (Acts 1:13-14). It is a group that includes women and men and it is foundational of the early Christian communities. Mary, who was actively engaged in the birth of Jesus in the context of a familial kinship group is now actively engaged with the birth of the movement grounded in Jesus but this time in the context of a new kinship group that includes female and male disciples who have been companions with Jesus in his ministry.

The language of John 19:25-27 points to the symbolic aspect of this final scene before the death of Jesus. It is a scene that could be paralleled with the miracle of Cana (John 2:1-11). In the account that opens the ministry of Jesus, Mary is identified as "woman" [John 2:4, omitted in the REB], a figure of the people, the remnant who call forth Jesus' liberating powers symbolized in the abundance of rich wine. In the Jewish Scriptures, the people are often identified symbolically as "woman" [Isa. 26:17-18; Jer. 2:2; Ezek. 16:8]; at times as "unfaithful woman" who must be brought back to God [Hos. 1-3; Ezek. 23:2-4]. Jesus' use of the title "woman" for Mary in both the Cana and Passion encounters [19:26 REB has "mother"] places her symbolically at the beginning of his earthly ministry and at the beginning of the new movement within Judaism that would center around the memory of Jesus the crucified and raised prophet and revelation of God.

At the level of the narrative, Jesus speaks powerfully poignant words from the cross to the two people with whom he is most intimately connected: "There is your son. . . . There is your mother" (John 19:26, 27). From a cultural point of view, this would have been understood as an act of love and care for Jesus' mother who could have been left destitute by the death of her son. Symbolically, it links familial kinship and new kinship within the movement that would be born from the pierced side of Jesus crucified.

The story of Mary of Nazareth has been virtually lost to us. The hints in the biblical narrative, however, have resourced Christian imagination down through the centuries and can continue to resource that imagination today. With other women, she is the woman of passion and compassion standing at the foot of the cross. As faithful kinswoman, she stands with her kinspeople and is called by Jesus into the new kinship of the reign-of-God movement. Beyond the death of Jesus she continues in fidelity with the new kinship group, participating in the inauguration of that movement. As woman of fidelity, passion, and compassion, she places all women at the heart of the Christian movement, her memory challenging in our day all that hinders their full participation in the ongoing movement.

## Retelling the Story

All these with one accord were constantly at prayer, together with a group of women, and Mary the mother of Jesus, and his brothers. . . . And there appeared to them flames like tongues of fire distributed among them and coming to rest on each one. They were all filled with the Holy Spirit and began to talk in other tongues, as the Spirit gave them power of utterance. (Acts 1:14; 2:3-4)

## Anne Hutchinson (1591–1643)

Anne Hutchinson's husband, William, was a cloth merchant. He had prospered since his wife convinced him to follow their minister, John Cotton, from England to the Massachusetts Bay Colony. Anne had quickly taken up nursing the sick and helping the poor.

Anne was surprised to discover that in the colonies John Cotton was only an assistant to a small-minded, arrogant minister named Wilson. Wilson was a boring speaker whose discourses were often confusing. Anne began holding religious discussions in her home. At first the only people who attended were women Anne had assisted in childbirth.

At church meetings, men had the right to stand up and speak out if they had a question. Women were never allowed to speak in public. Anne explained to the women what Minister Wilson's sermons were about. She encouraged them to ask questions and participate in discussions.

As the weeks went by, more and more people came to listen to the discussions, men as well as women. At first Anne only expounded on Minister Wilson's sermons. The conversations became deeper, and Anne began to share her own beliefs with the group.

> When the crowd calls Jesus "son of Mary" (Mark 6:3), they are apparently uttering an insult according to the mores of the day, whereby calling a son by the name of the mother only was to imply illegitimacy, especially in Jewish society. Mark, the storyteller who tells this story, thus has the hometown crowd insulting Jesus, leading to Jesus' conclusion: "A prophet never lacks honour except in his home town, among his relations and his own family" (6:4). Since Mark has no birth story, this reference to illegitimacy does not seem to be a veiled reference to a virgin birth. It could refer to a pre-Markan tradition that Jesus was illegitimate, but it could just as likely be used here as a typical (and presumably unfounded) slur one would expect from a hostile crowd.

She said, "No matter what Minister Wilson tells you, there is something more important than the laws of the church. You can have a personal relationship with our heavenly Father. If you seek God, God will speak to you and make his will known to you. He will send you the gift of the Holy Spirit."

The idea that one could expect to commune directly with God was a foreign one in the Massachusetts Bay Colony. Wilson taught that God had communicated directly with the apostles of the past, but now all communication with God could happen only through God's ministers. Those who attended Anne Hutchinson's discussions began to ask questions of Minister Wilson that made him angry. He told Governor Henry Vane, "This woman is dangerous. She has more people resort to her for counsel about matters of conscience . . . than any minister in the colony."

Governor Vane thought he should hear her message for himself, so he attended Anne's discourses. He appreciated her message and became one of her strongest supporters. Many prominent members of the colony agreed with her and began to turn away from the ministers. Instead they communicated with God directly and sought the gift of the Holy Spirit.

The ministers felt their power over the colony eroding. They organized the conservative merchants to remove Governor Vane and elect former governor John Winthrop. He was a harsh man who could be depended upon to oppose all change in the colony. He immediately demanded that Mistress Hutchinson cease all meetings in her home, but Anne followed her conscience and continued. William Hutchinson knew he should remove his family from the jurisdiction of the ministers, so he left Boston searching for a new home for his family.

As soon as William departed, Anne was arrested. The ministers were afraid of her supporters in Boston, so she was tried in Roxbury. Governor Winthrop himself presided at her trial. "You are called here as one who has troubled the Commonwealth and the churches," Governor Winthrop said. "You have traduced the ministers. . . . You held meetings at your house after these meetings had been censured as not comely or fitting for your sex."

Deputy Governor Dudley read from the charges against her. "Within half a year of her coming, she has created factions and parties with her preachings of the covenant of grace and the covenant of works." Then he turned to Anne and demanded, "What do you mean? Whence comes your authority?"

"What do I mean, sir?" answered Anne. "I mean what the Scriptures teach. Does it not say in the Good Book that salvation cannot be obtained by good works? Salvation is a gift, a gift of grace. Not one of us can earn it or be deserving of it. But we can ask God for it, and in his mercy God will grant it to us. And with it comes the gift of the Holy Spirit. That is my authority, the Holy Spirit. I pray to God and God talks to me. I often receive revelations of God's will in that way."

"Revelations . . . the last word of Satan!" burst out Governor Winthrop.

Deputy Governor Dudley added, "A devilish delusion!"

Governor Winthrop quickly delivered sentence. "You are banished from our jurisdiction as being a woman not fit for our society. You are to be imprisoned until the court sends you away."

Joseph Weld held her as a prisoner in his house. Although he was a wealthy Roxbury merchant, he spent no funds on Anne's care. She was always cold and often hungry. When she became ill, her sickness went untreated. Throughout the long, hard winter, the ministers badgered her constantly to admit that no one could commune with God directly.

Then she was summoned to a second trial, this one to be held in Boston itself. Word was circulated that the ministers had written out a list of her errors, and she would be forced to admit them publicly. The church was crowded. Many of those present were ones Anne had nursed through illness or tended in childbirth. Each of them knew too well the dangers of being driven out of the colony into the wilderness, and so they sat in silence because they were afraid.

Anne knew that Minister Wilson hated her and would try to humiliate her. Her only comfort was the certainty that her old friend John Cotton would defend her. But only her son-in-law rose to speak on her behalf. Anne was shocked when John Cotton rebuked him. Then Cotton turned to the women and said, "Take heed of her opinions . . . withhold all countenance and respect from her." His sharp words cut through Anne like a knife.

She was to be kept a prisoner at the Cottons' until the next session of her trial. The walk from the church to the Cottons' took Anne past her own home. Her youngest children came running out because they had not seen their mother in several months. Mrs. Cotton kept tight control of Anne and would not allow her to speak to her own children.

John Cotton gave her no peace. He hammered away at her day and night to take back what she had taught. "Think of your children," he said. "If you admit you were wrong you will be forgiven. You will be allowed to stay here in the colony."

Finally Anne took his advice. She was ill and exhausted from her ordeal. She wrote out a paper admitting to the errors of which she was accused. When she tried to read it in court, she was too weak to make her voice heard. John Cotton took the paper from her and read it aloud.

Minister Wilson wanted to humiliate her before the crowd. He asked her, "Will you now admit before this company that no one can commune directly with God?" Anne pulled herself to her feet and said in a loud voice, "No! My judgment is not altered although my expression is changed."

Minister Wilson pounced immediately upon her answer. "Pride is at the bottom of this trouble," he said in a cruel voice. "You would set yourself up above others, so that you might be called a prophetess. We would sin before God if we did not put from us a woman guilty of such evils. In the name of the church I do cast you out; and in the name of Christ I do deliver you up to Satan."

She had been excommunicated. She now was an outcast.

The crowd sat in stunned silence. Many of the women began to weep. Anne Hutchinson walked down the aisle of the church with her head high. One of the women toward the back dared to speak to her. In a whisper she said, "The Lord sanctify thee." Anne smiled at her. Then Anne's voice rang out through the church, "The Lord judges not as men judge!"

Her husband, William, returned from the wilderness. He had wonderful news for Anne. "I have found a new home for us. We will be welcome in the new colony of Rhode Island. Everyone there is welcome to worship as their conscience dictates."

Anne Hutchinson would be remembered as the mother of religious freedom in America. *(Elizabeth Ellis)*

Mark refers to brothers and sisters of Jesus, indicating he was unfamiliar with the tradition of Mary's perpetual virginity. That idea seems to have developed in the second century C.E. The apocryphal *Infancy Gospel of James* (or Protevangelium of James; ca. mid-second century C.E.) is perhaps the most influential exponent of this doctrine. The story begins with Mary's miraculous birth to a formerly childless couple, Joachim and Anna, and her subsequent dedication to God. Her childhood is marked by a life of absolute purity, and at twelve she becomes the ward of Joseph, who, in this story, is already an old man with children. The story of conception follows the model of Matthew and Luke, but takes the idea one step further. In this story, after Jesus is born, Mary is checked manually by two midwives who find that she is still a virgin, that is, her hymen is still intact. The second of these, Salome, vows, "As the Lord my God lives, unless I insert my finger and examine her, I will never believe that a virgin has given birth." She then approaches Mary with the words, "Mary, position yourself for an examination. You are facing a serious test." But when Salome does examine her, she is punished for her disbelief by her hand being consumed by flames. When she asks for forgiveness and worships the child, however, she is healed (19:18–20:11). (Miller, 373-89)

# Anna, the Prophet

*The voice of Anna, the prophet, resounds in the Temple in praise of the child, Jesus.*

## The Story

There was also a prophetess, Anna the daughter of Phanuel, of the tribe of Asher. She was a very old woman, who had lived seven years with her husband after she was first married, and then alone as a widow to the age of eighty-four. She never left the temple, but worshipped night and day with fasting and prayer. Coming up at that very moment, she gave thanks to God; and she talked about the child to all who were looking for the liberation of Jerusalem.

## Comments on the Story

In three short verses, the reader is introduced to the extraordinary prophetic woman, Anna. She is introduced into the Lukan narrative as the female member of a typical Lukan pair, the Zechariah/Mary comparison preceding this second pair of Simeon and Anna. The contrasts focus aspects of Anna's story. She is named prophet or prophetess (2:36) while Simeon is simply called an "upright and devout" man (2:25). She remains constantly in the temple worshiping, fasting, and praying day and night. Simeon, on the other hand, comes to the temple in response to the prompting of the Spirit on a single occasion. Simeon, however, is given prophetic voice, recognizing the mission of the child, Jesus, as connected to the salvation or redemption of Israel but it is, like his visit, a voice that is single and linked to this particular occasion. We do not hear Anna's prophetic words but are told by the narrator that she continued to speak about the child to those seeking a liberating figure in Israel, symbolized in Jerusalem, its holy city (2:38). Even though the narrator silences her voice, readers can allow it to resound in their imagination—the voice of the woman prophet ringing out in the Jerusalem temple, proclaiming liberation! The seemingly amazing aspect of Anna's story is that she is a woman in the public space of the temple, a woman whose voice is heard in this public place. The tragedy of the narration is that we do not hear her words. Simeon's voice, on the other hand, does not seem, according to the narrative, to be raised in public proclamation but rather in prayer (2:29-32) and in conversation with Mary (2:34-35). There is, however, no narrative account of the encounter between the two prophetic women, Anna and Mary, as there was between Elizabeth and Mary. One wonders about the possible recognition by each of the prophetic insight of the other as the aged and possibly childless widow and woman of prayer and fasting met and recognized the young mother of the child whom both prophetically knew to be the liberator of God's people (1:46-55; 2:38).

Anna is the only widow of the many encountered in Luke–Acts who is named (Luke 4:25-26; 7:11-17; 20:47; 21:1-4; Acts 6:1 and 9:39, 41). She is also identified according to her own genealogical line rather than that of her husband as was Judith, the ideal of the Israelite widow (Jdt. 8:1). She was widowed young, merely seven years after her marriage and hence, possibly in her early twenties. If her story is characterizing ideal widowhood, then this aspect of her story would be intended to speak to young widows. But she is not only young widow, she is also faithful widow through decades, not seeking remarriage but demonstrating the characteristics of the pious and ascetic widow, remaining in the temple continually, worshiping through fasting and prayer night and day (2:37). It is the prophetic single-mindedness of this single woman that enables her to recognize the child's liberating life mission and to proclaim this to all those open to a message of liberation.

Anna's short story leaves many questions unanswered. Was she a poor widow, reliant on begging in the temple or on temple funds for the meager upkeep that she would have needed for her ascetic lifestyle or was she, like Judith, a woman of wealth, which enabled her to support her choice of a life of piety and devotion when she was freed from the demands of marriage? Did she represent an institution of widows or institutional care of widows within Judaism or an emerging institution within early Christianity that would develop later into an order of widows (1 Tim. 5:3-16)? Does her choice of an ascetic lifestyle and her being named as prophet represent some of the life directions being chosen by women within early Christianity whose widowhood left them in an ambivalent position economically and socioculturally but with greater freedom to participate in the reign-of-God movement? Does the Lukan silencing of her voice represent an attempt to control the prophetic powers of holy women like Anna as the early Christian communities encounter the restrictions being placed on women within the empire toward the end of the first century? The imaginative answers we give to these questions raised by the story of Anna will determine how we fill in the gaps contained within her story as told by the Lukan narrator. Her story, however, provides glimpses into some of the liberating possibilities open to at least a few women within early Christianity. As we listen to Anna's story together with the other stories of widows within the Lukan writings, we recognize both powerlessness as well as potential. A recognition of this ambivalence may enable us today to be prophetically attentive to both the same powerlessness and yet potential in the lives and contexts of women and to seek the signs of liberating possibilities. The short story of Anna provokes prophetic possibilities far beyond her years, long though they were, in the Jerusalem temple. Her voice resounds today in women's prophetic consciousness.

## Retelling the Story

There was also a prophetess . . . who had lived . . . alone as a widow to the age of eighty-four. She never left the temple, but worshipped night and day with fasting and prayer. (Luke 2:36-37)

## Peace Pilgrim (?–1981)

You might have seen her as you sped past in your automobile—a small, gray-haired woman walking at the side of the road. If you were in a terrific hurry to get to your next appointment, you might not have noticed her at all. There would have been nothing to catch the attention of one so busy as you. Nothing but the tunic. On the back, in white letters, it declared,"25,000 miles on foot for peace." Was it possible that this diminutive, grandmotherly woman with her hair in a bun on the top of her head had really walked twenty-five thousand miles? Yes, and more. What would cause a woman to attempt such a thing?

As a widow, Anna personifies the characteristics of the office of the faithful widow that developed in the early church, as described in 1 Tim. 5:3-16. Anna fits the age requirement, being over sixty years of age, and the requirement not to remarry (1 Tim. 5:9). She also follows the pattern of devotion to God as one who "continues in supplications and prayers night and day" (1 Tim. 5:5 NRSV). (Brown, *Birth of the Messiah*, 467)

She grew up on a farm in the eastern part of the United States with no formal religious training at all. As a young woman she began to explore traditional religious teachings, and to develop a deeper sense that God had great work for her to do. For many years she did volunteer work with peace organizations. She also took time to work with people who had problems—physical as well as mental and emotional.

She came to believe that the key word for our time was "practice." She said, "We have all the Light we need. We just need to put that Light into practice!" And she set about doing that herself. Like Anna in the temple, she spent all her time in prayer and fasting. It helped her distill a message that could be easily understood by everyone. "This is the way of peace—overcome evil with good, and falsehood with truth, and hatred with love." She vowed to remain a wanderer until humankind had learned the way of peace.

On January 1, 1953, the woman set out walking across the United States. She would walk as a prayer. Walking would give her the opportunity to talk about her message of peace to everyone she met. To schoolchildren in playgrounds, men at construction sites, and women at the Laundromat, she brought the message: "Love casts out fear. Peace begins within. Seek the real Source of Peace and use the ways of peace in your relationships with others."

She walked alone and penniless. She belonged to no denomination, and had no organizational backing. If someone she met on the road offered her something to eat, she shared it with gladness. If no food was offered, she fasted. If people gave her a place to rest for the night, she was grateful for their hospitality. If no one offered, she slept under bridges, and on park benches, and under the wide night sky. She never asked for anything, always giving thanks for what God provided.

It was the height of the Cold War. People were terrified of the threat of Communism. They were searching for Communist sympathizers under every bed and in every closet. Senator Joseph McCarthy's investigations had the

Origen (third century C.E.) referred to Anna as an exemplar of virtuous womanhood: "Women, look on Anna's testimony and imitate it. If it ever happens to you that you lose your husbands, ponder what Scripture has said of Anna. 'For seven years from her virginity she lived with her husband,' and so on. For that reason she was a prophetess. The Holy Spirit did not dwell on her accidentally or by chance. It is a good thing, and first in value, if a woman can possess the grace of virginity. If she cannot do this, but she happens to lose her husband, let her persevere as a widow." (*Homilies on Luke* 17)

power to ruin people's lives just by suggestion and innuendo. Many powerful people considered it an act of treason to mention peace at all.

The woman knew that her mission would be misunderstood by some. A few people taunted her and made fun of her. She was occasionally arrested for vagrancy. Finally she was picked up for questioning by the FBI.

To protect her family from harassment, she refused to give her name. She said, "A pilgrim is a wanderer with a purpose. I am a pilgrim, a pilgrim for peace." When the authorities pressed her for her name, she said, "Your may call me Pilgrim for that is what I am. Peace Pilgrim. It is name enough for me." The FBI released her and she resumed her journey.

One day as Peace Pilgrim was walking down the road, an expensive car stopped beside her. The anxious driver told her he thought it was wonderful that she was following her calling. She replied, "I certainly think that everyone should be doing what he or she feels is the right thing to do."

The fretful man began to tell her what he felt he was being lead to do. It was a good thing that very much needed doing. She became very enthusiastic about his idea and took it for granted that he was already busy with doing this good work. She said, "That's wonderful! How are you getting along with it?"

The unhappy driver replied, "Oh, I'm not doing it. That kind of work doesn't pay anything!"

On another day, another luxury car stopped. The well-dressed couple inside began to talk to her about her work. When she explained to them that she was walking across the country talking to people about living more peaceful lives, the man in the car began to weep. He said, "You have done so much for peace, and I have done so little."

When she began her journey, she wore a navy blue tunic with letters that read, "Walking Coast to Coast for Peace." Later it would say, "Walking 10,000 Miles for World Disarmament." And then "25,000 Miles On Foot for Peace."

In Washington, D.C., in 1964, she decided to stop counting miles. She had walked more than twenty-five thousand miles in eleven years. She said she didn't want anyone to think she was bragging. She would walk for another seventeen years, criss-crossing the United States and Canada seven times, influencing the lives of hundreds of thousands of people.

On July 7, 1981, Peace Pilgrim died instantly in a head-on collision as she was being driven to a speaking engagement at a church near Knox, Indiana. People all over the world were stunned to hear this woman of wisdom and humor had been taken from us.

The day before her death, she was interviewed by Ted Hayes of radio station WKVI in Knox. In the interview he said to her, "You seem to be a most happy woman." Peace Pilgrim replied, "I certainly am a happy person. How could one know God and not be joyous?" *(Elizabeth Ellis)*

Anna is modeled after other female prophets in the Bible, such as Miriam (Exod. 15:20), Deborah (Judg. 4:4), Huldah (2 Kings 22:14), and Isaiah's wife (Isa. 8:3). Paired with Simeon, she also fulfills the biblical description of the messianic age, that both "sons and daughters will prophesy" (Joel 2:28, quoted by Luke in Acts 2:17). She is especially close to Judith, whose story is told in the apocryphal book of Judith (second century B.C.E.). Like Luke's story of Jesus, the book of Judith tells of God's deliverance of Israel not through the strong and powerful but through the meek and lowly. Like Anna, Judith was a widow who devoted her life to the service of God (Jdt. 8:1-8). After Israel was delivered, she gave thanks in a song of praise (Jdt 15:14–16:17), much like Anna does in Luke's story. (Brown, *Birth of the Messiah,* 441, 466-68)

# Peter's Mother-in-Law

*Peter's mother-in-law is healed and called to serve.*

## The Story

Jesus then went to Peter's house and found Peter's mother-in-law in bed with fever. So he took her by the hand; the fever left her, and she got up and attended to his needs.

## Comments on the Story

Apart from the brief reference to Mary in the Matthean infancy narrative, this is the first story of a woman within this narrative. It is located within chapters 8–9 of the Gospel which, in keeping with the Matthean narrative tendency to form collections of similar material, is a collation of ten miracle stories. This collection is, in turn, interspersed with small teaching sections between the first and second group of three miracles (8:16-22) and the second and third group that concludes with four miracle stories (9:9-17). This story of Peter's mother-in-law concludes the first group of three stories and provides one frame to the first of the teaching sections. It is, therefore, strategically placed in the narrative.

It is an exceptionally brief story—two verses only—and often it is virtually subsumed into the summary of healings and their interpretation in 8:16-17. It concludes a group of three healing stories—of a leper; a centurion's servant; and a woman. Readers/hearers are shaped, therefore, to understand this story simply as another healing and a brief one at that, which flows readily into the summary.

Those attentive to the telling of this story, however, may have noted some of its unusual features, especially Jesus' taking the initiative in this healing when usually the supplicant or others on behalf of the supplicant approach the healer or miracle worker. The story states explicitly that Jesus "saw" [REB: "found"] Peter's mother-in-law and responded by reaching out to touch her. Several verses later, the listener would have heard a similar pattern. Jesus "saw" Matthew sitting at the tax office and responded by calling him to follow (9:9). The pattern of these two stories is very similar except for the statement of the fever leaving the woman (8:15).

It would seem that we have a combination of two story-types and that the story of the healing of Peter's mother-in-law may have been told in different communities in different ways. The call story (4:18-22; 9:9) and the simple

47

healing story format (request; response; report) no doubt shaped the early stages of remembering Jesus and making meaning of that remembering. Whatever the event in Capernaum, it seems that some storytellers told of an encounter between Jesus and Peter's mother-in-law in terms of a call to discipleship—Jesus sees her; reaches out to touch her to call her forth; and she responds by arising and serving. Whether this was initially simply a call story and the healing aspect was incorporated later or whether it was told initially as a combination of story-types is almost impossible to establish. One imaginative conclusion we may draw, however, is that this story may have originated in women's storytelling circles and that the Matthean version of the story (Mark's and Luke's accounts differ in emphases and structure) has been faithful to their remembering a woman's call to discipleship.

For those who heard the story as a call story, it forms a fitting link between two healing stories and the healing aspect of this story (8:1-15) and the buffer section (8:16-22) that combines a summary and interpretation of Jesus' healing and stories of the cost of discipleship. The most extraordinary aspect of the choice of the call story-type, however, is that it is the only one of its kind—a woman called to discipleship using the formulaic story-type—in the canonical Gospels. Features of the story enhance its interpretation.

### Retelling the Story

He took her by the hand; the fever left her, and she got up and attended to his needs. (Matt. 8:15)

### Jane Addams (1860–1935)

Jane Addams grew up in the town of Cedarville, Illinois, near Chicago. Her mother died when she was an infant, so she and her father were very close. Her father was a banker and state senator. Everyone knew him, even Abraham Lincoln. He was a handsome man, too. Whenever little Jane went places with her father she was always careful to walk a little way behind him. She felt sorry that he had such a plain little girl. She hoped people would not realize she was his daughter. Jane had been born with curvature of the spine. Her back was bent and crooked, so she was badly pigeon-toed and held her head at an odd angle.

One day Jane and her father were riding together through the poorest section of Cedarville. She looked out the window at the run-down neighborhood. She thought about the lovely tree-lined street where she lived in the finest house in town. "Father," she asked, "why do these people live in such horrid little houses?"

"They live here because they are poor," her father replied. "These people work at jobs where they make very little money, or they have no jobs at all.

These little houses are the best they can get with the money that they have. Being poor makes life very hard. Not everyone is as fortunate as we are."

They rode together in silence for a while. Then Jane said, "When I grow up I am going to live in a great big house."

Her father nodded. "Yes, Jane, I imagine you will."

A beautiful smile transformed the little girl's plain face. "When I grow up I am going to live in a great big house in the middle of little ones like these, and I will invite everyone in the neighborhood to come and play in my nice yard!" Jane's father smiled, but he could not help wondering what his daughter's health would be like in the future.

When Jane finished college, she decided to become a doctor. She enrolled in the Women's Medical College of Philadelphia. The course work was very physically demanding. The curvature of the spine from which she had suffered all her life became more serious. She was in constant pain. At last she was sent to the hospital for surgery. It would be six months before she would be allowed to try to walk again.

Mr. Addams said, "Jane, I know you are heartbroken to give up your dream of becoming a doctor. But it is out of the question now."

Jane said, "Surely if I have some time to rest, I will regain my strength. Then I can return to school."

"No, Jane. The doctor says you must have two years of complete rest. Even then you will not be able to return to medical school. Any strenuous activity in the future and you will become crip-

When first-century listeners heard this story, would they have thought it normal or extraordinary for Peter's mother-in-law to serve Jesus? That is to say, was it common for a matron of the house to serve men at the guest table in a private home? In a wealthy Roman household the wife was expected to oversee the preparation of food for the family (Columella, *De Re Rustica* 12.3.8 [ca. 60 C.E.]; from Fantham, 379). Serving at the table, however, was usually a task for servants. Listeners who heard this story might compare it with their own backgrounds. Those who came from upper-class backgrounds where household chores were done by servants would find the actions of Peter's mother-in-law to be extraordinary, because she was taking on the role of a servant. Those who came from more modest backgrounds in which household servants were not so common would find her actions to be admirable but not abnormal. In either case, she would represent a model of hospitality and, metaphorically, since she was serving Jesus, a model of Christian service. In either case, it should also be noted that she, not Peter, is the one whose role it is to serve at the table.

pled." He put his hand on her shoulder. "Jane, the doctor says you must resign yourself to the life of an invalid." Jane turned her face to the wall and wept.

Her father sent her to Europe to recuperate. Perhaps Jane would be strong enough to attend the opera or visit some museums. These things held no interest for Jane, however. She spent her little strength touring the slums and ghettos of each city she visited.

In London, she visited Toynbee Hall, the world's first settlement house. It was not a mission for handouts, but a center for the poor to better their lives through education. Jane came away with her head spinning with questions.

Later she would have a vision. God had work for her to do. The poor needed her. She was not to be Lady Bountiful, dispensing charity to those below her. She was not to do things for people, but rather with them. The only way to truly help people would be to share their lives as an equal. That would be her life's work: she would buy a house in the slums and live in it to be there with the poor. From that moment, Jane began getting well.

Jane returned to Chicago and began searching through the hovels and tenements for the right location. At 335 South Halsted Street she found it, a great barn of a house that had seen better days. Because it had once belonged to the Hull family, she kept the name and called it Hull House.

At first the neighbors were suspicious of Jane and her friends. What were they doing there? What did they want? Gradually they learned that these women could be counted on in emergencies, like being out of work or having a sick child or having to go to court. Jane had never worked harder in her entire life, but still her health improved.

She took time to think about how to be of real help to the poor. It was good to assist with emergencies, but why not put a stop to the causes of the emergencies? Where to begin? At the beginning, of course. A healthy baby would not become a sickly child. Jane started classes to teach mothers better infant care and well-baby clinics to provide preventive medicine. A person with skills to sell would not be out of work, so she began English classes and vocational training. Busy children did not break windows or laws. So she began clubs for boys and girls that offered interesting things to do. Little by little, she identified the needs of the neighborhood. More and more people supported her work with their money or their time.

Jane toured the neighborhood with her clipboard, taking note of all the uncollected garbage. She took her concerns to the city sanitation office, but the bureaucrats only laughed at her. No city really provided the services in slum neighborhoods that were available in the rest of the city! They ordered her to leave. She did, but only long enough to get herself elected garbage inspector. After that she would personally follow the trucks to see that every neighborhood was free of refuse. For the first time there was no stench in the neighborhood around Hull House.

Jane knew that a good education for every child was the way to put an end to the cycle of poverty. However, her experience with the schools was not much different than her experience with the garbage collectors. In the area around Hull House there were three thousand more children of school age than there were seats in the schools. "Why bother providing them desks?" the school leaders asked her. "Most of the kids in a neighborhood like this don't deserve to come to school anyway." Jane responded by running for the Chicago School Board. She would spend years raising the level of education for all the city's children.

As the interest in Hull House and its programs grew, Jane turned her attention to changing laws that effected the lives of the poor. She pressured the Illinois state legislature to enact laws ending child labor. She worked to pass schooling laws. She worked for factory safety standards, sanitary codes, day nurseries, adult education, free employment bureaus, and juvenile courts. There was hardly a reform not propelled by the endless energy of Jane Addams.

By now more than a hundred thousand people a year were being served at Hull House. Judges and social workers would live there for months at a time to learn to work with people.

Jane Addams spent her last years working for peace and women's rights. She would come to think of them as two sides of the same coin. The Great War of 1914–18 shocked her. She asked, "How could men be so violent? Thousands of children are homeless and hungry. Didn't anyone think about the children when they started their stupid war?"

She was told, "No. Men don't think that way."

But Jane knew women did. She said, "Women should have the right to vote because they will think about the children. Women will not be so eager to

> Archaeological excavations in Capernaum have uncovered what some have identified as Peter's house. The original structure was a modest private house that was in use in the first century, at the time of the story. In the fourth century, at the time when Constantine was supporting the development of sacred sites in the Holy Land, the structure was renovated for use as a Christian memorial sanctuary. In the fifth century C.E. it was extensively remodeled and enlarged as an octagonal church. According to literary records, the fourth- and fifth-century structures were venerated by pilgrims as the site of the original house of Peter. There is no archaeological evidence to connect the original first-century house with Peter or even with Christianity. But to the fourth-century pilgrim it would still have served that purpose. Since this story is the primary biblical reference to Peter's home in Capernaum, it is quite likely that it was told or recalled by fourth- and fifth-century pilgrims who came to the site. (White, 2.152-59)

begin wars. Women will vote for peace." Jane organized the Women's International League for Peace and Freedom.

In 1931 she received the Nobel peace prize. Theodore Roosevelt called her "America's most useful citizen." Labor leader John Burns said, "She is the only saint America has produced." That was a high tribute, but to Jane it was more important that settlement houses patterned after Hull House had sprung up all over the United States. *(Elizabeth Ellis)*

# The Woman with a Hemorrhage

*A woman breaks with convention to seek healing and becomes an example of faith.*

## The Story

Just then a woman who had suffered from haemorrhages for twelve years came up from behind, and touched the edge of his cloak; for she said to herself, 'If I can only touch his cloak, I shall be healed.' But Jesus turned and saw her, and said, 'Take heart, my daughter; your faith has healed you.' And from that moment she recovered.

## Comments on the Story

Ancient storytellers, aware of the power of their art, must have recognized some of the significance of combining into a single story by way of intercalating one into the other, the healing of the woman with the hemorrhage and the raising of the synagogue leader's daughter. The young woman's restoration to life frames the older woman's restoration to health. The combined story immediately follows the second buffer story (9:9-17), which concludes with the image of new wine requiring fresh skins for preservation. The reader/hearer comes to the double miracle story, therefore, with expectations of newness, new constructs, new images in which to receive the vision of the reign of God.

One way in which newness is portrayed is by reversal of expectations. The woman with the hemorrhage is introduced into the story in the same way as is the male supplicant, father of the young woman who has just died. The focalizing word, "behold" or "look" (absent from the REB translation) is followed by a description of the person and their entry. They are contrasted, however, in a way that characterizes their own appropriation of social expectations. The synagogue leader, aware of his social status and power but also his need, comes in and kneels in front of Jesus. The woman, on the other hand, approaches from behind, seeking to mask her presence in the public arena. The male addresses Jesus directly, recognizing that if he should lay his hand on his daughter, she would live (9:18). The woman, on the other hand, makes her affirmation to herself, assuring herself that if she but touches his cloak, she would be made well (9:21). The synagogue leader then disappears from the story as he leads Jesus to his house, but the woman's story is concluded with her transformative encounter with Jesus. There is no story of the synagogue leader's transformation.

Whereas the previous story of a woman being healed in Matthew's Gospel

(8:14-15) had Jesus taking the initiative, in this story, it is the woman who takes the initiative to instigate her own healing. She steps out into the public arena, the arena that was considered the space of male power and male negotiations; and she takes action in this public space—she touches the fringe of the cloak of the Jewish teacher surrounded by eager listeners (9:18). She has broken through sociocultural and religious barriers that would render her powerless. The restriction of women to private space (which may have worked more as a culturally controlling expectation than practice for many poorer women who needed to take their place in the market or other workplaces in order to survive) is subverted by this woman's presence in the public arena, among the crowd around Jesus. She crosses gender barriers by reaching out to touch the fringe of the male teacher's cloak (9:20). If her bleeding is vaginal (which the story does not make clear), then she has also subverted ritual purity boundaries that render her and all she touches unclean. She is a woman of courage whose desire for healing empowers her to reach across cultural and religious boundaries to claim healing for her own body.

The Matthean story is brief by comparison to that of Mark and Luke, and the reader must fill in the gaps toward a coherent narrative. This is particularly so in relation to the response of Jesus. As narrated, he simply turns and sees her just as he saw Peter's mother-in-law in the previous healing. This woman, however, has taken the initiative and crossed the boundaries that create the space in which Jesus too can cross similar boundaries. He recognizes and acknowledges the extraordinary power of the woman's faith and proclaims that it is her faith that has made her well. He does not pronounce healing words that take the power to himself, but simply acknowledges the power of female faith. The story concludes with the simple statement "and instantly the woman was made well" (9:22 NRSV; REB: "recovered").

Three times in these three short verses, the verb "to save" or "to liberate" is used and translated as "healed" and "recovered." The narrative, therefore, focuses attention on the process of healing or saving from bodily affliction. It is an action normally attributed to Jesus [see 1:21 where the name of Jesus is explained as the one who will save]. In this story, however, it is a power claimed by a woman whose gender and status governed by socioreligious and cultural restrictions should have rendered her powerless. And yet she claims her own healing by way of a courageous and dangerous act in the public arena and it is this action that is named faith by Jesus.

The vision of the reign of God or God's kingdom recognizes women's power and their right to participate fully in all that leads to life. Jesus, representative of the divine in the midst of the people (1:23) is presented as the direct source of salvation for women's movement toward wholeness. Jesus does not require the woman to present an offering to the priest as he does the leper (Matt. 8:4; cf. Lev. 15:28-30). She is simply made well or saved.

While the story is silent in regard to reactions to such a healing, one can imagine that it was actions such as this that rendered Jesus a *skandalon* or stumbling block to the religious leaders. His vision of the reign of God and his actions toward actualizing it challenged and even broke open religious and culturally constructed boundaries. In the case of this story, it is the woman with the hemorrhage, the suffering one, who demonstrates to Jesus that such boundary breaking is both possible and indeed necessary for God's vision for humanity to be realized.

### Retelling the Story

But Jesus turned and saw her, and said, 'Take heart, my daughter; your faith has healed you.' And from that moment she recovered. (Matt. 9:22)

### Elizabeth Cady Stanton (1815–1902)

The whole Cady household was hushed with grief. Eleven-year-old Elizabeth had never felt such sorrow. Her only brother Eleazer was dead. Nothing the doctors tried had been able to save him. Elizabeth was greatly moved by the sight of her father sitting in the dark, with his head in his hands, broken down with grief. She knew how much he had loved his only son. She knew that he planned to take him into his law practice.

She felt moved to do something to comfort her father. She slipped silently up to his chair and put her arms around his neck. For a moment, he held her close and stroked her hair. A long anguished moan came from his lips, and he said, "Oh, my daughter, I wish that you were a son."

"I will try to be all my brother was," she cried out.

Eleazer had been a college student, so Elizabeth decided to continue her education. Since she had completed what little education was offered to girls, she asked her minister to teach her Greek and mathematics. She found her father's office was an agreeable place to study. She loved to sit there for hours poring over her books and listening as he advised his clients. Nearly all of them were men. Occasionally women would

It is likely that the hearer of this story would have identified this woman's condition with the state of uncleanness described in Lev. 15:25: "If a woman has a prolonged discharge of blood not at the time of her menstruation, or if her discharge continues beyond the period of menstruation, her impurity will last all the time of her discharge; she will be unclean as during the period of her menstruation." This meant that anyone who touched her would also be rendered unclean. (Lev. 15:19-24)

come to her father's office. When they did they always seemed to leave in tears. Elizabeth couldn't help wondering why.

One morning Elizabeth was surprised to see a prominent woman named Flora Campbell enter her father's office. She knew Mrs. Campbell because Elizabeth had accompanied her mother on social calls to Mrs. Campbell's home.

Mrs. Campbell came straight to the point. "Mr. Cady, I am in desperate need of your legal advice. As you know, I brought considerable wealth to my marriage, but it is gone now. My husband has spent everything. He drinks and gambles, and has used the money so foolishly. Now he says he is going to sell my parents' house. It is all I have left. I came to ask you to help me keep him from doing that. There must be some way you can stop him!"

"Unfortunately, there is not," the lawyer replied. "The law is very clear. A married woman owns nothing. Her husband controls everything. Even the clothes on her back are his to do with as he will."

Elizabeth saw a tear streak down Flora Campbell's face. "What am I going to do?" she asked. "He won't even give me money to buy food for the children."

"I am sure my wife would be able to use some help with the washing and the housework. That at least would give you money to buy food. But you should try to keep him in the dark about it for as long as possible, for the law says he is entitled to possession of all your earnings." Flora Campbell began to weep in earnest. Mr. Cady rose and walked with her toward the door. "I am sorry I am not able to be of greater assistance," he said.

Elizabeth's father returned to his office to find her ripping pages out of his law books. "What are you doing?" he demanded.

"Every woman who comes here to see you always leaves in tears," his daughter replied furiously. "If the laws are so unfair to women, I want to tear them out of the books."

"Tearing up my law books will not help the women. The only way to do that is to get the state legislature in Albany to change the laws." Daniel Cady would soon forget what had been said that day, but it would burn in Elizabeth's mind for years.

Eleazer's school, Union College, refused Elizabeth admission because she was female. It was a bitter blow because she had worked so hard to learn all the necessary requirements, excelling at both Greek and Latin. It was the first of many such rejections. She was unable to find any college that would admit a woman.

Restless and bored with life at home, she became a frequent visitor in the home of her cousin Gerrit Smith. His house was always filled with thoughtful earnest folk who supported new ideas like temperance and the abolition of slavery. It was there she met reformer Henry Brewster Stanton. Love bloomed quickly between them.

Their wedding trip took them to London to attend the World Antislavery Congress, where Henry was a delegate. Elizabeth was eager to observe the proceedings, and excited to learn there would be seven women delegates from the United States in attendance. The organizers, however, were horrified by the women's presence and refused them admittance. A furious debate raged on the convention floor. Many of the male delegates believed that admitting women would open them up to public ridicule. Others believed it was hypocritical to address the rights of Negroes while denying the rights of women. Finally the women were admitted. They had to sit in the balcony behind a screen that made it difficult to see or hear, and they were not allowed to speak out during the proceedings.

The men who banished them to the balcony had no idea of the opportunity they were creating. Delegate Lucretia Mott and Elizabeth Cady Stanton had never met; now they would spend days together behind that screen discussing the need to reform the laws that restricted the lives of women. Before they left London they had pledged to hold their own meeting.

In 1848 in the small town of Seneca Falls, New York, Elizabeth and Lucretia organized the Women's Rights Convention, the first in the history of the world. Elizabeth read the Declaration of Sentiments that she had patterned after the Declaration of Independence. "We hold these truths to be self-evident, that all men and women are created equal. . . ." Revolutionary ideas were addressed: women should have the right to control their own money and property; they should share in the guardianship of their children; education and careers should be open to them. At the end of the meeting, Elizabeth proposed an idea that shocked even Lucretia Mott: women should be given the right to vote.

Newspapers ridiculed the women. Ministers denounced them from the pulpit. Elizabeth's father was so upset that he came to her home to see if she had suffered a mental breakdown. While he was relieved to see that she was still sane, he told her, "My child, I wish you had waited until I was under the sod before you had done this foolish thing!" He disinherited her.

Elizabeth was greatly upset by her father's actions, but she put all her energy into raising her family and working to gain acceptance for women's rights. One by one, other states began to hold women's rights conventions. More and more women supported her ideas.

In 1854, Elizabeth was asked to address the New York state legislature on the need for changes in the laws. She received a sternly worded letter from her father to stop at his house on her way to Albany. He told her, "If you persist in this folly you will embarrass me publicly. No decent woman would wish to speak before a group of men. The idea is unthinkable." When she refused to give in, he lost his temper.

Elizabeth responded, "You are to blame. I am what you made me. You are the one who taught me to follow my conscience. You are the one who first made me aware of the terrible inequities in the law."

Judge Cady stared at her for a long time when she finished speaking. Finally he said, "Read me your speech." With a wavering voice she shared with him what she had written. He nodded his head, "It is a good speech. Well written. But we will need to close up some loopholes." Her father proceeded to give her exact legal statutes to cover every issue she had raised.

She would have to appear before the legislature a second time, but this time they would agree to give women everything she requested: the rights to own property, to collect wages, to sue and be sued, to share in the management of their children. They would give women everything she requested . . . except the right to vote. She would spend the rest of her life trying to accomplish that.

When she was eighty-seven years old, she wrote a letter to President Theodore Roosevelt urging him to be the leader who would open the door for women. She died while writing it. It would be eighteen more years before the Nineteenth Amendment would be ratified, but it would never have occurred without Elizabeth Cady Stanton. *(Elizabeth Ellis)*

> This woman later became famous in Christian lore. Eusebius, the church historian (fourth century C.E.), says she was from Caesarea Philippi and that a statue of her still stood there in his day along with an herb growing at its base that possessed healing powers (*Ecclesiastical History* 7.18). In *Acts of Pilate* 7 (third century C.E.), she is identified as Bernice, or, in Latin, Veronica. This same Veronica is then said to have been the woman who wiped sweat from the brow of Jesus when he stumbled while carrying the cross through the streets of Jerusalem. Later she found that the image of Jesus had been miraculously imprinted on the cloth she used. (Davies and Allison, 2.127 n. 20)

# The Official's Daughter

*A young girl is restored to life.*

## The Story

EVEN as he spoke, an official came up, who bowed before him and said, 'My daughter has just died; but come and lay your hand on her, and she will live.' Jesus rose and went with him, and so did his disciples.

· · · · · · · · · · · · · · · · · · · · · · · · ·

When Jesus arrived at the official's house and saw the flute-players and the general commotion, he said, 'Go away! The girl is not dead: she is asleep'; and they laughed at him. After turning them all out, he went into the room and took the girl by the hand, and she got up. The story became the talk of the whole district.

## Comments on the Story

One of the contrasts between the woman suffering from the hemorrhage (Matt. 9:20-22) and the official's daughter (Matt. 19:18-19, 23-26) is that the hemorrhaging woman is an active character in the narrative while the young woman is passive except for her final action of rising up from her deathbed (9:25). The two women are, on the other hand, paralleled with the bleeding woman being described as having "suffered from haemorrhages for twelve years" (9:20) and the young woman as having "just died" (9:18). In a similar vein, the hemorrhaging woman says to herself that if she takes the action of touching the cloak of Jesus she will be healed, while the young woman's father says to Jesus that if he takes the action of laying hands on his daughter then she shall be made to live. The two stories are clearly paralleled and one interprets the other even though Matthew does not include the Markan parenthetical reference to the young woman being "twelve years old" (Mark 5:42), which parallels the twelve years of the woman's hemorrhage.

One of the ways in which this story may be read is in terms of its pointing toward and helping to interpret the death and resurrection of Jesus. One sees aspects of that death written on the body of this young woman (and the bleeding woman with whom her story is associated).

In the father's request, there is a belief that it is possible that Jesus, who has demonstrated that he shares in God's healing and life-restoring powers, is able to restore his daughter to life. In a similar way, Jesus will indicate that he will be put to death and then raised on the third day (16:21; 17:22; 20:18-19) by the

59

same life-restoring power of God in which he shares. Just as Jesus follows the official to his house where his daughter has just died, so too Jesus is led away after the soldiers (and possibly also Simon of Cyrene) to the place of his own death (27:31, 32). Those around the place of death mock Jesus as he interprets the young girl's death as sleeping (9:24) just as others will mock Jesus and his interpretation of his own death (27:40, 42-43, 47-49). The young girl's story prefigures and configures the death of Jesus.

Another interesting aspect of this story from the point of view of the young woman (which is not given in the story and which we have to construct) is that she is introduced to the story under the care of her father who seeks her restoration to life. In the Matthean story, however, her restoration to life does not necessarily entail her restoration to her patriarchal family, under the authority and control of her father. She stands alone in the story. The narrator simply says that the young girl "got up." Just as the hemorrhaging woman was not incorporated into the ritual system following her cleansing, so too the young woman is not incorporated back into the familial or kinship system. This image would have been a strong one in a culture in which women, in particular, were deeply embedded in a kinship system regardless of the religious affiliation of the group to which they belonged. While early Christianity was not able to radically change the culture of the Greco-Roman world in which it made its home, it did seek in its storytelling to offer alternative images to the prevailing culture—images that arose either from an alternative imagination or from alternative practices within their emerging house-churches or both.

Another aspect of this text to explore is its transmission within the context of women's storytelling. It seems that the story may have been retained within the Matthean communities in its early starkness of telling, not accumulating many of the narrative details that both this and its intercalated story of the woman with the hemorrhage have in both Mark and Luke. The starkness of the story lies in its image of female resurrection or resuscitation. In a male-centered culture in which incarnation and resurrection were both associated with maleness, the story of the restoration to life of a young woman offered more inclusive imagery to the community, especially to its women. To tell of the restoration of a life is to claim the value and meaning of that life. The restoration of the young woman's life and her standing alone before the rest of her life could have functioned for women as a very powerful symbol of the value of their lives. It may have been told by them, therefore, in its simplicity and starkness in order that its message might not be obscured.

This is another story of a woman without a name, this time a young woman perhaps no more than twelve years of age, a woman at the dangerous and anomalous stage of moving into availability for marriage, which, according to the patriarchal culture, will mean a transition from the house of her father to the house of her husband. In her own body, it means the transition from childhood to womanhood. Transitions were considered dangerous periods and in this story the transition is associated with death itself. Jesus the healer restores the young woman not only to life but to a life symbolized by her aloneness at the close of the narrative as freed from cultural confines. Her story, together with that of the woman freed from the hemorrhage, were life-giving stories for women in early Christianity and for men who also sought to bring about the new structures that Jesus and the reign-of-God movement envisaged as possible.

## Retelling the Story

> When Jesus arrived at the official's house and saw the flute-players and the general commotion, he said, 'Go away! The girl is not dead: she is asleep'; and they laughed at him. (Matt. 9:23-24)

### Laura Bridgman (1829–1889)

Mr. Bridgman was a prosperous farmer and not one to be taken lightly, but he was in awe of the famous visitor now sitting in their parlor. He cleared his throat nervously before he began. "As you know, our two older daughters died in the scarlet fever epidemic back in 1831. Laura here was only two at the time. Her fever was so high for such a long time, she lost her powers of sight, hearing, and speech."

Dr. Samuel Gridley Howe, the director of the famous Perkins Institute for the Blind, nodded. "That is what I understood from the newspaper article I read about your daughter. How old is Laura now?" He looked curiously at the little girl sitting on the floor at her mother's feet. She was silent and still, but there was an unmistakable intelligence about her face.

"She is seven now," responded Mr. Bridgman.

"I have come to ask you if I might take Laura to my school. I believe I

The flute players and others causing a "general commotion" when Jesus arrives were the mourners, most of whom would have been women. Women had major roles to play in the funeral ritual. They were charged with the task of washing the body and laying it out for the mourning, a process that had evidently already taken place in this story. They also took primary responsibility for the mourning process itself. Indeed, the wailing of women mourners, often accompanied by tearing at the hair, was a centuries-long custom throughout the Mediterranean. Flute players, who provided music for the funeral dirge, were also usually women, although in this story Matthew uses a masculine term for flute players. (Davies and Allison, 2.130-31)

may be able to communicate with her. Perhaps I can even teach her to communicate with others."

Mr. Bridgman stood up abruptly. "Doctor, don't be silly. Look at the child. She cannot be taught. She cannot understand anything. She follows her mother around the house all day, holding an old boot! She does not even understand that it is not a fit plaything."

Dr. Howe replied, "I know it sounds impossible. There have been many cases where people have tried to reach children like this. I admit to you that all of them have failed. But, I have corresponded with many of these teachers. I believe that I can take the best of their ideas and add some of my own. Perhaps the Lord will show me a way to succeed where others have failed."

Laura's father was pacing about the parlor in a state of agitation. "Doctor Howe, the child cannot be controlled here in her own home. How could she possibly go to your school? I do not mean to be disrespectful to a gentleman as distinguished as yourself, but what you propose is ridiculous."

Laura's mother had been listening so quietly, both men were startled when she spoke. "You say I lost two daughters in the scarlet fever epidemic. I say I lost three. A child who cannot hear or see or speak might as well be dead! Every day I watch Laura drift farther and farther into the blackness and silence that is so much like a tomb. She has withdrawn from our world completely."

"She still responds when I stomp my feet on the floor in front of her," Mr. Bridgman said angrily.

"True," replied his wife. Then softly she added, "But, for how much longer?"

Doctor Howe seized the moment. "I cannot promise you that I can help her, but please let me try."

Slowly Mr. Bridgman nodded his consent.

When Dr. Howe returned to the Perkins Institute for the Blind, Laura went with him. She was quite bewildered at first by the change in her environment. After a short time, she grew content and began the process of exploring her new dwelling. Doctor Howe wrote to her mother, "Her little hands are continually stretched out, and her tiny fingers are in constant motion, like the feelers of an insect."

The teachers at Perkins did everything they could to stimulate Laura and try to reach her. When she did something well, they patted her on the head. When she made a mistake, they tapped her elbow. There was no Braille or sign language as yet, so they put raised letters on all the objects in Laura's new environment. Every fork and piece of furniture were labeled. Before long Laura could match the labels to the objects although she seemed to have little understanding of what it meant. One day, after only a few weeks, she made the connection. Doctor Howe watched in awe the look of wonder and delight that crossed her face.

He ran to her and began to pat her head. "Yes, Laura, yes," he said out loud. "They are words! They mean something!" Then he realized that he was patting her head too hard in his enthusiasm. He began to gently stroke her hair, and then the learned doctor began to weep.

Doctor Howe wrote, "She perceived that here was a way by which she could make herself up a sign of anything that was in her own mind, and show it to another mind; and at once her countenance lighted up with a human expression. It was no longer a dog or parrot—it was an immortal spirit, eagerly seizing upon a new link of union with other spirits!"

Laura learned to write on grooved paper. After that, she wrote to her family regularly. It took years, but she learned to write poetry and even wrote an autobiography. She learned life skills, too: cleaning, sewing, and knitting.

Although she often went to visit her family, she lived the remainder of her life at the Perkins Institute; first as a student, then as a teacher. On open house days at the Institute, crowds of people would come to visit the school just to watch Laura sew or write letters.

One of the people who came to visit Laura was the English author Charles

The official requests that Jesus "lay [his] hand on her" to heal his daughter (9:18). Healing by touch was a common feature in ancient miracle stories, for it was thought that touch transferred power in some way from the healer to the one being healed. The first-century pagan miracle worker Apollonius of Tyana healed by touch (Philostratus, *Life of Apollonius* 4.45 [third century C.E.]) as did Pyrrhus, whose "divine power" was said to be transferred by the touch of his foot (Plutarch, *Pyrrhus*, 3.7-9 [second century C.E.]). In the Gospels touch is used by Jesus to heal fever (Mark 1:31), leprosy (Mark 1:41), dumbness (Mark 7:33), blindness (Mark 8:23), as well as the hemorrhaging of the woman in the previous story, and, in the story of the official's daughter, death. In Mark's version of this story, words of healing are also spoken. Here in Matthew it is the touch alone that heals. (Theissen, 62)

Dickens. His book *American Notes* was published in 1843. In it, he wrote of her: "Self-elected saints with gloomy brows, this sightless, earless, voiceless child may teach you lessons you will do well to follow. Let that poor hand of hers lie gently on your hearts."

People all over the world came to know Laura Bridgman through the articles Dr. Howe wrote about her. Her progress was followed with great interest by educators in America, Canada, and Europe. Many of them began to use the methods of the Perkins Institute in their own work with disabled students.

Even after her death from pneumonia at the age of sixty, Laura continued to influence the education of children with special needs. A doctor conducted an anatomical study of her brain that was cited in textbooks for decades. One of the students who would learn much from Laura's case during her own training at the Perkins Institute was Anne Sullivan—who would go on to work with an even more famous student: Helen Keller. *(Elizabeth Ellis)*

# MATTHEW 14:1-12

# Herodias and Salome

*Herodias and Salome use their power as women to bring down a rival:*
*John the Baptist.*

### The Story

I⊤ was at that time that reports about Jesus reached Herod the tetrarch. 'This is John the Baptist,' he said to his attendants; 'he has been raised from the dead, and that is why these miraculous powers are at work in him.'

Now Herod had arrested John, put him in chains, and thrown him into prison, on account of Herodias, his brother Philip's wife; for John had told him: 'You have no right to her.' Herod would have liked to put him to death, but he was afraid of the people, in whose eyes John was a prophet. But at his birthday celebrations the daughter of Herodias danced before the guests, and Herod was so delighted that he promised on oath to give her anything she asked for. Prompted by her mother, she said, 'Give me here on a dish the head of John the Baptist.' At this the king was distressed, but because of his oath and his guests, he ordered the request to be granted, and had John beheaded in prison. The head was brought on a dish and given to the girl; and she carried it to her mother. Then John's disciples came and took away the body, and buried it; and they went and told Jesus.

### Comments on the Story

Herodias and her daughter (named Salome in Josephus's *Antiquities* 18.5.4) are deeply embedded characters. They are embedded first of all in a story about Herod and his desire to put John the Baptist to death. They are also embedded within the Herodian familial structure. Herodias is introduced as his (Herod's) brother Philip's wife (14:3); and the language of John the Baptist's disapproval denotes possession—"It is not lawful for you to have her" [14:4 NRSV; REB: "You have no right to her"]. Salome, on the other hand, is a more ambiguous character in the story, and is linked to Herodias as her daughter; but she too is embedded in the patriarchal familial structure by this very relationship.

The story in Matthew's Gospel, as in Mark's, is a flashback during the developing ministry of Jesus, which recounts the earlier beheading of John the Baptist. The beheading is incorporated into the Gospel story by way of Herod's supposition that the reports he is hearing of Jesus' ministry suggest that John, whom he put to death, has been raised from the dead. The key characters in the story, therefore, are Herod, John, and Jesus. The readers are given Herod's per-

65

spective and that of the narrator, and it is Herod who desires to put John to death, not Herodias as in the Markan story. Herodias and Salome are embedded, therefore, in a story of male dominance and power, in this instance, over other males. Matthew 14:1-12 is a story of male political power and honor and its effect in the life of John which, in turn, prefigures the effect of the same type of power in the life of Jesus. As John's fate was in the hands of Herod, Jesus' fate will later lie in the hands of Pilate, and in that story as in this, a woman's word is introduced (14:8; cf. 27:19). The Matthean author seems to have established a parallel between the two.

Herodias, in the Matthean account, does not even appear in the narrative but is a shadow character behind the scenes, the mother who prompts her daughter and who receives the head of John the Baptist on a platter (14:8, 11). In some ways, this enhances the construction of female characters in this story. She represents the female Other, the power that can destroy a man, even bring him to death. She is behind the scenes and although one does not even hear her voice, the effect of her power is deadly. Her daughter, Salome, on the other hand, is more ambiguous as a character. She dances before Herod's company and this pleases Herod, but it is not clear whether this is an innocent dance of a young girl forced to perform by her powerful stepfather or the sensuous dance associated with woman as deceiver using her sexual powers to betray the male.

Herodias and Salome are depicted as women of power who use female power to bring about an effect they desire in the public arena that is culturally reserved as the domain of male political power. Readers would readily recall other such women in Israel's sacred story. Esther, like Salome, was able to please Artaxerxes and thereby influence him to execute Haman, thus bringing salvation to her people. Likewise, Judith used her influence to enable the beheading of Holofernes. They were, however, idealized women whose power was in the service of God's saving work in Israel. Salome and Herodias, on the other hand, symbolize negative female power in the political arena, power like that of Jezebel.

Herodias and Pilate's wife are the only two characters in the Matthean narrative who represent the public power of influential women and in each instance that power is embedded in their relationships with their husbands. Neither, however, appears as a character in the story. Herodias's words are conveyed through her daughter's request and the words of Pilate's wife are brought to him presumably by a messenger. The words of one bring about the death of John the Baptist, the words of the other fail to prevent the death of Jesus. Women's public or political power is represented in shadow and portrayed as negative or ineffective.

It is important to note by way of contrast that to this point in the story, women in the public arena have been women in need. Mary's departure to Israel and return (2:14, 21) was a necessary escape from the destructive political designs of Herod the Great, the father of Herod Antipas depicted in this story. The woman with the hemorrhage sought contact with Jesus' healing power (9:21); and later in the story another woman and daughter will enter, but but this time without power and in need, the daughter needing healing (15:22, 25).

While it could be argued that the Gospel story critiques the political power symbolized in Herod and Pilate, whether it is held by men or women, the attentive reader is aware that there is a different male public or political power that is valorized in the narrative—that of John the Baptist, Jesus, and his male disciples. There is, on the other hand, no equivalent female public political power explicitly valorized, although the attentive reader can recognize its echoes in this story and others that present the male perspective on female power.

The significant question that arises from such an attentiveness is how the women's stories would be told if we were able to hear their own voices. What would Herodias and Salome tell us of the power that was exercised over them, of the way they were used to cloak Herod's own destructive power, and of the impact on their lives of belonging to a Herodian court and being the chattel passed between brothers? What was Salome's experience of being daughter to a mother who was so used and abused? These and other questions cause us to draw on our creative imagination in order to tell the story from a different point of view, that of Herodias and Salome, and not that of Herod or a narrator with an androcentric perspective.

### Retelling the Story

Now Herod had arrested John, put him in chains, and thrown him into prison, on account of Herodias, his brother Philip's wife; for John had told him: 'You have no right to her.' (Matt. 14:3-4)

### Eleanor Roosevelt (1884–1962)

Eleanor Roosevelt took the arm of her famous uncle Theodore and waited for her bridesmaids to walk down the aisle. "I wish your father were alive to

There was a well-known oft-repeated story about a Roman proconsul that bears remarkable resemblance to the story about Herod. It illustrates how widespread were such stories about unpopular rulers, and how common was the idea that a loose woman at a banquet could generate such mischief. "Flamininus, when proconsul, was once asked a favor by a whore while dining. She said she had never seen a man's head being cut off. He had a condemned criminal killed." (Seneca, *Controversiae* 9.2 [first century C.E.]; from Corley, 41)

see this glorious day," he said. Eleanor tried to smile, but thinking of her parents always made her sad. Losing them when she was still a child had caused her childhood to be lonely and full of fear, although she realized she had been given every advantage. The Roosevelts were people of wealth and power, the cream of American aristocracy. After all, Uncle Teddy, her father's older brother, had been president of the United States for most of her childhood. Her grandmother, however, had been austere and demanding, rarely showing Eleanor any real affection.

"Your dress is lovely," continued Uncle Teddy. Again Eleanor tried to smile. She noticed he had not said she looked lovely. She had never heard anyone say that. All the members of her family were graceful, attractive people. She had been called "ugly duckling" all her life. She well knew that she had no chin; her teeth were too big; her ears protruded.

"Franklin is a fine fellow. He has a great future ahead of him," Uncle Teddy remarked. Eleanor looked toward the altar where her distant cousin Franklin Roosevelt stood. This time her smile was sincere. It lit her entire face. She was still amazed that someone so handsome and full of life had asked her to marry him. Now she would have someone to protect her and take care of her. She tightened her grip on Uncle Teddy's arm and started down the aisle toward her husband and her future.

For the most part, Eleanor would be happy in her new life. She and Franklin would have five children. Her mother-in-law would prove to be harsh and domineering, but Eleanor had many years of practice in dealing with difficult older women. She threw all her heart into her family. Slowly some of her childhood fears began to disappear.

Uncle Teddy was right about Franklin's future. It wasn't long before people began to talk about Franklin's running for public office. In 1911 he had been elected to the New York state senate. By 1913 Woodrow Wilson had appointed him assistant secretary of the navy. In 1920 he and his running mate James Cox lost the presidential election to Harding and Coolidge. His supporters were disappointed, but they vowed it was just a matter of time until he was president.

In July of 1921, Eleanor and the children traveled to Campobello Island, off the northern tip of Maine. Franklin wound up some political business and joined them a few days later. This had become their favorite time of the year. They could be together with time for leisurely reading and conversation. The hectic demands melted away, leaving Franklin free to swim and explore with the children.

One morning Eleanor watched through the window as Franklin walked back to the house from his morning swim. The cold water always made him stiff for a few minutes afterward. But this morning, the stiffness did not seem to be leaving him. There was something about his gait that startled Eleanor. She ran out on the porch, calling out, "Franklin, is something wrong?"

He replied, "My legs ache. I feel so tired. I think I'll take a nap." In all the years they had been married, she had never known her energetic husband to lie down in the daytime. Suddenly, she was afraid.

Within hours Franklin could not move his limbs. The athletic thirty-nine-year-old was paralyzed. Doctors swarmed to Campobello and confirmed Eleanor's worst fear: Franklin had polio.

Eleanor accompanied her husband back to New York. During the next two months she would rarely leave his hospital room. The doctors' prognosis was bleak. Even a partial recovery was doubtful. Slowly it became clear that Franklin would have to use a wheelchair for the rest of his life.

One morning in September, Franklin's longtime assistant, Louis Howe, came to talk to Eleanor. "We have to get Franklin back into politics. If we don't he will dry up like an old cornstalk."

"Back into politics?" Eleanor questioned. "That's impossible! Who would vote for a man who is crippled?"

"He may be crippled, but he is still the greatest man I have ever known," responded Louis. "This illness has affected his legs but not his mind. He can still be president."

"Just how do you propose to do that?" quizzed Eleanor.

"Franklin will grow stronger. He will be able to run the country from his wheelchair," replied Louis.

"But, that could take years. By then people would have forgotten Franklin," sighed Eleanor.

"You can't let that happen," responded Louis. "You must be actively engaged in politics immediately so no one will have a chance to forget Franklin."

"Oh, Louis," said Eleanor, "I could never do that. I am very shy and self-conscious. I would be far too afraid to make a speech in public."

"You owe it to your husband," answered Louis. It was a gut-wrenching decision for Eleanor, but she agreed. Soon the Roosevelt home in New York was filled with important visitors. Political dinner parties and strategy sessions were scheduled weekly. Eleanor presided over it all while Franklin participated from his wheelchair. In a few weeks Eleanor was involved in both the state Democratic Party and the Women's Trade Union. Louis Howe arranged for her to make speeches at political events. Eleanor was so frightened she thought she might faint. Her first efforts were dismal failures, but gradually she became more skilled. With greater skill came increased confidence. Eventually her plain face became a familiar one in New York political circles, but she never felt comfortable being in the spotlight.

In 1928 Franklin was elected governor of New York. Eleanor was his scout and his messenger. In 1932, in the midst of the Great Depression, Franklin Roosevelt was elected president of the United States. A newspaper reporter asked Eleanor if there would be any problems because the new president was crippled. "None," replied Eleanor. "I will be his legs."

She was as good as her word. She was everywhere: in work camps, in slums, in the factories. She came to know the country's poverty and its problems firsthand. She understood the plight of the farmers in the dust bowl and the mothers who had no food for their children. She felt the pain of the African Americans living in segregation. She could not pass or sign legislation. But she could report back to Franklin, giving him needed data. She always put a human face on it.

Mine and factory owners called her a snooper. Slum lords called her a spy. Racists throughout the nation called her names that were even worse. She was fiercely opposed by powerful men who felt she would harm the president politically. Minorities and workers, however, looked to her for help and called her friend. Slowly Franklin Roosevelt began to pull the country out of the worst depression in its history.

Marian Anderson, the most celebrated singer of her day, had appeared before the crown heads of Europe. In 1939, she was making a concert tour across the United States. Howard University decided to sponsor one of her concerts and tried to book Constitution Hall in Washington, D.C. The Daughters of the American Revolution denied them use of the hall because of Marian Anderson's race. Many fair-minded Americans were outraged, but no one seemed to know what to do about it.

Eleanor Roosevelt, a direct descendant of a signer of the Declaration of Independence, had been a member of the Daughters of the American Revolution all her adult life. Now she resigned from the D.A.R. in a letter printed in newspapers across America. The headlines announced: MRS. ROOSEVELT

> This story draws on prototypes from Jewish stories about conniving women. In the story of Esther, for example, the king is so entranced with her beauty at a banquet that he promises her anything she wants, up to half his kingdom, much like the rash promise of Herod in this story, and eventually he executes her enemy, Haman (Esth. 5:3; 7:8-10). In the story of Judith, a foreign king who is threatening the Jews is beguiled by the beauty of Judith at a banquet and, after he falls into a drunken stupor, she beheads him and thereby saves her people (Jdt. 12:10–13:10). These two women are national heroines, but in a third story, the story of Jezebel, the deceitful woman is an enemy of the prophet Elijah, just as Herodias and Salome are enemies of the new Elijah, John. Jezebel is not successful in killing Elijah, although she is responsible for the death of Naboth. She then meets a violent end appropriate to her villainous life (1 Kings 19–21; 2 Kings 9). (from Anderson and Moore, 127-30)

TAKES A STAND! She arranged for Marian Anderson to sing from the steps of the Lincoln Memorial on Easter Sunday. Over seventy-five thousand people would attend this historic musical event: half of them black, half of them white. Eleanor Roosevelt had beheaded bigotry in America.

In her autobiography, she wrote, "And having learned to stare down fear, I long ago reached the point where there is no living person whom I fear, and few challenges that I am not willing to meet." *(Elizabeth Ellis)*

# Justa, the Canaanite Woman

*A woman challenges Jesus to extend his ministry beyond religious and cultural convention.*

## The Story

JESUS then withdrew to the region of Tyre and Sidon. And a Canaanite woman from those parts came to meet him crying, 'Son of David! Have pity on me; my daughter is tormented by a devil.' But he said not a word in reply. His disciples came and urged him: 'Send her away! See how she comes shouting after us.' Jesus replied, 'I was sent to the lost sheep of the house of Israel, and to them alone.'

But the woman came and fell at his feet and cried, 'Help me, sir.' Jesus replied, 'It is not right to take the children's bread and throw it to the dogs.' 'True, sir,' she answered, 'and yet the dogs eat the scraps that fall from their master's table.' Hearing this Jesus replied, 'What faith you have! Let it be as you wish!' And from that moment her daughter was restored to health.

## Comments on the Story

This extraordinary story of a woman who challenges Jesus and through that challenge broadens Jesus' own vision of his ministry, is told in both the Markan and Matthean communities. In both narratives it is placed within a similar block of material [The "Bread Section" in Mark 6:30–8:36 and Matthew 14:13–16:12] and it immediately follows Jesus' challenging of those "traditions of the elders" or "ancient tradition" not in accord with the commandments of God (15:1-20). The story is, however, significantly developed in the Matthean retelling and it is that account that will be the focus here.

The encounter between Jesus and the woman identified geographically as Syro-Phoenician in the Markan narrative and ethnically as Canaanite in the Matthean narrative takes place on the margins, the boundaries—in geographical, ethnic, and in this story, gender demarcations. It is, therefore, a story fraught with the tensions of such a location.

The woman is introduced by the typical Matthean phrase that draws readers' attention to a person or action—"behold" or "look" (omitted in the REB). In this story she is not given a name (the extracanonical tradition calls her Justa, the just or righteous one), but she is identified as "Canaanite." This is an anachronistically ethnic designation that categorizes her as both ethnic and religious outsider from the perspective of the storyteller steeped in Israel's sacred story and from the perspective of the other characters in the narrative,

72

Jesus and the disciples. She is also a woman alone in the public arena, general-ly recognized as the arena of male activity within first-century Mediterranean culture. She is not located within a patriarchal family structure where women belong to or are within the control of either father or husband and hence are no danger. Moreover, this woman dares to raise her voice, to cry out, within this public male space. Indeed, her very story is characterized by voice, hers and Jesus' raised in dialogue or debate—a most extraordinary development within the story since this is the first time that a woman's voice has been heard [the woman with the hemorrhage simply speaks within herself; Matt. 9:21].

The cry of the woman—"Son of David! Have pity on me" (15:22)—paral-lels that of the two Jewish men seeking sight (9:27). Her statement of need—"my daughter is tormented by a devil"—echoes that of the centurion who says to Jesus, "my servant is lying at home paralysed" (8:6). What is extraordinary in this story, however, is that Jesus is portrayed as refusing to respond to the woman's plea. When this story was being told in the Matthean community, it is likely that such a response reflected a heated debate between households about women's leadership and participation in the group's liturgical life. The opposi-tion of Jesus to the woman's appeal would have reflected a position of opposi-tion to women's roles in the community's house-churches. From a narrative point of view, Jesus' ignoring of the woman shocks the reader to question whether Jesus' vision is limited by the ethnic and gender boundaries of his sociocultural and religious location. The story and its literary context (15:1-20) would certainly lead to an affirmative response to such a question, which is further confirmed by the subsequent statement of Jesus—"I was sent to the lost sheep of the house of Israel, and to them alone" (15:24, cf. 10:6).

This story highlights not only the voice given to Justa, the so-called Canaan-ite woman, but also the profound struggle that predominates. Jesus' initial rebuff by way of silence, a failure to engage with and respond to the woman, is augmented by the request of the disciples to send her away because she is cry-ing after them. In the narrative, both Jesus and the disciples, gendered within the narrative as male, stand over against the woman. The verb "to cry out" used in verse 23 and used to introduce Justa's speech in verse 22 may have evoked women's religious ritualization, which was, in some situations, charac-terized by such a crying aloud, a further indication of the genderization of this story, especially in the Matthean rendering. A third opposition is heaped upon the two already noted when Jesus highlights the boundaries of his ministry within the "house of Israel" (v. 24). This, however, creates further tension in the narrative since the story of the healing of the foreign centurion's servant has already been evoked in which Jesus points to ethnic outsiders being incor-porated into the reign of God/kingdom (8:10-13). Why not this woman and her daughter? This heaped-up and seemingly uncharacteristic resistance serves to highlight further the courageous and persistent demand of the woman. She is not intimidated by the force of male power set against her but she once again begs to be heard. Her request is in the developing theological and liturgical formulae of the community—*Kyrios* ["Lord" or REB: "Sir"] and "help me," language of the psalms. The urgency of her demand and the courage of her stand is amplified further when she refuses to be intimidated or cowered by the proverbial statement Jesus uses against her— "It is not right to take the children's bread and throw it to the dogs" (v. 26). In the context of the debate that characterizes the story, she very skillfully turns the saying back upon Jesus— "yet the dogs eat the scraps that fall from the table of their *kyrioi* [masters]" (AT). This is a skillful play upon the title given to Jesus.

The location of Jesus' vision as presented in this story within the "ancient tradition" or "traditions of the elders" (see 15:2) both in relation to ethnicity and gender boundaries is challenged by this woman who is considered outsider or foreigner. In light of the woman's challenge and the immediately preceding teachings (15:1-9), Jesus must consider what is merely human tradition and what is the word or the law of God. The response of Jesus to the woman in the language of the Matthean traditioning highlights the significance of this woman. She is of great faith in contrast to the little faith and lack of understanding of both Peter and the disciples (14:31; 16:8). What she desires on earth, Jesus sees as being in keeping with what God desires in heaven (cf. 6:10; 26:39), with the divine vision for human wholeness and life.

Justa's story stands at a pivotal point in the Matthean narrative. She significantly advances what is one of the subplots of the narrative, namely women's participation in the *basileia* (reign-of-God) mission of Jesus and their discipleship in this mission. Mary, the mother-in-law of Peter, the daughter of an unnamed official, and the woman with the hemorrhage have all been silent. The only female voice heard by the reader to this point in the story is that of the daughter of Herodias in what seems to be a traditionally genderized story of female power that threatens the political and social power of the male. While Justa's daughter is silent in the narrative, her mother speaks on her behalf. In her speaking, she gains access to the power of the *basileia*/kingdom vision as well as a place at its center for herself and her daughter and her daughter's daughter. Hers is an alternative voice, in a predominantly patriarchal narrative. Reading against the grain of this narrative, however, Justa can function not only as foremother to those outside Israel who would share in the *basileia* vision but also to those women who are claiming their own voice and their place at the center and not on the margins.

## Retelling the Story

His disciples came and urged him: 'Send her away! See how she comes shouting after us.' (Matt. 15:23*b*)

## Dorothea Dix (1802–1887)

When Dorothea Dix heard there was a man downstairs in the parlor asking to speak with her, curiosity gave wings to her feet. She trotted down the boarding house stairs as quickly as decorum would allow. There stood John Nichols from her church. Dorothea extended her hand in greeting, "Mr. Nichols, what brings you out on such a cold day?"

"I have come to ask something of you," Mr. Nichols responded. "It is an unusual request. Would you consent to lead a women's Sunday school class tomorrow?"

Dorothea chuckled, "I hardly see anything unusual about your request. As a teacher and a minister's daughter, I have been leading Sunday school classes for most of my forty years."

"It is the location that is unusual, Miss Dix. These women are prisoners in the Cambridge jail." Mr. Nichols shifted his weight nervously from one foot to the other while he waited for her response.

A jail? It was a great deal to ask. Respectable women would never go to such a place. There would be a great deal of gossip about it, Dorothea was sure of that. She smiled. "Mr. Nichols, God loves all his children," she said. "Those who have done wrong have an even greater need to hear the Word of God. I will be happy to lead the class for you."

John Nichols looked grateful and turned toward the door, but Dorothea's next question pulled him back. "Are there insane people at the Cambridge jail?"

"I have not seen them, for they are not kept with the other prisoners, but they are there," he replied.

"Oh, Mr. Nichols, I am so happy to hear that they are not housed with the prisoners. . . ."

He broke in before she could continue. "I think you misunderstand my meaning. They are not kept with the other prisoners because they are not treated nearly as well. If a person from a wealthy family is insane, they can be cared for at home by attendants or given a bed in one of the few private hospitals for their treatment. But the poor do not have those choices. They are shut away in prisons or jails. The conditions in which they live are unbelievably horrible. Everyone wants to forget about them. No one speaks out on their behalf."

Dorothea would think about his words long after he departed.

Sunday dawned, unseasonably raw for March. Dorothea dressed as warmly as possible and made her way to the forbidding stone entrance to the prison. She shared her carefully prepared Bible service with the women prisoners. The jailer was ushering her from the building when she asked to see the women who were insane.

The jailer laughed at her request, and kept moving her toward the exit. She asked again. This time his refusal was more adamant. "You want to see the crazies? What on earth for? Why, a lady like yourself shouldn't even be coming to a place like this."

Dorothea begged him. "Please," she said. "What can it hurt?"

"You don't understand," the huge jailer responded. "They are possessed. It's unnatural. It's evil."

Dorothea would not let her request be denied. Finally, the jailer shrugged and began leading her to another building at the rear of the prison. Just inside the front door, he stopped. He searched a huge ring of keys and inserted one into a trapdoor in the floor. He unlocked it and heaved it open. "Down here," was all he said.

There was no light coming from within the gaping hole in the dungeon floor, but there was a stench so strong it made Dorothea nauseated. The jailer grinned wickedly at her discomfort. That was all she needed to strengthen her resolve. He lit a torch, and she followed him closely down the stone stairs. The noise of the people shrieking and groaning became as overwhelming as the odor.

"Open one of the cells," said Dorothea.

"No," the jailer responded. "I can't do that."

Again Dorothea insisted until the man gave way. He unlocked the closest cell and stepped aside. Before her Dorothea saw a tiny cell with a mud floor. It was so cold, half the floor was covered with ice. There were two rough wooden cages. In each of them Dorothea could see the half-starved figure of a woman clothed in rags. Each woman's face was covered in dirt and her own filth. One of the women let out a scream. Dorothea jumped, her heart beating wildly. The jailer laughed. "Not a pretty sight, is it?"

When Jesus mentions casting bread to dogs, the ancient listener would not think of throwing out the trash after the meal, but rather would think of feeding the dogs under the table. Numerous meal representations in ancient Greek and Roman art show dogs present under the table even at a formal banquet. They were there evidently to eat whatever scraps fell from the table. The woman in the story picks up on the image, accepting her role as one who is not yet accepted at the table, but who nevertheless has access to table scraps. She plays the classic role of trickster in the story. That is, she overcomes her given position as the "underdog" in the story through her cleverness, a ploy practiced in countless traditional trickster tales. Well-known examples of the trickster genre include the Coyote tales in Native American tradition and the Brer Rabbit stories from the African American tradition. Trickster tales are also found in the Old Testament. (see examples in Niditch)

"Are the others that are kept here like these two?" Dorothea asked.

"Some are better," he replied, "and some are worse. Most, I guess, are about the same."

"Can't you give them some light and some heat?"

"No. If we did they'd probably set the place on fire." He shook his head at the stupidity of her question. "Besides, light and heat cost money. Who'd pay for that stuff?" And then he took her firmly by the elbow and began escorting her toward the exit. "Stupid woman," he thought to himself. "Why didn't she go home and mind her own business?"

Dorothea did go home, but she was unable to forget what she had experienced at the Cambridge, Massachusetts, prison. It was there waiting for her each time she bent her head in prayer. These poor people had done nothing wrong. They had broken no laws, but they were imprisoned like convicts, treated worse than animals. There was so much shame attached to having a family member who was mentally ill, even their own relatives had forsaken them. They had no one to speak for them.

Dorothea kept thinking about the passage from her Bible that read, "Inasmuch as ye have done it unto one of the least of these my brethren, ye have done it unto me" (Matt. 25:40 KJV). Surely these pitiful creatures were "the least of these." Dorothea would speak for them.

She spent the next eighteen months going into places most genteel women did not want to know existed. She traveled the length and breadth of the state of Massachusetts searching out the mentally ill, cataloging them and the conditions in which they were kept. No jail or prison or poorhouse was omitted. She found the mentally ill in cells and cages, closets and cellars. Powerful people tried to prevent her investigation; she refused to be stopped. Many people tried to deny the truth of her findings. She was called a busybody, a do-gooder, a liar, an immoral woman. Like the Canaanite woman in the Gospels, she refused to be sent away. She refused to be stilled.

In 1843, when no proper lady would

The Canaanite woman became famous in early Christian lore and legend under the name of Justa; her daughter was named Bernice. According to the *Pseudo-Clementine Homilies* (third to fourth centuries C.E.), she became an exemplary church woman. Upon their conversion to Christianity, she and her daughter were cast out of their home by her husband, a non-Christian. She did not remarry but remained a "widow." She was a woman of means, but gave her daughter in marriage to a Christian man who happened to be poor. Because she was a widow, she was unable to have more children, so she adopted two sons. They fell in with the archheretic Simon Magus, but were brought back to the truth by Zacchaeus and then renounced Simon. (2.19-21)

77

call public attention to herself, Dorothea presented a report of her findings to the Massachusetts state legislature. It caused such an uproar, the lawmakers voted to add two hundred beds to the only hospital in the state for the mentally ill.

Far from being satisfied, Dorothea moved on to Rhode Island and began her investigations there. She was scorned by society matrons, criticized by newspaper editors, and condemned by the clergy. Dorothea kept crying out and would not be silenced. When her work was finished in Rhode Island, she turned her attention to establishing New Jersey's first hospital for the mentally ill. In her lifetime she would work in fifteen different states, and her influence would be felt nationwide. Until her death, at age eighty-five, she continued to cry out for those—"the least of these"—who could not speak for themselves. *(Elizabeth Ellis)*

# The Poor Widow

*A poor woman provides a model of extravagant giving.*

### The Story

As he was sitting opposite the temple treasury, he watched the people dropping their money into the chest. Many rich people were putting in large amounts. Presently there came a poor widow who dropped in two tiny coins, together worth a penny. He called his disciples to him and said, 'Truly I tell you: this poor widow has given more than all those giving to the treasury; for the others who have given had more than enough, but she, with less than enough, has given all that she had to live on.'

### Comments on the Story

This very small story (4 verses) is sandwiched between Jesus' controversial debates with the Jewish leaders in the Temple (11:27–12:40) and his final teaching of his disciples about the destruction of the Temple as symbol of the end times (13:1-37). It shares a similar context to those stories that frame it, namely the Temple itself (11:27) or a place from which the Temple is visible and is the focus of attention (12:41; 13:1, 3). The literary setting and context interact, therefore, to give meaning to the story of the poor widow and her contribution to the Temple treasury.

Generally this story is understood as an exemplary story and the brief reference to the widow and her action in 12:42 is subsumed into Jesus' saying, which constitutes two verses: 12:43-44. Focus on the woman and her action and Jesus' interpretation as descriptive of the woman's action, however, allows us to explore two possible ways of understanding the brief glimpse we have of this woman.

The widow in Israelite society, as in many other neighboring cultures in the Mediterranean region, was vulnerable. Unless a widow had a son to offer protection and advocacy, she lost this security upon the death of her husband. In the wealthy strata of society, material resources could ensure the widow had some of the protection she needed and at a time when women had more freedom to dispose of their inherited property, she could choose how to use her resources. For the poor in society, however, widowhood could often mean destitution because even if she had a son, he may not have been able to support her as well as his own family. The Markan story identifies the woman as belonging to this category of widows and it was these women whom the prophetic ethic of Israel deemed in need of protection and support (Isa. 1:17, 23; Jer. 7:6; 22:3; Deut. 10:18). The Temple, as place of redistribution of tithes and other contributions as well as taxes, ought to have been providing the sustenance this poor widow needed, not taking it from her (Deut. 14:29).

The poor widow who ought to have been receiving from the Temple treasury comes and puts in "all that she had to live on" as her contribution to the welfare of others. As such she could be seen to represent the giving of one's very life for others. This is a two-edged virtue, especially when predicated of women. It is the virtue that has led to the absolute negation of women's selves, the loss of their woman-identity and the construction of an identity always embedded in others. On the other hand, such a gift, especially as it is presented in the Markan Gospel, represents the ultimate in identity, which enables the free gift of oneself for others. This is the story of Jesus and this is the action that the poor woman performs. She models Jesus' self-gift and hence models ideal discipleship of Jesus.

Such an interpretation seems to fail to take account of the Markan context unless one sees the woman in contrast to the scribes described in the preceding verse (12:40). Given the critique of the Temple and its officials that surround the story, however, the reader recognizes that the woman's gift is not going to contribute to others who are as destitute as or more destitute than herself. Rather it merely contributes to a corrupt system that "eats up the property of widows" (12:40). Jesus the Jewish prophet, in line with Jeremiah before him, critiques the Temple system of redistribution, which was intended to provide for the poor but which was co-opted at points in its history merely to serve its entrepreneurs, the Temple servants or officials. Jesus points to its destruction (13:2) as did Jeremiah, for whom the oppression of the widow was likewise a sign of Temple corruption (Jer. 7:1-20). In this light, the action of the poor widow is not seen as exemplary but as ironic. She gives all she has to live on to a corrupt system that is about to be destroyed. The words of Jesus then too become ironic. The gift of the wealthy to a corrupt system is not so costly. They have "more than enough" and hence will not be as harmed by the destruction of the system. She, however, who has "less than enough" loses her very livelihood to the system. The extent of her gift merely highlights the extent of the corruption.

This poor widow whose story is used by Jesus and has been used by interpreters to provide an example either of unique self-giving or of the destructive power of the corruption of religious institutions deserves a voice. We have Jesus' interpretation of her actions and the narrator's description of it but it seems that we do not have here the memory of a woman or women's remembering of her and women's telling of her story. Her voice or that of her sisters in early Christianity needs to be heard so that she is not locked into stereotypical female representations of absolute self-giving or of gullibility. Did she

80

make a choice to give "all that she had to live on"? What could have prompted such a choice? Was it an act of compliance with the system or resistance to the system by giving her small amount? These questions enable us to reimagine her story and to place it within the storytelling of Jewish women within the first century who were telling the story of Jesus and their memories and their meaning-making in relation to that story and their own.

### Retelling the Story

'She, with less than enough, has given all that she had to live on.' (Mark 12:44*b*)

### Mary McLeod Bethune (1875–1955)

John Williams took out his handkerchief and mopped the sweat from the back of his neck. It might be September already in the year 1904, but there was no break in the heat. Not yet. He thought to himself that he was crazy to agree to meet anyone out here in the middle of the day. But the prospect of renting a run-down house that had stood empty for an entire year had made him forget the soaring temperature.

He watched as a Black woman walked down the road toward him. Her face broke into a smile as she called out, "Hello there. You must be Mr. Williams, the real estate agent." She extended her hand. "I am Mary McLeod Bethune. Thank you for agreeing to show this property to me on such short notice."

John Williams opened the door. "Well, as you can see, Mrs. Bethune, the place is not much to look at." He took in the uneven floorboards and peeling paint with one glance. Perhaps a

This story assumes that widows could be recognized by their appearance. Apparently widows at this time, as in Old Testament times, indicated their status by their dress. In the Old Testament, Tamar is said to wear "widow's clothes" (Gen. 38:14) as does Judith, whose widow's garments especially include "sackcloth" and represent mourning for her husband (Jdt. 8:4-5). (Stählin, 445)

little salesmanship was in order. "But, I was told you have limited funds to work with, and the rent on this place is only eleven dollars a month."

Mary McLeod Bethune looked the place over carefully. "It will smell a lot better in here when I've had the chance to scrub it, Sir. It will do nicely," she smiled.

The woman's smile was contagious. John Williams found himself smiling in response. "Great," he said. "When are you and your husband going to move in?"

"My husband Albertus teaches at a school in Georgia. My little boy and I came down here to Florida alone. We do not see Mr. Bethune very often. We are staying with Susie Warren. I am not interested in using this house as a dwelling, Sir. I am going to open a school. A school for Negro girls. And I must hurry if I am going to have classes this term. I plan to open in one week."

John Williams snorted. "You won't be able to open a school here in one week. It will take months of backbreaking work to get this place fixed up."

"One week is all the time I have," she said emphatically.

"Well, what you do with the place is your business, lady, so long as the rent gets paid."

With no hint of embarrassment, Mary McLeod Bethune said, "I do not have the money now. If you give me permission to use the building, I will have the money when the school opens in a week."

John Williams stared at her. "Well, it has been sitting empty this whole past year, so I guess I could settle for half of it now."

"I do not have five-fifty now. I will give you the entire eleven dollars when the school opens," she responded.

John Williams shook his head. "There aren't any schools for Black children anywhere around here. And I reckon that's exactly the way the White folks want it."

Mary McLeod Bethune nodded her agreement. "I was teaching at the mission school in Palatka when I got a message to come here to Daytona Beach and start a school for these children."

John's face brightened. "A message? To come here? Who sent for you?"

"God did, Sir," was her only reply.

"Most of the families who live around here are not going to be able to pay you any money to educate their children. They are too poor to be able to pay tuition. How are you going to raise the eleven dollars?" asked the real estate man.

Mary McLeod Bethune responded confidently, "Mrs. Susie Warren has given me a bushel of sweet potatoes."

"A bushel of sweet potatoes! Lady, you're not going to be able to open a school with a bushel of sweet potatoes! That won't be enough!" he sputtered.

The calmness of her response silenced him. "It will have to be enough, Sir. It is all I have."

John Williams agreed to wait a week for the rent to be paid, and Mary McLeod Bethune set to work. She rolled up her sleeves and chopped wood. She spent many hours each day laboring over a wood-burning stove. The bushel of sweet potatoes was transformed into delicious sweet potato pies. The men working nearby to build the Florida East Coast Railroad proved to be eager consumers of her homemade delicacies. Nickel by nickel, the needed amount was accumulated.

On October 3, 1904, the Daytona Literary and Industrial School for Training Negro Girls began classes. Five little girls proudly entered the clean and tidy building to sit at desks made of boxes that Mary McLeod Bethune had scrounged from the town dump. Mary worked hard to give the children the best education possible. She knew it was the only chance they had to better themselves. John Williams had been right about opposition to the school from the White community. The Ku Klux Klan often threatened her and tried in other ways to intimidate her, but Mary McLeod Bethune never wavered.

In two years, the enrollment of her school had grown to over two hundred fifty students. A new location was badly needed. Once more Mary McLeod Bethune enlisted the aid of John Williams. Although she sometimes began the day with no idea how she would feed the students their evening meal, she told Mr. Williams she wanted to buy a piece of property. By this time, he knew not to argue with her faith. He drove her around the area in a buggy, looking at land that was for sale.

Toward the end of the day, they drove by the town dump. "Stop!" called out the teacher. She examined every aspect of the land on which the dump was located. Then she said, "This is it!"

"Are you sure?" questioned Mr. Williams.

"Quite sure," answered Mrs. Bethune. "Make them an offer of thirty dollars for it."

"Thirty dollars? I don't think that will be enough to satisfy the owners."

"It will have to be enough," replied Mary. "It's all I have."

On that site in 1923 the Daytona Literary and Industrial School for Training Negro Girls merged with a school for boys to become Bethune-Cookman College, with Mary as its first president. The graduates of the school came to be a blessing to everyone in the United States, Black and White. Mary McLeod

The idea that the gifts of the poor might be more acceptable to God than those of the wealthy was a convention in pious storytelling in the ancient world. In a play of Euripides, for example, a character observes: "Often I see that poor people are more wise than the rich, and with their own hands offer small gifts to the gods and [one sees in them] more piety than those who bring oxen to the sacrifice" (Danae, fragment 329 [fifth century B.C.E.]). Similarly, from the rabbinic tradition: "Once a woman brought a handful of fine flour, and the priest despised her, saying: 'See what she offers! What is there in this [for the priests] to eat? What is there in this to offer up?' It was shown to him in a dream: 'Do not despise her! It is regarded as if she had sacrificed her own life.' (Leviticus Rabbah 3.5) (Boring, nos. 244 and 246)

Bethune would become one of the most respected and beloved women in America. She would serve in both the Department of Education and the Bureau of Negro Affairs.

When Franklin Roosevelt died in office, his funeral was an magnificent affair of state. Beside his grave there were four chairs reserved for special mourners. The first was for his wife Eleanor. The second was for Harry Truman, who was president of the United States now that Roosevelt was dead. The third was for the prime minister of Great Britain, to honor our closest ally of World War II. The fourth chair was reserved for a representative of all the American people. They could not have chosen better, for in that chair sat Mary McLeod Bethune. *(Elizabeth Ellis)*

# The Woman Called Sinner

*An outcast woman shows Jesus true hospitality.*

## The Story

One of the Pharisees invited Jesus to a meal; he went to the Pharisee's house and took his place at table. A woman who was living an immoral life in the town had learned that Jesus was a guest in the Pharisee's house and had brought oil of myrrh in a small flask. She took her place behind him, by his feet, weeping. His feet were wet with her tears and she wiped them with her hair, kissing them and anointing them with the myrrh. When his host the Pharisee saw this he said to himself, 'If this man were a real prophet, he would know who his woman is who is touching him, and what a bad character she is.' Jesus took him up: 'Simon,' he said, 'I have something to say to you.' 'What is it, Teacher?' he asked. 'Two men were in debt to a moneylender: one owed him five hundred silver pieces, the other fifty. As they did not have the means to pay he canceled both debts. Now, which will love him more?' Simon replied, 'I should think the one that was let off more.' 'You are right,' said Jesus. Then turning to the woman, he said to Simon, 'You see this woman? I came to your house: you provided no water for my feet; but this woman has made my feet wet with her tears and wiped them with her hair. You gave me no kiss; but she has been kissing my feet ever since I came in. You did not anoint my head with oil; but she has anointed my feet with myrrh. So, I tell you, her great love proves that her many sins have been forgiven; where little has been forgiven, little love is shown.' Then he said to her, 'Your sins are forgiven.' The other guests began to ask themselves, 'Who is this, that he can forgive sins?' But he said to the woman, 'Your faith has saved you; go in peace.'

## Comments on the Story

The story of the woman who anoints Jesus has been told in different ways by the different Gospel-writing communities (Matt. 26:6-13; Mark 14:3-9; Luke 7:36-50, and John 12:1-8). In Matthew, Mark, and John, it is an anointing just prior to Jesus' passion whereas the Lukan story is situated much earlier in Jesus' ministry in Galilee. Mark and Matthew have an anointing of Jesus' head while in John and Luke it is the feet of Jesus that are bathed in tears and anointed with ointment. In each instance, it is a woman who anoints. It has been suggested that the origin of the story lay, therefore, in women's struggle to give meaning to Jesus' death in gatherings in their women's spaces. They

85

named Jesus as Anointed One by way of a female ritual of anointing. The Lukan storyteller stands firmly in the line of development of the tradition that shifts the context from women's gathering and ritualizing to a much more traditionally acceptable male gathering or meal, the context of male meaning-making. The story of the woman's anointing is co-opted into and services their meaning-making.

If we focus on the woman in this story rather than on the interaction between the two males and their table companions, which frames and even dominates her story, we find that the story points back to Luke 7:34 and the claim that Jesus is friend of tax collectors and sinners, and points forward toward the women who are healed and serve Jesus (8:2-3). The woman is called "sinner" and her association with the city has led many interpreters to consider her a prostitute. The text does not explicitly make this connection but the combined phraseology in verse 37 introducing the woman seems to suggest to readers that she has been a grave sinner. It is important to note that the verb is used in the past tense—the woman was one who was known to the city's inhabitants as a sinner.

The actions of the woman and the later narrating of them by Jesus (7:38, 44-46) draw attention to the lavishness of the woman's deed. Hers is a spontaneous act but it is the act of a servant or of one who has received pardon. Jesus first interprets her act as one of service: washing and drying his feet, kissing them and anointing them with ointment (much more extravagant, in fact, than the normal courtesies offered to one invited to a banquet), in contrast to the lack of hospitality offered him by Simon. Her service is interpreted as a critical corrective to the lack of service offered by Simon as host and of his consequent challenge to Jesus' honor. The kissing of Jesus' feet and anointing them with ointment, the actions beyond hospitality requirements, point to a recognition of pardon received. The one who had received pardon would fall at the feet of the one granting pardon and kiss this person's feet. The anointing with ointment is here too a further extravagance. What then is the meaning of the extravagance of anointing in this story as it is recounted in Luke? It seems to point to the woman's great love. The woman comes into the house as one who has been a sinner but the later words of Jesus in verse 47 indicate that she does not come seeking forgiveness, but rather that her having been forgiven leads her to show much love. Her extravagant outpouring is her offer of love. She has been forgiven by God but she recognizes in Jesus one who mediates the divine and she seeks the reassurance of what she already knows, of her forgiveness. In this, she, like Simon, challenges Jesus' honor. Will he recognize and acknowledge God's forgiveness in her extravagant act of loving service? Simon failed to recognize and to correctly interpret the woman's action or the nature of Jesus' prophetic activity. He assumed that if Jesus were a prophet he would have recognized the woman as a sinner whereas the prophetic insight of Jesus was to recognize that she was one who had been forgiven much and hence was able to show profound love to the prophetic one who represented to her the source of her forgiveness. In this too, she provides a critical corrective to Simon: the one who has been forgiven little or knows no need of forgiveness, loves little (7:47).

The first words that Jesus addresses to the woman are a reiteration or reaffirmation of her own conviction, namely that she has been forgiven (7:48). The questioning of those at table indicate that they too have failed to recognize that Jesus simply affirms what God has wrought in this woman's life. She is, however, commissioned to "go in peace," a commission that is also given to the woman with the hemorrhage in a subsequent story (8:48). Both women have reached out to touch Jesus (7:38; 8:44); both have had the healing that had taken place within them (cf. 8:44) affirmed by the proclamation that it was their faith that saved them (7:50; 8:48); and both are commissioned to go in peace.

Their stories interact with the account in 8:2-3, which immediately follows the story of the anointing woman. A number of women who have been healed of many evil spirits and infirmities accompany Jesus and other followers and minister to the group out of their resources. From the perspective of the male storyteller, women are recipients of male benefaction which, in turn, leads to their benefaction of Jesus in accord with Jesus' own pattern of benefaction. Women are presented as being in need of either the forgiveness of their sins— imaged in possible female guise as sexual sin—or in need of healing of female infirmities and demon possession. From the point of view of the women benefactors in the Jesus movement, their making meaning of Jesus as anointed one and as servant leader needs to be freed of its confines within androcentric storytelling and enabled to find its original voice. Their focus is on Jesus and who they recognized him to be rather than on their need of healing for service according to the male perspective. Jesus is the prophetic Anointed One who can, indeed, give meaning to situations according to God's perspective.

### Retelling the Story

> A woman who was living an immoral life in the town had learned that Jesus was a guest in the Pharisee's house and had brought oil of myrrh in a small flask. (Luke 7:37)

I don't belong here.

They call this the house of God but they think it belongs to them—the "good" folks, the ones who know they'd never have gotten into my kind of trouble. They seem to talk a lot about forgiveness here, but there's always that look, that disgusted little breath of air that escapes from those clenched-teeth smiles, reminding me that although I may be forgiven I will never be accepted.

The actions of the unnamed woman in this story betray her as a woman of questionable reputation, as suggested by Cicero's list of the stereotypical characteristics of a courtesan: "If a woman without a husband . . . is in the habit of attending dinner parties with men who are perfect strangers . . . if, in fact, she so behaves then not only her bearing but her dress and her companions, not only the ardour of her looks and the licentiousness of her gossip but also her embraces and caresses . . . proclaim her to be not only a courtesan, but also a shameless and wanton courtesan." The storyteller seems to be intentionally portraying this woman according to the stereotype, then provides a surprise ending when Jesus gives her his approval. (Cicero, *Divinatio in Caecilium* 20:44-49 [first century B.C.E.]; from Corley, 61)

Sometimes it seems as though they're just waiting for me to fail, to fall back into old habits, an old life. "A leopard can't change his spots, you know" I hear whispered not so softly behind me.

I want to run, but I won't. I clutch my bottle of perfume more tightly. It's six ounces of Chanel #5 and it's mine. I paid top dollar for it. It took me a long time to get it. The cost was a year of sobriety and being clean of everything, but I made it. I earned it. I am worth something. I AM somebody and this proves it. I brought it with me to show them, to say THERE! See? I did it! This is MY testament to my new life and the God who showed me how to find it! It's funny. They're the ones who are always talking about God. I wonder if they ever had to rely on God the way I have.

Ever since I heard that preacher that day at the storefront church, I thought, just maybe, God could love *me,* too. Just maybe, God would forget who I was long enough to help me. That preacher—he was different from the rest. I saw him really talk to someone I had known—in my "other" life. I saw him care for her like she was a real person, and then I saw him heal her in God's name. You could tell God lived in him. There was real power there! That's when I knew I had to turn my life over to this God. So I did.

And now he's here. When I heard he was going to be here, I had to come. I had to SHOW him. It's not that I need his healing; I need him to know I've been healed! I don't know any other way to let God know except through that preacher. And God needs to know.

I can't give my message through these others. They're the ones who picketed me, who crossed over to the other side of the street to avoid my stench. They still keep their distance. I think they're afraid of catching something from me. No, I can't get to God through them . . . yet.

So here I am. And there he is, speaking again of love and forgiveness. He's looking right at me. I find myself drawn toward that accepting, loving face.

Suddenly I'm aware that the prize in my hand is not a prize after all. It's me. It's something of value and so am I. This God he speaks of values me. I want to shout out my love, my thanks, but no words come. What can I do to show my God I understand? I can give . . . me. The perfume is me.

I rush forward and find myself pouring it at his feet. The tears come; I can no longer hold them back. Tears of a lifetime now flow freely and his feet are bathed in fragrance, sorrow and joy, regret and hope. I, who have never been at a loss for words, kneel, soundless.

I look up into his eyes. He knows. His hand rests lightly on my head and I receive from him grace, a grace these good people around me will never understand.

"Go in peace," he says. And now I can, knowing the peace I feel at this precious moment will last forever. *(Phyllis Williams Kumorowski)*

Among the women heroines of the early Christian faith and legend were several who were identified by their former lives as prostitutes. Among these were Saint Pelagia the Harlot and Saint Mary the Harlot, both of whose stories were being circulated in the fifth centures C.E. *The Life of Saint Pelagia* the Harlot tells how she was a famous harlot of her day known for her seductive beauty. But when she hears Bishop Nonnus preach, she repents of her sins and devotes the remainder of her life to ascetic solitude, disguised as a monk. *The Life of Saint Mary the Harlot* tells how she was an orphan who was raised in a pious household by her uncle who was a holy man. But an evil monk seduced her, and, in her despair over her sin, she took refuge in a brothel. Her uncle then seeks her out and assures her she can do penance for her sins. She then repents and devotes the remainder of her life to ascetic piety. Such stories were popular forms of morality tales in the fifth century, though part of their popularity derived from the lurid adventures of their heroines before they turned in penance back to the true faith. (from Kraemer, *Maenads, Martyrs, Matrons, Monastics,* nos. 125 and 126)

# Mary Magdalene

*Mary of Magdala emerges as one of the leading women of the Jesus followers and one of the women who first witnesses the Resurrection.*

## The Story

AFTER this he went journeying from town to town and village to village, proclaiming the good news of the kingdom of God. With him were the Twelve and a number of women who had been set free from evil spirits and infirmities: Mary, known as Mary of Magdala, from whom seven demons had come out, Joanna, the wife of Chuza a steward of Herod's, Susanna, and many others. These women provided for them out of their own resources.

. . . . . . . . . . . . . . . . . . . . . . . .

By now it was about midday and a darkness fell over the whole land, which lasted until three in the afternoon: the sun's light failed. And the curtain of the temple was torn in two. Then Jesus uttered a loud cry and said, 'Father, into your hands I commit my spirit'; and with these words he died. When the centurion saw what had happened, he gave praise to God. 'Beyond all doubt', he said, 'this man was innocent.'

The crowd who had assembled for the spectacle, when they saw what had happened, went home beating their breasts.

HIS friends had all been standing at a distance; the women who had accompanied him from Galilee stood with them and watched it all.

Now there was a man called Joseph, a member of the Council, a good and upright man, who had dissented from their policy and the action they had taken. He came from the Judaean town of Arimathaea, and he was one who looked forward to the kingdom of God. This man now approached Pilate and asked for the body of Jesus. Taking it down from the cross, he wrapped it in a linen sheet, and laid it in a tomb cut out of the rock, in which no one had been laid before. It was the day of preparation, and the sabbath was about to begin.

The women who had accompanied Jesus from Galilee followed; they took note of the tomb and saw his body laid in it. Then they went home and prepared spices and perfumes; and on the sabbath they rested in obedience to the commandment.

BUT very early on the first day of the week they came to the tomb bringing the spices they had prepared. They found that the stone had been rolled away from the tomb, but when they went inside, they did not find the body of the Lord Jesus. While they stood utterly at a loss, suddenly two men in dazzling garments were at their side. They were terrified, and stood with eyes cast down, but the men said, 'Why search among the dead for one who is alive? Remember how he told you, while was still in Galilee, that the Son of Man must be given into the power of sinful men and be crucified, and must rise again on the third day.' Then they recalled his words and, returning from the tomb, they reported everything to the eleven and all the others.

The women were Mary of Magdala, Joanna, and Mary the mother of James, and they, with the other women, told these things to the apostles. But the story appeared to them to be nonsense, and they would not believe them.

## Comments on the Story

Mary Magdalene is presented in a variety of ways within the Gospel traditions and in even greater variety in the development of traditions beyond the Gospels. This section will take account of her characterization in the Lukan narrative and her position vis-à-vis other women among whom she is named and with whom she is associated.

In the two references to Mary Magdalene in Luke's narrative, she stands at the head of a group of three women (8:2-3; 24:10). She is not identified by way of her association with a significant male (cf. Joanna in 8:3 and Mary in 24:10) but rather is distinguished from other Marys by way of her location: Magdala. This may mean that she was not restricted by patriarchal marriage relationships and was of sufficiently independent means to make the decision to join the Jesus group. The group of three named women in 8:2-3 and 24:10 may function in the same way as did similar groups of three named male disciples in pointing to an inner circle as representative of a larger group. This is so in both instances as mention is made of "many others" and "other women." Mary Magdalene is named at the head of such lists of female disciples not only in Luke, but elsewhere (Mark 15:40; 16:1; Matt. 27:56; 28:1). The only exception is John 19:25 where the focus is on Mary, the mother of Jesus, at the foot of the cross. Mary Magdalene is, however, present. This may indicate that Mary Magdalene was indeed seen as a leader among the female disciples or the leading female disciple as later tradition will develop even to the point in the Gospel of Thomas of presenting her leadership as a challenge to that of Peter (Logion 114).

There is an ambiguity surrounding the women of Luke 8:2-3, including Mary Magdalene. They are characterized as all having been set free from evil spirits and infirmities. It is this that is the catalyst for their possible itinerant discipleship of Jesus in a similar way to the miraculous experience of Peter, James, and John leading to their following of Jesus (5:1-11). It is interesting to note, however, that the miraculous experience of the men is exterior to their bodily person while that of the women is profoundly bodily. Even though the Lukan narrator is not able to escape cultural stereotyping, it is significant that

91

both women and men experience the miraculous, are recipients of Jesus' bene-faction, and become part of his movement—a new fictive kinship, as a result. For women, the receipt of benefaction is greeted with a return of benefaction characterized as following and serving. For men, the response is simply to fol-low. In the Gospels, they are not presented as benefactors of the movement. Perhaps this prepares the way for the later role given to the male disciples of replacing Jesus as the benefactor who heals and teaches.

The description of the ongoing response of Mary Magdalene, Joanna, Susan-na, and the many others healed is that they provide for Jesus, and presumably the Twelve, out of their own resources. Since it is unlikely that numerous wealthy women joined the Jesus' movement or even were benefactors in the later expansion period after the death of Jesus, many suggest that the women put together what they had in a way that foreshadowed the sharing of resources in Acts (2:44-45; 4:32-35). The verb used to describe the women's providing is generally translated "to serve." In the Lukan writing up to chapter 12, it is used only in relation to women (4:39; 8:3; 10:40). Subsequently, it is used in texts that exhort disciples to be like one who serves (12:37; 17:8), and Jesus at his last meal with the disciples invites them to serve as he has served (22:26-27). The women who have received the benefaction of Jesus become benefactors, in their turn, and as such are exemplary of disciples of Jesus and leaders in the Jesus movement, mirroring the role Jesus left to his disciples.

It can be assumed that the women who followed Jesus from Galilee (Luke 23:49) and who stood by the cross with all Jesus' acquaintances, included the women named in 8:2-3. They continued to follow, seeing the tomb and return-ing to prepare spices used to carry out the burial rites that beloved disciples would render to their leader whose death they mourned. These women, who included Mary Magdalene, are depicted a second time in discipleship terms. They follow Jesus from Galilee together with the male disciples whose initial response to Jesus was that of following (5:11).

Mary Magdalene, together with the other women, experiences the empty tomb and encounters the two messengers who appear to them. The words of the messengers are revealing in relation to the women's participation in the movement. The messengers remind the women of Jesus' prediction of his being handed over to be crucified and that he would be raised on the third day (24:7). The narrator says that the women remembered Jesus' words, which points to their participation not just in domestic service and providing for phys-ical needs, but in the teaching of Jesus and the expectations of his promises. It is the women's fidelity that brings them to the cross and tomb, but when they return to tell the apostles what they had experienced, the men did not believe them, and considered their words an idle tale (24:11).

Women's discipleship is hidden beneath the Lukan narrative, to be uncov-ered only by those who read against the grain of the androcentric narrative. For these, however, there is a rich seam of female discipleship that is paralleled to that of male discipleship. For the reader unaware of the Lukan depiction of the women characters under traditional female guises, the Lukan text is dangerous, and Mary Magdalene—leader of female disciples, faithful follower of Jesus to the foot of the cross, and first witness to the resurrection—will be read as healed sinner whose testimony could not satisfy male disciples who are portrayed as authentic disciples despite their betrayal of Jesus and denial of his leadership. For the resistant reader, however, she will emerge in the multiple perspectives that she and other female disciples manifest.

### Retelling the Story

> With him were the Twelve and a number of women who had been set free from evil spirits and infirmities. (Luke 8:1*b*-2*a*)

Mary of Magdala bent lovingly over the gnarled woman, softly dabbing a moist, cool cloth on her wrinkled and fevered brow. She laid down her cloth to briefly massage her own stiffened back. It had been a long night.

The woman had been a thorn in the side of the small band of disciples for a long time. She lived in a small earthen house near their meeting place, but seemed to dwell in the doorway. Always when they gathered together, there she was, frowning, scolding them, calling out, "Who ARE you people? Why do you still follow?" When she had taken ill, most of the group found reason to be elsewhere, but Mary lingered. Now she sat alone beside the ailing woman. Another voice, a voice from the past, floated across her mind.

"Mary, why do you follow?"

It hadn't been more than a week or two before they entered Jerusalem that Jesus, reclining on the couch after supper, had thoughtfully asked her that same question.

"I don't know," she had answered. "I think you need me."

"Yes, I do," he had replied, "but how did you know?"

In various writings of early Christian literature, Mary Magdalene and Peter are represented as competitors for Christian leadership. Logion 114 in the *Gospel of Thomas* (ca. late-first century C.E.) deals with this conflict in a novel way: "Simon Peter said to them, 'Make Mary leave us, for females don't deserve life.' Jesus said, 'Look, I will guide her to make her male, so that she too may become a living spirit resembling you males. For every female who makes herself male will enter the domain of Heaven.' " In this version of the early Christian heresy known as gnosticism the heavenly realm was represented by the male and the earthly realm by the female. (Miller, 322)

She had shrugged and continued with her tasks. "A woman knows. God puts it on our hearts."

"You have a heart for God, Mary."

"Where is your head, woman?"

The shrill voice of the bedridden grandmother jolted her back to the present. The woman was delirious, talking to no one, yet unable to rest. Again, Mary moistened her cloth. Placing it gently on the woman's forehead seemed to quiet her. Mary held it there a few moments before again slipping into her reverie. "A heart for God," he had said.

"And I have a heart for you," she had softly replied.

She remembered how the dual statements had struck her as odd. She had even mentioned it to him.

"Lord, so many times it seems that the love I have for you is the same as that which I feel for God. Can you explain that to me?"

According to the gnostic *Gospel of Philip* (third to fourth century C.E.), Mary Magdalene was venerated as the companion of Jesus, the one whom Jesus "loved more that all the disciples, and he used to kiss her on her [text unclear] more often than the rest of the disciples. They said to him, 'Why do you love her more than all of us?' The savior answered, saying to them, 'Why do I not love you like her? If a blind person and one with sight are both in the darkness, they are not different from one another. When the light comes then the person with sight will see the light, and the blind person will remain in the darkness' " (63.34–64.8). Here the love between Jesus and Mary is presented as a metaphor for spiritual illumination. (Schüssler Fiorenza, ed., *Searching the Scriptures* 631)

The Master/Servant had leaned forward intently. "I think I can. Are you ready to hear it?"

She remembered the slight chill she had felt tingling down her back. How she wished she had said, "Yes! I am not only ready to hear it, I NEED to hear it—from you, right now!"

If only she had listened, if only she had been willing to be the disciple he called her to be and to hear every truth he was ready to reveal, then maybe some of the pain of the time that followed could have been prevented. But she had not. Her faith had not found its footing yet. Her confidence as his spokesperson lay smothered under centuries of admonitions about "a woman's place."

"I am not ready yet," she had answered. "Let my heart and hands learn to return your love first. Then, when you think I'm ready to hear it, I will sit at your feet."

"When you are ready," he answered, "you will know."

Their time together had passed so quickly. How she longed to have it back again.

"Woman, why do you care for me?"

The question came, not from a memory, but from the tired voice of the one outstretched before her. Mary's gaze met hers.

"What did you say?"

The old woman shifted slightly. "I asked why you stayed, what made you come here to care for me."

"Perhaps," the woman of Magdala replied, "because the Master once asked me if I was prepared to care for his sheep after he had gone."

The old woman looked thoughtful. "You speak of the Nazarene—of Jesus."

"Yes."

"And what was your reply to him?"

Mary closed her eyes and once more she was sitting beside her Lord. "I told him I was prepared to care for his sheep; I was not prepared for him to go."

"Am I one of his sheep?"

"Hannah, you are like a lamb that has separated itself from the flock and is now hurt—needing help and yet afraid to return. You need a shepherd; you need THE shepherd. His hands could not be here to touch you, so I must be here for him."

Hannah leaned back on her pillow. The peace that had eluded her for so long enveloped her at last. "You are his hands."

And when Hannah closed her eyes, she knew she had returned, like a lost lamb returning to the flock, and she gave thanks for the one who had remained to be the hands of her shepherd. *(Phyllis Williams Kumorowski)*

Although the New Testament presents Mary Magdalene as a respectable woman of some means and a leader among the disciples, later Christian imagination merged her with other New Testament women, most notably the sinful woman who anointed Jesus in Luke 7. Eventually Mary Magdalene became known as the redeemed prostitute and a model of Christian repentance. Gregory the Great's homily on Luke (ca. 591 C.E.) exemplifies this development: "She whom Luke calls the sinful woman, whom John calls Mary, we believe to be the Mary from whom seven devils were ejected according to Mark. And what did these seven devils signify, if not all the vices? . . . It is clear, brothers, that the woman previously used the unguent to perfume her flesh in forbidden acts. What she therefore displayed more scandalously, she was now offering to God in a more praiseworthy manner. . . . She turned the mass of her crimes to virtues, in order to serve God entirely in penance, for as much as she had wrongly held God in contempt." (*Homilies* XXXIII; from Haskins, 96)

# Women at the Cross and Tomb

*Among all Jesus' disciples, it is the women who witness successively the cross, burial, and resurrection.*

## The Story

Jesus again cried aloud and breathed his last. At that moment the curtain of the temple was torn in two from top to bottom. The earth shook, rocks split, and graves opened; many of God's saints were raised from sleep, and coming out of their graves after his resurrection entered the Holy City, where many saw them. And when the centurion and his men who were keeping watch over Jesus saw the earthquake and all that was happening, they were filled with awe and said, 'This must have been a son of God.'

A NUMBER of women were also present watching from a distance; they had followed Jesus from Galilee and looked after him. Among them were Mary of Magdala, Mary the mother of James and Joseph, and the mother of the sons of Zebedee.

When evening fell, a wealthy man from Arimathaea, Joseph by name, who had himself become a disciple of Jesus, approached Pilate and asked for the body of Jesus; and Pilate gave orders that he should have it. Joseph took the body, wrapped it in a clean linen sheet, and laid it in his own unused tomb, which he had cut out of the rock. He then rolled a large stone against the entrance, and went away. Mary of Magdala was there, and the other Mary, sitting opposite the grave.

. . . . . . . . . . . . . . . . . . . . . . . . .

A BOUT daybreak on the first day of the week, when the Sabbath was over, Mary of Magdala and the other Mary came to look at the grave. Suddenly there was a violent earthquake; an angel of the Lord descended from heaven and came and rolled away the stone, and sat down on it. His face shone like lightning; his garments were white as snow. At the sight of him the guards shook with fear and fell to the ground as though dead.

The angel spoke to the women: 'You', he said, 'have nothing to fear. I know you are looking for Jesus who was crucified. He is not here; he has been raised, as he said he would be. Come and see the place where he was laid, and then go quickly and tell his disciples: "He has been raised from the dead and is going ahead of you into Galilee; there you will see him." That is what I came to tell you.'

They hurried away from the tomb in awe and great joy, and ran to bring the news to the disciples. Suddenly Jesus was there in their path, greeting them. They came up and clasped his feet, kneeling before him. 'Do not be afraid,' Jesus said to them. 'Go and take word to my brothers that they are to leave for Galilee. They will see me there.'

**Comments on the Story**

Stories of women faithfully standing by the cross of Jesus, keeping watch at the tomb, being first to witness the empty tomb, and encountering the risen Jesus are characteristic of the four canonical Gospels. The variety with which the stories are told, however, is as extraordinary as their presence at the culmination of the Gospel stories. There are certain sociohistorical and religious considerations that give rise to the claim that the inclusion of these stories of women is extraordinary in narratives that have seemed to minimize their participation in the reign-of-God or Jesus movement generally. First, women were considered less reliable witnesses than men and the absence of the male disciples, who have fled in fear, leaves only the women's witness to the Crucifixion and empty tomb as the foundational source for early Christian memory and meaning-making around what became the core of the *kerygma*. Second, if resurrection appearance stories developed around issues of leadership and authority in the early house-churches and communities of followers of Jesus, then women's leadership and authority must have been recognized at least in the Matthean (Matt. 28:9-10) and Johannine communities (John 20:11-18).

In relation to the origins of the traditions that have developed into the stories being considered here, it seems reasonable to imagine that one significant source may well have been women's remembering, women's meaning-making, following the death and resurrection of Jesus. It is particularly women's faithful presence at the foot of the cross and the absence of the named male disciples that seem to be a tradition that it is difficult to imagine the early church constructing. Indeed, there is a tendency in the later development of the tradition in Luke and John to seek to rehabilitate the disciples who had fled (Luke 24:11; John 20:1-10). The presence of the women may, therefore, have been an authentic remembering and storytelling around that remembering. Their presence at a distance (which has received a variety of interpretations to lessen the significance of the women's presence) may simply have been a reality in that the crucified Jesus would have been surrounded by soldiers who either would have kept the crowd at bay or whom the women would not have wished to encounter.

As the Matthean story of women at the cross is told, they are said to have followed Jesus from Galilee and ministered to him or "looked after" [REB]/"provided for" him according to some translations. These two words, in the context of the entire Gospel narrative, are discipleship words. It is disciples who leave all and follow Jesus (Matt. 4:20, 22; 8:22; 9:9; 16:24). It is clearly only faithful disciples who will have followed Jesus from Galilee to the very place of crucifixion; and such discipleship for women in the sociocultural and religious context of first-century Galilee would have been extremely dangerous. The second descriptive designation given to the women of this story is

97

that they have "ministered" to or "served" Jesus (the REB's "provided for" carries connotations of satisfying domestic or food service only). This verb, as we have already noted earlier, can refer to table or domestic service but it is never used in this way in the Matthean Gospel. Indeed, it is a verb that is used in Matthew 20:28 to characterize the ministry of Jesus and that developed within the early church as a description of active participation in the life of the house-churches. Women following to the foot of the cross and ministering to Jesus narrates faithful discipleship and not only faithful but also passionate discipleship, which becomes compassion in the face of the death of the beloved one. And so the women likewise keep faithful watch at the tomb (27:61) in contrast to the aggressive watch of the soldiers (27:36).

At the heart of the Matthean account of the empty tomb is the two-fold commissioning of the women disciples. In the Matthean story, the women do not come to anoint Jesus because that has already been performed by another woman prior to the death of Jesus (Matt. 26:6-13). They come as witnesses to "see" or "look at" the tomb. They have little time, however, to function as witnesses of a tomb because they immediately encounter an earthquake, a sign of the presence of divine power, which removes the stone from the entrance to the tomb. What they now encounter is a divine messenger interpreting for them what they have experienced—that Jesus who had been crucified has been raised. The divine power manifest at the crucifixion of Jesus (27:51-53) now opens the tomb so that it can be made known that Jesus has been raised, the prediction has been fulfilled as Jesus had told his faithful disciples and as the angel now brings to mind for these faithful women disciples in face of the trauma of Jesus' death (28:6).

But the women are immediately directed away from the empty tomb to go and to tell that Jesus has been raised. They are to become the first to proclaim the *kerygma* that the crucified one has been raised (28:7). And further, they are to direct the disciples who have deserted Jesus in his most difficult hour to go to Galilee to be reconciled to Jesus. The women are mediators of this reconciliation because of their fidelity. Their response to this commission in fear and great joy brings them to encounter the risen Jesus who reiterates the commission to direct the eleven to Galilee.

The image with which the women's story closes is the open road to Galilee, the journey away from the empty tomb, from all places of death and confinement, toward the possibilities that the open road to Galilee holds. It is encounter with Jesus, who cannot be grasped or held, but who will continue the commission begun with the divine messenger's instruction to the women—go and tell—in a cyclical movement that is to encompass all nations (28:19). The women's fidelity to the cross and tomb and the open road to Galilee is not eclipsed by the commissioning of eleven male disciples on a mountain in Galilee, but must be continually read in conjunction with it so that in fidelity to the Matthean storytelling, open road and mountain of authorization together with female and male discipleship may be kept in the creative tension in which we find them at the close of this Gospel. It is only then that women disciples today will be authorized with men to "go and tell," to reconcile and proclaim a story that is open-ended—Jesus has been raised and is going ahead into. . . .

### Retelling the Story

> The angel spoke to the women: 'You', he said, 'have nothing to fear.' (Matt. 28:5*a*)

The ugly orange flames seared the night as they shot up through the disintegrating stone and wood that had once been a house of God. Emmanuel AME Church had been the center of the Black community, that which bound them together and to the larger family of God. It was a place of solace for the disheartened, of hope for the hopeless, and of grace for the overburdened. Now it stood as a stark testimony to hatred.

Almost everyone had gone now. Only a few firefighters remained, mostly to make sure the wind didn't carry the flames anywhere else. The building was beyond salvage. In the dimming light of the few persistent flames, three women huddled together, their ebony faces stained by tears. Filled with anguish, they were determined to remain there until the last.

The others had gone. They left in defeat as that which held them together crumbled before them on a windy Friday night. They left in anger at the triumphant injustice. They left in fear, wondering if those who would deliberately set a torch to a place of worship would not hesitate to harm those who worshiped there.

"We can never rebuild." "We can never be the same." "Everything we ever believed in is gone." Their beaten voices echoed in their absence.

Only these three faithful women remained to give testimony to the love they had discovered within those walls. And yet they, too, grieved.

"How can God allow this kind of ignorance and uncontrolled power to

> Ancient Judaism did not consider women qualified to be witnesses: "From women let no evidence be accepted, because of the levity and temerity of their sex" (Josephus, *Antiquities* 4.219). In the second century, Celsus, the pagan critic of Christianity, discounted the validity of the empty tomb story by arguing that it came from "a half frantic woman" (Origen, *Contra Celsum* 2.59). In such a cultural atmosphere, it is remarkable that the empty tomb story was given such weight in the Gospels. (Davies and Allison, 3.662)

destroy us?" one wailed. Joanna was a kind woman who could not imagine seeing anything but good in another human being.

Mary, the acknowledged matriarch of the community, wrapped her coat more tightly around her sister in Christ. "Hush, Joanna; it's true they've destroyed a building, but they cannot ever destroy us, because they can't destroy the One whose spirit is in us!"

Maggie, the youngest of the three, wept in silence.

The fire chief approached them hesitantly carrying the small brass sign that had hung over the doorway. He wiped it gently with a clean linen cloth and handed it to Mary. "I am truly sorry, ma'am. I've done everything I know to do. I guess we just need to let it rest. Why don't you all go home now and get some rest yourself?"

Mary took the plaque from him. It was burnished now, and still warm. "Thank you, Joseph," she said.

At daybreak Sunday morning, Mary and Maggie were back. Neither knew exactly why they felt the need to be there; they just wanted to go see their church one more time. They spoke in whispers, anxious about what they might find. It occurred to them that it could be dangerous for them to be there. What remained of the building was certainly unstable, and worse, they had heard that the chief of police had posted a guard there, supposedly to prevent further trouble. Those guards would be in a foul mood for sure after spending a cold night out on what was left of the church grounds.

To their relief, however, when they arrived the guards were gone. The back door was buried in debris, so they walked around to the front. Maggie gingerly tried the massive front door. It was lodged in place, stuck fast.

"Well, I guess there will be no going inside today," Mary announced.

As Maggie turned to answer her she heard a distant rumbling, and felt the ground move beneath her.

"Earthquake!" she shouted to her friend, and they clung tightly to each other, frozen by fear. After what seemed like an eternity, the rolling movement and the rumbling stopped.

When the flying dust and ashes at last settled, Mary touched her friend's shoulder lightly and pointed toward the church. No sound escaped their lips as the two stared in amazement. The front door, which had been so tightly wedged closed, now stood wide open in front of them. The two women cautiously made their way inside. They moved slowly, their eyes unaccustomed to the darkness within.

When they could finally discern shapes, they found that there was nothing to see. All around them was nothing but the charred remains of the hollow shell that had been their church home. Blackened glass crunched under their feet between sodden papers that had once been pages of Scripture, or music for a joyful praise choir. If possible, the devastation was even worse than they had imagined it would be.

"Oh, Mary," Maggie whispered, her voice dried within her throat. "I had wanted so much for there to be some sign of hope here, something that said, 'We will survive this!' But there is nothing left at all. Nothing." She sagged onto the stump of what had been a pew.

"But there is, Maggie." Mary's voice held wonder and awe in it, and Maggie looked up to where her friend's gaze was fixed. She gasped as she saw it. How could she have missed it before? There, high up in the wall at what had been the front of the sanctuary, the small circular stained-glass window remained, intact.

It was impossible. The heat had been far too intense, the destruction too complete. Part of the roof above it was gone. Yet there it remained. Soot covered, yet whole, the figure of the risen Christ still pronounced blessing on this place and this people.

Then, as they watched in disbelief, the sun came up full behind it, and the force of its powerful rays penetrated even the soot and ash on the glass, creating a glow—then a rainbow that permeated the sanctuary. Brighter and brighter it grew until they felt bathed in its light! Then a beam of light burst forth from the window and illuminated a charred piece of paper on the floor. They looked and saw it was a page from the Bible, and the words that were illuminated were these: "He is not here; he has been raised . . . go quickly and tell his disciples."

Mary Magdalene came to be the most celebrated of all the women who were named as witnesses to the empty tomb, and thus, stories about her proliferated. In the noncanonical Gospel of Mary, in an event that takes place after the Resurrection, she recounts to the other apostles a special revelation she received from Jesus about the nature of the soul. Peter becomes jealous and says, " 'Has the Savior spoken secretly to a woman and not openly so that we would all hear? Surely he did not wish to indicate that she is more worthy than we are?' Then Mary wept and said to Peter, 'Peter, my brother, what are you imagining about this? Do you think that I've made all this up secretly by myself or that I am telling lies about the Savior?' Levi said to Peter, 'Peter, you have a constant inclination to anger and you are always ready to give way to it. And even now you are doing exactly that by questioning the woman as if you're her adversary. If the Savior considered her to be worthy, who are you to disregard her? For he knew her completely and loved her devotedly' " What is represented here in story form is evidently a continuing controversy in early Christianity about the role of women in the leadership of the church. (*Gospel of Mary* 10.3-10 [ca. late-first to early-second centuries C.E.]; from Miller, 359)

The women began to smile, then to laugh for joy, for suddenly they understood! It was a message from God, telling them that their church was not dead, for its Christ was alive! They would not be conquered by hate and prejudice! They would begin anew!

Then as quickly as it came, the beam of light faded as the sun rose higher in the sky. The moment was gone, but its effect lingered with the women. They no longer felt alone; in fact, they knew they would never truly be alone again. They strode, arm in arm, out into the sunlight. They saw the open road ahead of them. A way had been opened. A message of hope and reconciliation had been given. The way was before them. They would make it straight before their Lord. *(Phyllis Williams Kumorowski)*

# Mary and Martha of Bethany

*Mary and Martha exemplify contrasting styles of discipleship, which leads to tension between them.*

### The Story

While they were on their way Jesus came to a village where a woman named Martha made him welcome. She had a sister, Mary, who seated herself at the Lord's feet and stayed there listening to his words. Now Martha was distracted by her many tasks, so she came to him and said, 'Lord, do you not care that my sister has left me to get on with the work by myself? Tell her to come and give me a hand.' But the Lord answered, 'Martha, Martha, you are fretting and fussing about so many things; only one thing is necessary. Mary has chosen what is best; it shall not be taken away from her.'

### Comments on the Story

Tension characterizes the story of Martha and Mary of Bethany as it is told by the Lukan community. There is tension within the text as the two women are pitted against each other around the character of Jesus. There clearly was tension around its transmission as there are a number of variants to the concluding verse in particular, which seek to soften the stark dichotomy it creates. And finally, there has been tension within and created by its history of interpretation in which the story has been used to denigrate women's work, especially domestic and familial service, in favor of quiet contemplation. It is reasonable to assume, therefore, that this story, this tradition as transmitted by Luke, developed in controversy (the Johannine tradition of Martha and Mary, found in John 11:1-44; 12:1-11, having developed quite differently). Reconstructing this development, it would seem that a tradition of Martha and Mary of Bethany, a tradition of key female participants in the continuation of the reign-of-God or Jesus movement beyond the death of Jesus, was used in the Lukan community not only to address a very controversial issue around women's active diaconal or public ministry in their midst but also to denigrate such ministry. There are, however, traces of the earlier memories of these two women and their ministry within the story but also these have been overshadowed by the pitting of the women against each other in the final layering of the story.

The first two verses introduce the reader to Martha and Mary. Martha is clearly presented as a leader of a house-church and she performs the function of such a leader by welcoming the itinerant missionary group into her home. The verb used here is one favored by the Lukan writer to characterize such hospitality and such a reception of Jesus and those who continue his missionary preaching (cf. Luke 9:5, 48; 10:8, 10). It would be the leader of the house-church who would perform such a role. Mary is presented as the sister of Martha, connoting for readers either familial ties (this would seem to be the strength of the tradition) or membership within the new fictive kinship or reign-of-God household. She is engaged in what is an equally important aspect of response to the ministry of Jesus, namely listening to the word he proclaims. Already in the Gospel the crowds are presented as listening to Jesus' word (5:1, 15, 17). There is, however, another developing thematic in the story: response to Jesus, according to Jesus' own teaching, is not characterized simply by listening but also by doing (cf. 6:46-49; 8:11-18; 21; and subsequently 11:27-28). This will be an important consideration in the development of this story. At the outset, however, the two women are presented within a setting symbolizing a house-church, carrying out the functions of those engaged in ministry and leadership within such a setting.

In verse 40, Martha is characterized as being engaged in *diakonia,* a word used within the emerging Christian church for ministry or service within the reign-of-God community and for the sake of the continuation of the gospel of Jesus. This public ministry is characterized in the Lukan text as problematic: it is a distraction according to some interpretations or the weight of much *diakonia* is a concern to Martha. From the point of view of a community that might be seeking to move women from the public ministry that Martha symbolizes, the presentation of it as distraction and then dragging Martha away from the "better part" is a powerful rhetorical device. From the point of view of women in such ministry, if the community was presenting another option to women— that of quiet reserved and private listening—then the weight of the public ministry would be falling on fewer women. Martha is narrated as presenting this problematic situation to Jesus for resolution.

One of the very subtle rhetorical devices in this story is that it pits the women over against each other around Jesus as the authoritative teacher. The use of *kyrios* or Lord with its connotations of both divine authority as well as the authority of the male head of a household, both by Martha (10:40) and by the narrator (10:41), gives greater authority to Jesus' pronouncement that closes the story. Jesus rebukes Martha with words that indicate that this is not just a personal issue between two sisters but rather that there is a public disturbance. Martha's public ministry is designated as the cause of the disturbance and is compared unfavorably to that of Mary.

Turning to the image of Mary, which closes the narrative and which is proclaimed as the "better part," the reader is left with a woman who, according to the story, simply listens to Jesus—a private rather than public role—and there

104

is no indication of her actively doing the word. Such an image is quite contrary to the Gospel response already noted above, which has Jesus proclaim that true discipleship consists in hearing and doing. What may have been a very active ministry of hearing and doing remembered in relation to Mary of Bethany has become a form of discipleship that renders women's ministry private, inactive, and contrary to the Gospel invocation to hear and do. It is interesting in this regard that in 8:21, Luke designates the "mother and . . . brothers" of Jesus as those who hear the word of God and do it. Matthew and Mark include in this same tradition, "brother and sister and mother" (Matt. 12:50; Mark 3:35).

A reclaiming of the story of Martha and Mary beyond the androcentric controversy of a first-century Christian community and beyond the history of a patriarchal tendency to pit women against women will recognize the significant ministry of both Martha and Mary in a house-church at Bethany. They will be remembered as welcoming others into the household, learning the traditions of Jesus, and then proclaiming and doing them. This doing will not be in silence and privacy but in the public arena of that house-church or even beyond in the marketplace or in gatherings where women continued to prophetically shape the memories of Jesus and of their participation in the reign-of-God or Jesus movement.

### Retelling the Story

> Now Martha was distracted by her many tasks, so she came to him and said, 'Lord, do you not care that my sister has left me to get on with the work by myself? Tell her to come and give me a hand.' (Luke 10:40)

The house was beginning to quiet down. Jesus and just a few of his disciples remained up on the roof, talking beneath the evening's starlight. Beneath them, inside the house, two sisters met, somewhat shyly, to make amends. As usual, it was Martha, the older of the two, who spoke first.

"Mary," she blurted out, "I feel so bad about what happened this afternoon. Of course you wanted to hear Jesus, and I know we had agreed that you could go be with him first, but I wanted to hear him, too, and it looked like there was so much that needed to be done that I would never get my chance. Please forgive me."

Her younger sister breathed a little sigh of thanks. It was always so hard for her to find the right words to say, and so she often just remained silent. She had worried all afternoon about what she would say when she finally was alone with the sister she adored.

"Martha, I'm sorry, too. I was so wrapped up in hearing him, that I paid no attention to how late it was getting. Did you hear what he said, though? We were so worried about whether he would allow us to learn, to sit at his feet and listen to his words! It was almost as if he understood our concerns when he said that while there were many ways women could serve, this was not only acceptable, but could sometimes be the better way! I couldn't believe how he accepted us equally with his other followers! I've never met anyone like him before!"

She and Martha embraced. They never had been able to be at odds with each other for very long. The two sisters had always been close; their newfound faith had drawn them even closer.

Martha thoughtfully patted her sister's shoulder. "You know," she said at last, "it bothered me a little when he said that what you were doing was better. It was like every other time I've had to hear a man express the feeling that "women's" work is insignificant compared to what they do—namely sit and talk. It hurt to think that, after all he's said, Jesus was, after all, just echoing what we've heard all our lives."

"Oh no, Martha! That's not what I heard at all! I think the reason it sounded something like a reproof is because you were complaining about what you were doing. Your heart wasn't in it and you made it very clear. You know what he's taught us about that. It's not *what* we do in his name, it's *how* we do it—

The household was generally considered the domain of women. Philo, the first-century Jewish philosopher, expressed a sentiment shared by Greeks and Romans as well: "The women are best suited to the indoor life which never strays from the house, within which the middle door is taken by the maidens as their boundary, and the outer door by those who have reached full womanhood. Organized communities are of two sorts, the greater which we call cities and the smaller which we call households. Both of these have their governors; the government of the greater is assigned to men, under the name of statesmanship, that of the lesser known as household management, to women. A woman then, should not be a busybody, meddling with matters outside her household concerns, but should seek a life of seclusion. She should not show herself off like a vagrant in the streets before the eyes of other men, except when she has to go to the temple, and even then she should take pains to go, not when the market is full, but when most people have gone home, and so like a free-born lady worthy of the name, with everything quiet around her, make her oblations and offer her prayers to avert the evil and gain the good." (*Special Laws* 3.169-71; from Kraemer, *Maenads, Martyrs, Matrons, Monastics,* no. 15). To many hearers of the story, therefore, normal propriety would suggest that since matters outside the home should not concern women, Mary was out of line.

with conviction and joy. Otherwise it's not a ministry, just a duty."

Martha smiled lovingly at her earnest younger sister. "I know. I was so distracted by all the demands I felt were being placed on me, I forgot why I was serving—I forgot *whom* I was serving. How basic can you get? No wonder he sounded so parental; how many times have we heard him say we should devote all our attention to the Lord and everything else will follow?"

"Oh, Martha." Now it was Mary who was being parental. "Don't berate yourself so much. I got so involved in hearing him that that's all I did—just sit there. And I haven't done much else since. You might have been complaining, but at least you were *doing* something. He's also mentioned more than a few times that our faith is to be a living, growing thing. How many times have we heard him remind us that we were blessed to be a blessing? All I did was sit there like a rock in the road."

Martha took her hand. "So do it now, little sister. Go out in his name and start serving."

Mary responded by taking Martha's other hand into her own. "And now you go out there and sit at his feet."

Martha squeezed her hand as they headed for the doorway. "It seems so clear when you look at it, doesn't it? Does everyone take this long to understand him, or is it just us?"

"I don't know, dear one. I just know that I want to serve him in any way I can, and no matter what shape that service takes, I know he'll receive it. That's good enough for me."

"Me, too." *(Phyllis Williams Kumorowski)*

> Household management, which was considered "women's work" by the ancients, included "looking after those who are preparing the food for the family" (Columella, *De Re Rustica* 12.1.6 [first century C.E.]; from Fantham et al., 379). Though Martha is presented in this story as an independent woman who is hosting the disciples in her home, she still has responsibility for food preparation. Contrast this with the story of the healing of Peter's mother-in-law, in which the two men, Jesus and Peter, must await the rising of Peter's mother-in-law from the sickbed to be served (Luke 4:38-39; see also chapter 5 above).

> Women had an ambiguous status at the ancient dinner table. Men always reclined at an ancient meal, and they always recline in the meal stories in the Gospels. According to the most ancient rules of a reclining banquet, respectable women should not be present at a reclining banquet, or, if they were, then they were to sit, not recline,

indicating their status relative to the men. The only women who would regularly recline along with the men were the prostitutes, whose presence at banquets was popularly portrayed on vase paintings of the era. While this custom had changed by the first century so that respectable women were found to be reclining along with men more and more, the old stigma still lingered. In this story, therefore, in an apparent attempt to preserve the "respectability" of Mary, she is specifically said to be "sitting" at the feet of Jesus. While this might be said to be an appropriate position for any disciple in the presence of the master, only Mary is so pictured; male disciples are always pictured reclining with Jesus. Thus the storyteller, in wishing to present Mary in a model role as a student of the master but also as a respectable woman, cannot avoid picturing her in a subordinate role relative to male disciples. (adapted from Corley, 137-38)

# The Woman with a Crippling Spirit

*A crippled woman is healed while worshiping in the synagogue.*

## The Story

He was teaching in one of the synagogues on the Sabbath, and there was a woman there possessed by a spirit that had crippled her for eighteen years. She was bent double and quite unable to stand up straight. When Jesus saw her he called her and said, 'You are rid of your trouble,' and he laid his hands on her. Immediately she straightened up and began to praise God. But the president of the synagogue, indignant with Jesus for healing on the sabbath, intervened and said to the congregation, 'There are six working days: come and be cured on one of them, and not on the sabbath.' The Lord gave him this answer: 'What hypocrites you are!' he said, 'Is there a single one of you who does not loose his ox or his donkey from its stall and take it out to water on the sabbath? And here is this woman, a daughter of Abraham, who has been bound by Satan for eighteen long years: was it not right for her to be loosed from her bonds on the sabbath?' At these words all his opponents were covered with confusion, while the mass of the people were delighted at all the wonderful things he was doing.

## Comments on the Story

Like the previous story, this story of the woman with the spirit that had crippled her for eighteen years (13:11-13) is profoundly interwoven into the Lukan narrative and the issues of the community. It is contextualized in a synagogue and on the sabbath (13:10) and is followed by a controversy between Jesus and the leader of the synagogue. Hence, there is a danger that the healing of this woman and her liberation from years of possession by the spirit that crippled her is silenced by the male voices of controversy. We turn first, therefore, to the woman's healing.

First, the story places the woman in the synagogue on the sabbath. Her presence does not seem surprising in the narrative, which may indicate that she, like other women of her time, regularly took part in the synagogue worship and indeed some of her sisters may even have been leaders of the synagogue. She is there with others to worship, to pray, to offer fidelity to the God of the Torah. The description of her illness makes her presence even more poignant. Hers may well have been the prayer of the psalmist who laments affliction borne but then places trust in the God who can relieve such affliction.

This same description—with a spirit "that had crippled her for eighteen years [so that] she was bent double and quite unable to stand up straight"— provides an insight into the symbolic universe of first-century Mediterranean peoples. Supreme power belongs to the most high god and was shared with lesser gods, other good spirits, and angels or divine messengers. These all had power over human beings as did the demonic spirits who could cause illness, and in this case, severe curvature of the spine.

Because the story is so brief, we do well to try imagining the experience of the woman, to be severely bent over for eighteen years. All she would see would be downward rather than out in front of her. She would not be able to stand straight to greet, to see, or even to rejoice. As the story is recounted, it seems that she does not see Jesus. Rather, he sees her and he takes the initiative in not only greeting her but also proclaiming her healing. In only two other healing stories does Jesus see and act without a request being made and each of them involves a woman—Peter's mother-in-law (Matt. 8:14-15) and the widow of Nain (Luke 7:11-17). The words of Jesus are significant in this instance— "you are rid of your trouble"—the verb being in the perfect passive indicating that Jesus simply recognizes the healing action that has been performed by God. It is the Most High God who has power over the demonic spirit who crippled the woman and Jesus is simply mediator of that power. The divine passive continues in the description of the woman being straightened consequent to Jesus' laying of his hands on her. And her response is to enter into an ongoing praise of the God who heals a woman so possessed by an oppressive spirit for eighteen years. While Jesus is the mediator, the focus of the story is on the woman healed and the God who heals. The woman is not victim in need of male deliverance but her oppression is recognized as demonic and her healing renders her alive to full participation in God's desire for fullness of life for all.

The controversy between Jesus and the leader of the synagogue shifts the reader's focus, however, onto the struggle between two male leaders over the woman and her healing. In either the context of the reign-of-God or Jesus movement at the time of Jesus or the Lukan context, the controversy would have been within Judaism and about authority to interpret the law. According to one interpretation represented by the leader of the synagogue, the focus was on the law forbidding work on the Sabbath, with healing being considered such a work. According to the other, that of Jesus, healing or loosing from bondage took precedence as in other instances cited by Jesus—the untying of a donkey or ox and leading it to drink on the Sabbath—as an act of compassion.

Subsequent Christian interpretation has characterized Jesus as representative of Christianity, a path of compassion, and rendered the leader of the synagogue representative of law-bound Judaism. This anti-Judaism that pits Judaism over against Christianity is as insidious as the pitting of woman against woman encountered in the story of Martha and Mary. Rather, just as such controversies developed within Judaism as it sought a prophetic way in the first century of the common era, so too have they characterized Christianity. Contemporary interpreters and storytellers must ensure in their retelling of this story that both the synagogue leader and Jesus represent tendencies within Christianity and not set Christianity over against Judaism.

Contemporary interpreters must also ensure that the story of the woman who has been bent over is not obscured by legal controversies and that women's voices and women's stories do not continue to be subverted to doctrinal controversies. So much Christian history and Christian storytelling has been written on the bodies of women. This story tells of the freeing of a woman's body from all types of demonic spirits that cripple it. This woman is symbolic of women's history generally and women's history within Christianity. Today's storytellers must ensure that with Jesus, they touch the woman's body with their words in such a way that she can continue to stand straight and that her voice might be heard praising God. How might she have named the God who healed her? What words would she say? In imagining and retelling her story, we may be able to free many other women who have been bent over for unnamed years so that they too can stand straight and name the God who heals them and take their place in the midst of the synagogue, the church, and the world and from there let their voices be heard.

### Retelling the Story

She was bent double and quite unable to stand up straight. (Luke 13:11*b*)

The steps were getting higher and the walk was getting longer every day, Esther was sure of it. For eighteen years it had continued to get worse. For eighteen years, she had been able to see less and less as she had to narrow her focus to the walkway beneath her. For eighteen years this . . . thing . . . within her had increasingly crippled her in body and in spirit. She was devoted to her Lord but it was getting so hard to show it.

The blue Judean sky and the tall beams of the synagogue hovered above her unseen. "Look down. Look out!" her mind called to her. "One step—

Until recently, studies of the ancient synagogue assumed that women were isolated from men in "women's galleries" such as were common in medieval synagogues. But more recent studies of the archaeology of first-century synagogues have disputed that view and pointed out that synagogues of this period do not, in fact, provide evidence that men were isolated from women. The synagogue where this story takes place seems to have been such a structure, for there is no indication in the story that the woman was restricted in her access to the synagogue in any way. (Brooten, 103-38)

that's it. Another step. Rest awhile. You can do it, Esther! If it's important, you can do it," she told herself.

She was aware that so many things went beyond her notice as she struggled to make her unyielding body obey her desire to press forward. She herself went beyond the notice of most of the scurrying people around her. She did, however, notice them, and felt the painful oblivion into which she was sinking. It was getting so hard. Did anyone really care anymore? Did God care?

"More people than usual today," she thought as she entered the synagogue. "Must be the nice weather."

"Ouch!" There went her back again. She stopped and tried to catch her breath. Oh, to be free of this never-ending pain! For that matter, to be free of all that held her in bondage. To be free to learn about the God she loved! To be free from the constraints of time and an unwilling body so she could do the work that needed to be done! To be free from the expectations of a society that conflicted with the expectations of her Lord! To be free to raise her tortured arms in praise once more!

Esther sighed. Apparently, it was not God's will or God's time for such dreams today. But the spirit of the Lord was within her and she would not allow her dreams to die yet. And so she pressed on.

She was inside the synagogue now. The muffled silence was broken as a man called to someone across the room. She froze as she realized he was calling to her! What could he want of her? Was she no longer welcome here either?

"Woman!" he called as he walked purposefully toward her. She could see his sandaled feet drawing closer.

"Woman, you are set free from your ailment."

Set free? What did he mean? What was he saying? Her heart pounded wildly within her as she saw his arm reach out toward her. She closed her eyes tightly, confused and fearful of what would follow.

Then she felt his gentle touch on her arm as the warmth of a hot summer sun coursed through her. It took her breath away!

As she gasped, she straightened, and found herself looking directly into his face. She, who had not been able to look into anyone's eyes for almost eighteen years now looked into the eyes of divine love.

She suddenly realized she was standing—straight and tall. A cry that was half a laugh, half a shout of joy escaped her lips as she did what she had been waiting for, dreaming of, for so long—she raised her arms and looked heavenward in praise to her God.

"Thank you, God of love! God of my parents and God of my heart, in you I am whole and I am free! I have looked into your eyes and felt your touch, and now I know!"

Healed! Able to stand tall on the day of the Lord in the house of the Lord! And she knew that at last she was, indeed, free. *(Phyllis Williams Kumorowski)*

Women were often quite prominent as benefactors and leaders of ancient synagogues. A third-century inscription from Phocaea in Asia Minor is dedicated to such a woman: "Tation, wife of Straton the son of Empedon, made a gift to the Jews of the house and the walls of the peristyle court which she had built from her own resources. The congregation of the Jews has honored Tation, wife of Straton the son of Empedon, with a gold crown and a seat of honor." Far from being relegated to a "women's gallery," this important woman was given a position of prominence in the synagogue assembly. (White, 2.324-25)

# The Woman Accused of Adultery

*A woman accused of adultery is saved from execution by Jesus.*

## The Story

AND they all went home, while Jesus went to the mount of Olives. At daybreak he appeared again in the temple, and all the people gathered round him. He had taken his seat and was engaged in teaching them when the scribes and the Pharisees brought in a woman caught committing adultery. Making her stand in the middle they said to him, 'Teacher, this woman was caught in the very act of adultery. In the law Moses has laid down that such women are to be stoned. What do you say about it?' They put the question as a test, hoping to frame a charge against him.

Jesus bent down and wrote with his finger on the ground. When they continued to press their question he sat up straight and said, 'Let whichever of you is free from sin throw the first stone at her.' Then once again he bent down and wrote on the ground. When they heard what he said, one by one they went away, the eldest first; and Jesus was left alone, with the woman still standing there. Jesus again sat up and said to the woman, 'Where are they? Has no one condemned you?' She answered, 'No one, sir.' 'Neither do I condemn you,' Jesus said. 'Go; do not sin again.'

## Comments on the Story

The traditional naming of this story as "The Woman Accused of Adultery" is quite telling since the focus of the narrative is not on the woman and her story at all but on a challenge to Jesus' honor proffered by the scribes and Pharisees. It is a story about male interaction and a struggle over male power, which has been written on the body of a woman, named as adulteress. She has no real name and so can represent the women of the first century and all subsequent centuries whose bodies have been symbolized and demonized as vessels of sin and who have been objectified before the male gaze.

Her story can function representatively in another way also in that according to tradition history, it is not found in the earliest manuscripts that contain the Johannine Gospel and when it is found in later manuscripts, it is located at different points in the narrative. It is not affected by literary context, therefore, but can be read alone. While she is one woman without name or location or even literary context, she is also many women who share the same fate. The history of her story is indicative also of the fragile inclusion of stories of

114

women within narratives constructed at a time in the first century when patriarchy was being reinstated not only in early Christianity but also in the Greco-
Roman world.

If we see this woman through the eyes of the scribes and Pharisees, she is
symbol of sin, "caught committing adultery." She is an object to be pointed to
and she is described in terms of sin and law (8:4-5). On reading the law, however, one becomes aware that both Leviticus 20:10 and Deuteronomy 22:22-
24, which deal with such a case, state that both the woman and the man who
have offended by committing adultery are to be put to death. The serious omis-
sion in this story is the other party to the act. This highlights even more strongly the symbolic nature of woman as intimately connected with sin in the eyes
of those who condemn her. To purge a society or community of the female sinner is assumed to purge it of sin.

Verse 6 is very telling in relation to the story—they said this to test him, so
that they might have some charge to bring against him. This verse is situated
near the midpoint of the story and focuses the story for the reader. The woman
for whom this is a life and death situation is, for the scribes and Pharisees, a
pawn in a "game" of challenge and riposte in the public arena of male struggles for honor and power. They certainly do not write the woman's story but
they write their words, their definitions, their power struggles on her body, the
object of their gaze. For contemporary storytellers there is a warning here: that
the struggle between different first-century Jewish and Jewish-Christian groups
over issues of law not be retold in terms of anti-Jewish polemic but that the
scribes and Pharisees can represent a long history of Christian men writing stories of sin and violation of laws governing sexuality on the bodies of countless
women held up before the male public gaze—heretics and healers, witches and
sorcerers, prophets and poets.

Jesus' first response is to the scribes and Pharisees but his words move the
focus from the woman as object and sinner to the entire gathered crowd and
especially the woman's accusers—"Let whichever of you is free from sin
throw the first stone at her" (8:7). Jesus attaches sin not just to a woman but to
men as well, and challenges a law that gives a right over the life of another so
that only those who are without sin themselves can cast life-threatening stones
at another.

Only then does Jesus turn to the woman, addressing her with the title,
"Woman" (absent from the REB translation), which he uses for his mother
(2:4; 19:26) and for Mary Magdalene (20:15). There is a formality about this
address, rather than it connoting relationship, and yet in those other instances
the relationship is most intimate. Jesus, therefore, encounters the woman as
human subject, not as object. He does not condemn her as sinner but challenges her as he does men also to work against sin in her life (8:11; cf. 5:14).
In the story, she has been moved from objectified other to participating subject

in the invitation to God's *basileia* or kingdom vision, which Jesus preaches, a vision of humanity freed from the bondage of human sin.

But what of the woman's story—how would she tell it? We do not hear her voice; we are not given her perspective nor that of her sisters, the women storytellers of the early Christian era. She might tell of her stand of defiance before those who singled her out and failed to bring her supposed accomplice before their justice or she might equally speak of the false accusation and the way she was being used within a round of power games. She might also tell of her dread as she faced accusers whom she knew had the power to put her to death without any court of appeal on her part. Linked to this dread was the shame of being a public spectacle.

How would she describe those moments of tension when Jesus stooped to write on the ground—was he another and even more powerful figure that she was brought before him? Why the delay—was he seeking simply to prolong her agony? She does not name Jesus as does the Samaritan woman; she does not recognize his power as extraordinary. She does not make theological claims, but simply answers his question—"Has no one condemned you?" Readers are left to speculate on her response to Jesus as human subject, incorporated now into the community of women and men who know sin and are invited by Jesus to free their lives of that sin. She is not singled out nor does the encounter with Jesus make her unique, but returns her to her human community and invites her to participate in the extension of God's *basileia* by avoiding sin. She is truly representative and stands as challenge to all who objectify not only women but also men and to anyone who usurps power over the life of another.

This story was not originally found in John. It does not appear in the earliest manuscripts of John or any of the other canonical Gospels. But in later manuscripts it is sometimes found in Luke and sometimes here in John. Thus it appears to have circulated independently of any of the Gospels. It became quite popular in Christian storytelling circles, so much so that it was deemed appropriate for placement in the canonical Gospels by many Christian scribes. Where to place it, however, varied from scribe to scribe.

### Retelling the Story

Making her stand in the middle they said to him, "Teacher, this woman was caught in the very act of adultery. (John 8:3*b*-4)

I never intended to offend anyone. My husband had beaten me—again. I know the law allows it, but I couldn't allow it anymore. I just had to get away, at least for a while. So I left. I just wanted to be alone. Then he came along.

I had only gotten a little ways outside of town when he came by. I've known

Though according to Jewish law men and women were both held responsible for adultery, storytellers often preferred to dwell on the punishment of women. A similar story, which may, in fact, be a model for this one, is that of Susanna found in the apocryphal addition to the book of Daniel. Susanna was a beautiful, righteous Jewish woman married to a prominent Babylonian. In the story, two "elders" of the community spy on her while she is at her private bath in the garden and threaten to accuse her of adultery if she does not submit to them. When she responds by raising a clamor, the elders then make their accusation. They claim to have been "in a corner of the garden" when they saw Susanna "shut the garden doors and [dismiss] her maids, and then a young man, who had been in hiding, came and lay with her. . . . We saw them in the act, but we could not hold the man; he was too strong for us." When Susanna is brought forward for punishment, Daniel intervenes in the case with the help of God and proves the accusers guilty and deserving of God's punishment. This they summarily receive by being put to death by the people (Susanna [third to first century B.C.E.]). Women accused of adultery did not always escape, however. In the Mishnah there is a story of a priest's daughter who is said to have been caught in the act of adultery and is put to death by burning her alive (*Sanhedrin* 7.2). (See Brown, *Death of the Messiah*, 1.369)

Mark all my life. We played together as children and celebrated each other's marriages and children's births. He's always been there for me. He's known how my husband has treated me over the years. He's seen the welts; he's heard the screaming. Somehow he has always found a way to let me know that I'm not alone, that someone cares—that God cares.

And he let me know that again this time. We sat by a stream where he washed the blood from my face and he held my hand.

I didn't mean to begin weeping that way, but so many years of pent-up hurts just seemed to burst to the surface. He held me in his arms until the sobs faded away. Then he very tenderly kissed my tear-stained face. Time and space seemed to drift away from us both. We didn't even notice anyone else was there until they were upon us.

Savagely they tore us apart, shouting obscenities at us. We tried to explain, but no one would listen. I guess it didn't matter to anyone. A married woman should never have been in another man's embrace—for any reason.

After that, it got so confusing. Some were shouting horrible things. "Stone her! Death to the whore!" These were my people, my friends, my neighbors! I was struck dumb by their fury and their violence. They were all around me. Then there was a lull of a kind as some of my accusers huddled together. The

117

crowd seemed to be tensely awaiting a verdict. I don't know how to describe the way those men looked at me when they turned around. It was almost a triumphant, glowing leer, as though they had won some sort of victory.

"Ha!" one of them shouted. "Now we have him!"

I didn't know what they were talking about. Were they talking about Mark? He was nowhere in sight. I remember wondering whether they had already killed him, or had simply forgotten about him as they seized upon the errant wife. Perhaps they felt no need to get rid of us both—but then, who were they talking about?

I had little time to think about it, though, for again they turned on me and began dragging me toward the opposite end of town. I tried to talk to them, plead with them for understanding, for mercy. No one listened. No one cared. They were more interested in proving a point, in purging an evil from their midst. I was nothing to them. My "friends" remained silent, or joined right in the mob, shouting with all the rest. I couldn't believe it. The woman who had lived next door to me all my life spat on me. I saw my husband bend over and pick up a large rock.

Onward and onward we went until finally I was thrust to the ground. I lay there waiting for it to happen. I knew they were going to stone me to death, there on the street where I had taken my first steps, where I had watched my children play with their children. Life wasn't worth much anymore, anyway. I closed my eyes and hoped the blow that would take me from consciousness would come quickly.

Nothing happened. I became aware that the noise had quieted. Cautiously, I opened my eyes. A man that I had seen briefly that afternoon stood before me. It was that prophet from Nazareth—the one who had caused all that commotion when he came into town. I noticed his clothes—simple homespun, not very impressive for a prophet. What struck me most, though, was his demeanor. His very presence seemed calming. I allowed myself to breathe.

Then one of the town leaders strode forward. As a couple of other men wrenched me to my feet, he spoke to the prophet, loud enough so all could hear. "Teacher, this woman was caught in the very act of committing adultery. Now, in the law, Moses commanded us to stone such women. What do you say?"

My shame was complete. Not only did I need to die for my error, my weakness, but they were going to make a sport out of my humiliation before my family, all those who had known me, and this holy man. I had suspected God had abandoned me long ago. Now I would just have to hear him pronounce officially that it was so and that death would bring me no peace, either. I waited for his condemnation, hoping it would be brief; what remained of my strength and composure was failing rapidly.

Yet he did not respond. He looked at me with the most compassionate eyes I have ever seen and then he knelt down. "Well, here it comes," I thought. "He's getting a rock. He cares, but he will enforce the law."

But he didn't pick up a rock. He just remained kneeling there. What was he going to do? Was he going to pray first? In my twisted state, I even envisioned him jumping up and throwing a cloud of dust in front of them, calling for me to run, to escape. I briefly tensed my muscles.

Then, as the crowd pushed closer to see, he began writing in the dirt. I couldn't tell what he was writing, for his back was to me. I think he must have been naming their darkest secrets, if such a thing is possible, because as they came forward to question him, the looks on their faces were something to behold! As they came forward, they would look down, and their faces would blanch—every one of them! Then they would cast their eyes down and move away, or slink back into the crowd. I've never seen anything like it.

He stood then, and said—gently, but so that all could hear, "Let anyone among you who is without sin be the first to throw a stone at her." Then he knelt and continued to write on the ground.

In later Christian lore, the adulterous woman comes to be identified with the woman who is a sinner in Luke 7:36-50, and both stories are said to be about Mary Magdalene. This is not at all true to the biblical text, where Mary Magdalene is never identified with these two stories. Nor do the two stories in any way indicate they are about the same person. Yet Christian imagination makes that connection, and Mary Magdalene comes to be venerated in Christian piety as the archetypal sinner who repents. She becomes a popular figure in Renaissance art where she is repeatedly portrayed as a nude or partially nude figure in the act of repenting. (Haskins)

One by one, slowly and quietly, they left. Finally we were there alone. I could hear the sound of birdsong on the quiet street. He stood as though he were very tired and very sad, and said to me, "Woman, where are they? Has no one condemned you?"

I could hardly find my voice. I could only shake my head in numb disbelief as I said, "No. No one, sir."

"Neither do I condemn you," he said, very softly. "Go your way, and from now on, don't sin again."

I was a person to him, not a point of law, not a piece of property to be bartered, nor a piece of trash to be discarded. He never even asked my name; he raised his hand to hush me when I tried to tell him what had happened. I don't think any of the external things in which we place so much value were of any importance to him. He didn't care what I had done or not done; he only cared for me and for what I might become. So I will be "me" now, wherever that will take me. I don't know what it will mean exactly, but I know that whatever happens, God is with me. God does care. I know because I have felt God's mercy and seen God's face. *(Phyllis Williams Kumorowski)*

# The Woman Who Anointed Jesus at Bethany

*A woman anoints Jesus at a meal in a controversial act that is prophetic of his death.*

## The Story

JESUS was at Bethany in the house of Simon the leper, when a woman approached him with a bottle of very costly perfume; and she began to pour it over his head as he sat at table. The disciples were indignant when they saw it. 'Why this waste?' they said. 'It could have been sold for a large sum and the money given to the poor.' Jesus noticed, and said to them, 'Why make trouble for the woman? It is a fine thing she has done for me. You have the poor among you always, but you will not always have me. When she poured this perfume on my body it was her way of preparing me for burial. Truly I tell you: wherever this gospel is proclaimed throughout the world, what she has done will be told as her memorial.'

## Comments on the Story

This story and the traditions it represent are quite extraordinary in the Gospel narratives. The story depicts a woman active in relation to Jesus, who receives from her rather than having her be the recipient of his healing power or authoritative teaching or both, as is more typically narrated in the Gospels. It also belongs within a quite complex line of tradition development as already indicated when discussing the woman called sinner in the Lukan tradition (Luke 7:36-50).

It has been suggested that this tradition of an anointing woman originated in women's circles as they gathered to remember their companion and friend, Jesus, after his death, and in the process began the weaving of meaning around that death. In such a setting, women may have drawn on a woman's ritual of pouring sweets or good things over the head of a guest to welcome the person into her home and to give honor to the one so welcomed. The language of the story still retains echoes of this ritual action. As women gave meaning to Jesus as the anointed one, their ritual storytelling wove in a new thread of anointing with "costly perfume" indicating the lavishness of the action as well as introducing a prophetic note. Women's ritual meaning-making is woven into a woman's story and it is the story of a woman of action, a woman who crosses gender boundaries in recognition of a most sensitive and tragic moment in the life of Jesus.

As this story passed into circles of male meaning-making, it began to take on elements from its new context. These included indignation at such bold actions attributed to a woman and objections to the woman's prophetic meaning-making of Jesus as the anointed one. The developing tradition of a woman's anointing of Jesus must have been strong, however, and hence responses to the disciples' objections were attributed to Jesus.

Within the Matthean community's telling of the Jesus story, similar to the Markan, this story is placed at the beginning of the Passion narrative and incorporates a woman into the *dramatis personae* of the Passion narrative whom the readers meet within in its opening verses—the disciples (26:1), the chief priests and elders of the people as representative of Jewish leaders (26:3), Jesus, and in verses 6-13, a woman of action, who separates herself from the crowd and enters into what is most likely a male meal or *haburah,* to anoint Jesus. Her story parallels that of her sisters who enter the male public space at the foot of the cross to remain faithful witnesses to Jesus' death and resurrection. As we have already noted, they did not go to anoint Jesus' body because that action had already been performed by their sister who prophetically anointed Jesus for death.

This is one of the three highly structured interpretations of the woman's action given by Jesus, each introduced by the same conjunction (26:10-12). First, Jesus interprets her action as a good work done to him. Jesus' own ministry was characterized by its works (11:2, 5); and the disciple is one who is to do what is good rather than what is bad (7:15-20; 12:33). Indeed, in the last great parable of the final judgment just prior to this story, Jesus says that to do good or offer *diakonia* to the least one is to offer it to Jesus (25:40). This woman enacts that parable by recognizing in Jesus, as he faces his Passion, the one most in need of compassion.

Jesus' second interpretation affirms the woman's sensitivity to the time in Jesus' life, a moment when he faces the threat of death at the hands of those in power who plot against him (26:4). As such he is most in need and the objection that the perfume could have been sold and the money given to the poor is shown to be absolutely inappropriate as a discipleship response at this particular moment. This interpretation recognizes the woman's discipleship sensitivity to time and in no way, however, denigrates the demands of the poor.

The final interpretation that developed in the community and was attributed to Jesus was that this woman performed the ultimate act of discipleship, namely the preparation of the body of the beloved leader and friend for burial (cf. 14:12). For Matthew, she did not simply do "what lay in her power" as in Mark (14:8) but prepared the body of Jesus for burial and hence the women do not go to anoint the body (Matt. 28:1) but to see the tomb, an action that renders them witnesses to the events surrounding the resurrection of Jesus.

The most extraordinary element in this story is, however, the final words of Jesus in which the woman's action as narrated in this story is made a constitutive element of the gospel. It is to be told as part of the good news wherever it is proclaimed. Conversely, one could interpret this statement to mean that the gospel is not truly or completely proclaimed unless what she has done, her good work, her *diakonia,* is proclaimed. And its telling is to be "in memory of her," not of Jesus. The action of this woman, her courageous crossing of boundaries to minister as disciple and friend to the Jesus who faces death, is a mirror image of the action of Jesus both in life and in death. The breaking of bread and pouring out of wine "in memory of him" is paralleled by the breaking of boundaries and the pouring out of ointment "in memory of her." A woman's action at a supper and Jesus' own action at a supper are to be remembered as constitutive elements of the gospel story.

This story provides a significant challenge to today's community of believers who both tell and ritualize the memory of Jesus. One has to ask whether this woman's story and that of many other women of action in the reign-of-God or Jesus movement whom she represents, are told and ritualized as constitutive of the gospel. Or rather, do we remember the one who betrayed Jesus or the other who denied Jesus rather than the woman who recognized his vulnerability in facing his Passion? And in this remembering, does gender govern what is proclaimed rather than the words of Jesus of the Markan and Matthean Gospels? These and other questions must be faced by today's communities who continue the story of Jesus as well as the praxis of the reign of God.

## Retelling the Story

*What she has done will be told as her memorial. (Matt. 26:13b)*

People tend to think an inheritance is the money, the property—it's not; it's the memories.

Donna carefully lifted the old quilt from the massive trunk and smoothed it across her lap. It had been her mother's when she was a child, and her mother's mother before her. Donna's great-grandmother had created that piece of usable art stitch-by-stitch in her sod house on the Kansas prairie.

It was worn now, faded and fragile, but it had been a warm comfort to a little girl on a dark and frosty night, a refuge from the howling winds outside her bedroom window. Donna fingered Grandma's quilt lovingly.

"Saying the quilt" had become a bedtime ritual when she was young. When she had been tucked into bed and the quilt smoothed out over her, she would point to one of the colorful squares and ask, "Say that story. Would you tell me about that one again?"

Then her mother would snuggle down close to her and tell one of the stories of her heritage that had been sewn into her coverlet. "Oh! That one tells about how they crossed the frontier in their prairie schooner! See the horses pulling them?" Then would follow a wonderful story about great-grandmother as a little girl heading west with her brothers and sisters and Ma and Pa. She would hear of the courage and faith that they had, which had been passed down to her. Donna delighted in hearing the words repeated over and over, the same stories that her mother had loved as a child.

Her favorite story was about a mostly blue block near the corner of the quilt, showing a woman kneeling before a bearded man. "What's this?" she would ask, already knowing the answer.

"Why, that one tells us who we are! It was who Great-grandma was, and who Grandma was, and who I am and who you are, too. This was a woman who lived a long time ago in a faraway place called Israel. The man in front of her is Jesus. You know who Jesus is and how he gave the word of God and the love of God to each person he met. But on that day, it was not Jesus who gave love, but

> Ancient perfume was oil-based and was usually applied on the hair. It was a common courtesy to provide perfume for one's guests at a banquet. What appears objectionable in this case is the quality of perfume that is used. Athenaeus refers to the servants providing "sweet-smelling perfume in a saucer" for the guests at a banquet (11.462c-d). Josephus tells of a time when Agrippa used this custom to his advantage when appearing before the Roman senate: "On being summoned by the senate, he anointed his head with unguents as if he had arrived from a banquet that had just broken up" (*Antiquities* 19.239 [first century C.E.]).

this woman. She came right up to him at dinner one night and lavishly poured expensive perfume on him. She was filled with love for him and the fragrance of her gift of love filled the room for days. Some people there objected to her gift. They thought the money she spent on the perfume would have been a better gift. They just didn't understand that she was giving love—even when it was costly to her to do so. But Jesus understood. And just like with all gifts of love, her timing was perfect. Jesus needed that gift of love right then to sustain him through what was coming, just like you can go out and face anything because of the love that's been lavished on you!"

Donna tenderly ran her fingers across the embroidered lines. The quilt was a testimony to that kind of love. In this square it was a sacrifice of money and dignity when a costly perfume was given; in that square was the sacrifice of time as she viewed again the picture of a mother up at night with a sick child. There was the sacrifice of dreams as the family moved ahead after a death on the trail. In the quilt was a lifetime of choosing to give beauty, warmth, love, and grace in every way a woman could.

"Whatcha doin', Mom?" It was Donna's six-year-old daughter, Kim, who had silently entered the room and her thoughts.

"Hi, honey. I was just—remembering."

"That's Grandma's quilt, isn't it?" the child asked as she squirmed up into her mother's lap.

Donna held her close, wrapping the quilt around her. "Yes, it is, sweetheart. It's Grandma's quilt."

"Oh, good! Do we have to wait for bedtime, or can we say the quilt now?"

Donna caressed her hair and Kim thought she could see a trace of tears in her mother's eyes. "I would love to say the quilt with you. Which square would you like to hear about?"

The little girl did not hesitate as she pointed to her favorite—a mostly blue square with a woman kneeling before a bearded man. *(Phyllis Williams Kumorowski)*

Perfumes and spices were also used to anoint a body for burial. A basic description of this funerary ritual is found in the Jewish apocryphal work *Testament of Abraham* 20.11 (first to second century C.E.): "And they tended the body of the righteous Abraham with divine ointments and perfumes until the third day after his death. And they buried him in the promised land at the oak of Mamre." Lucian refers to the same custom among the Greeks and Romans: "Then they bathe them [i.e., the corpses] and after anointing with the finest of perfume that body which is already hasting to corruption, and crowning it with pretty flowers, they lay them in state, clothed in splendid raiment" (*de Luctu* 11 [second century C.E.]). As the Gospel story implies, the task of preparing a body for burial was usually delegated to the women.

# The Samaritan Woman

*A Samaritan woman meets Jesus at a well, converses at length on matters of theology, and becomes a model disciple.*

**The Story**

NEWS now reached the Pharisees that Jesus was winning and baptizing more disciples than John; although, in fact, it was his disciples who were baptizing, not Jesus himself. When Jesus heard this, he left Judaea and set out once more for Galilee. He had to pass through Samaria, and on his way came to a Samaritan town called Sychar, near the plot of ground which Jacob gave to his son Joseph; Jacob's well was there. It was about noon, and Jesus, tired after his journey, was sitting by the well.

His disciples had gone into the town to buy food. Meanwhile a Samaritan woman came to draw water, and Jesus said to her, 'Give me a drink.' The woman said, 'What! You, a Jew, ask for a drink from a Samaritan woman?' (Jews do not share drinking vessels with Samaritans.) Jesus replied, 'If only you knew what God gives, and who it is that is asking you for a drink, you would have asked him and he would have given you living water.' 'Sir,' the woman said, 'you have no bucket and the well is deep, so where can you get "living water?" Are you greater than Jacob our ancestor who gave us the well and drank from it himself, he and his sons and his cattle too?' Jesus answered, 'Everyone who drinks this water will be thirsty again; but whoever drinks the water I shall give will never again be thirsty. The water that I shall give will be a spring of water within him, welling up and bringing eternal life.' 'Sir,' said the woman, 'give me this water, and then I shall not be thirsty, nor have to come all this way to draw water.'

'Go and call your husband,' said Jesus, 'and come back here.' She answered, 'I have no husband.' Jesus said, 'You are right in saying that you have no husband, for though you have had five husbands, the man you are living with now is not your husband. You have spoken the truth!' 'Sir,' replied the woman, 'I can see you are a prophet. Our fathers worshipped on this mountain, but you Jews say that the place where God must be worshipped is in Jerusalem.' 'Believe me,' said Jesus, 'the time is coming when you will worship the Father neither on this mountain nor in Jerusalem. You Samaritans worship you know not what; we worship what we know. It is from the Jews that salvation comes. But the time is coming, indeed it is already here, when true worshippers will worship the Father in spirit and in truth. These are the worshippers the Father wants. God is spirit, and those who worship him must worship in spirit and in truth.' The woman answered, 'I know that Messiah' (that is, Christ) 'is coming. When he comes he will make everything clear to us.' Jesus said to her, 'I am he, I who am speaking to you.'

At that moment his disciples returned, and were astonished to find him talking with a woman; but none of them said, 'What do you want?' or 'Why are you talking with her?' The woman left her water-jar and went off to the town, where she said to the people, 'Come and see a man who has told me everything I ever did. Could this be the Messiah?' They left the town and made their way towards him.

MEANWHILE the disciples were urging him, 'Rabbi, have something to eat.' But he said, 'I have food to eat of which you know nothing.' At this the disciples said to one another, 'Can someone have brought him food?' But Jesus said, 'For me it is meat and drink to do the will of him who sent me until I have finished his work.

'Do you not say, "Four months more and then comes harvest"? But look, I tell you, look around at the fields: they are already white, ripe for harvesting. The reaper is drawing his pay and harvesting a crop for eternal life, so that sower and reaper may rejoice together. That is how the saying comes true: "One sows, another reaps." I sent you to reap a crop for which you have not laboured. Others laboured and you have come in for the harvest of their labour.'

Many Samaritans of that town came to believe in him because of the woman's testimony: 'He told me everything I ever did.' So when these Samaritans came to him they pressed him to stay with them; and he stayed there two days. Many more became believers because of what they heard from his own lips. They told the woman, 'It is no longer because of what you said that we believe, for we have heard him ourselves; and we are convinced that he is the Saviour of the world.'

## Comments on the Story

The image of the "woman at the well" or even more powerfully, the image of the woman who leaves her water jar at the well and goes back to the city to tell her people that she has discovered the Messiah, captures the Christian imagination. The strength of its symbolism renders the story of this woman a significant one, especially in the contemporary context of a reclaiming of women's stories in sacred texts. Unfortunately, however, this symbolism has been marred by an androcentric history, which sees the woman in the typical stereotype of the evil woman, the one who provokes sexually [an interpretation given to the Samaritan woman's encounter with Jesus] or whose insatiable sexual appetite ensnares men [the woman with five husbands].

The story of the Samaritan woman's encounter with Jesus is carefully placed in the Johannine Gospel, one whose symbolic quality is well attested, between the two Cana incidents, a series of stories of encounter with Jesus, which lead to the other person coming to believe in Jesus. It is also set in relationship to the story of Nicodemus, which precedes it, and the healing of the official's son, which follows.

Like the previous story in this volume, this one too seems to be less historical than symbolic within the context of the meaning-making of early Christian communities, not only in relation to Jesus but also in relation to their own developing self-identity. In this instance, the identity and value of the Samaritan mission is storied in this missionary woman who is more than a character in a story. She can be read as representative of that mission and the Samaritan community's struggle for identity in relation to the Jewish prophet, Jesus.

The entire tenor of the conversation between the woman and Jesus is religious and theological. The initial request for a drink is merely a catalyst, in the context of encounter between Jesus and a Samaritan, for an exploration of living water, which can no longer be found only in sources linked with ancestors in the faith—the well of Jacob where not only he but also Rachel and Leah, together with their family and their flocks, down through generations, had been satisfied. The center of the Samaritan community's life was being shifted and the woman faithfully represents to Jesus their core theological beliefs.

The conversation moves then to other areas central to Samaritan life and especially their ancestral claim to the north, or to Israel, as the place of preservation of the true tradition in the line of Moses rather than the Davidic kingdom and lineage associated with Jerusalem and the south. Once again, the woman faithfully presents the Samaritan belief while Jesus claims his own Jewish tradition and the centrality of Jerusalem, but he also moves beyond a claim on either Gerazim (the Samaritan mountain of worship) or Jerusalem, to a place where Jew and Samaritan can meet in worship and that is in the spirit (4:20-24). The conversation enables readers to glimpse the religious and theological shifts necessary for Jew and Samaritan to meet on the new ground of belief in Jesus.

The Samaritan woman's journey is representative of that faith journey for the Samaritans. She recognizes Jesus as a prophet and then as a messianic prophet who would open up a new future for the people as did Moses in the first great act of liberation. It is in this context that the dialogue about the five husbands must be situated. It is highly unlikely that a historical women would have, in fact, had five husbands. Rather, this section too must be understood in its representative aspect. In it, the reader can hear Jesus the prophet drawing on the prophetic imagery associated with the Israel that strayed or sinned, the imagery of the unfaithful wife. This imagery was most prominent in Hosea, a prophet of the north and hence of Samaria. Samaria's mingling of the Mosaic tradition with other religious traditions after the Assyrian invasion was considered a contamination of the pure Israelite tradition and hence, the Jewish rejection of Samaritans as unclean foreigners. In the history of interpretation of this text and of the Samaritan woman as one of loose sexual morality, one can see the inherent misogyny and danger in symbolizing infidelity in such a gendered way. Women have borne the weight of such symbolism down through the ages.

But another symbolism prevails in this story. The Samaritan woman is not only theologian but also missionary, signified first in the powerful symbol of leaving her water jar (just as other disciples left boats and tax offices) and going to the city where she tells all that she has experienced and come to believe. She is, therefore, the catalyst for all the inhabitants of the city going out to encounter Jesus for themselves and their coming to believe in him as a result of that encounter. This in no way lessens the symbolic value of the woman's mission. She was indeed true apostle-disciple because she led others to Jesus as did John the Baptist (1:35-39), Andrew (1:40-42), and Philip (1:43-51).

The disciples' astonishment (4:27) that Jesus was speaking with a woman is perhaps indicative of the challenging nature of this story within early Christianity. The mission to the Samaritans was by now a part of the history of the Johannine community, but a woman as symbol of the theological and religious shifts occurring in early Christian communities and of significant missionary activity was clearly still not fully accepted. The story of the Samaritan woman is, therefore, an important one to retell and reclaim so that it may today, as in the first century, authorize and symbolize women's active mission in proclaiming Jesus and the reign of God and women's competent participation in articulating theology. In doing so, however, we must take care not to reinscribe in our stories the misogynist imaging of women as the unfaithful ones as found in the prophets and in this Gospel story. It is not construct of the woman who has five husbands that is central to this story, but rather the image of the woman who leaves her water jar and goes to tell the city of the one whom she has encountered and who has changed her life, Jesus—prophet, messiah, and liberator.

### Retelling the Story

The woman left her water-jar and went off to the town, where she said to the people, 'Come and see a man who has told me everything I ever did. Could this be the Messiah?' (John 4:28-29)

"Deborah, Sarah, I am so glad to finally be able to *tell* someone exactly how it happened!"

The three Samaritan women, baskets and buckets strewn aside, huddled excitedly at the well.

"Slow down, Elizabeth, and tell us *everything*! I want to hear every detail! You say it happened right here? Yesterday afternoon?"

Elizabeth, daughter of Samuel the tentmaker, began to speak. "Yes. I was sitting right here on the edge of the well. Actually, I wasn't in a very good mood. It had been a terrible morning. Avram and I had had a terrible argument.

Then, as always, he just left in the middle of it to go wall wailing or read a good scroll or something manly like that, and I was left to do all those trivial little feminine things at home."

"Like scrubbing the floor," Deborah said with understanding.

"And loading up the wood for the fire," Sarah added.

"And preparing the supper, and getting the ground ready to plow," she pointed to the bucket at her feet, "and walking a half mile to haul water enough for us all."

Her friends nodded sympathetically and she continued.

"So there I was at the well, grumbling to myself when this man I'd never seen before walked right up to me. . . ."

"A man? Here? What was he doing here? They have their own space."

"A man? As in one of those 'I don't mind making my wife go all the way out there to fetch a heavy bucket of water, but I'd never be caught dead there myself' kind of people?"

"Exactly." Elizabeth was beginning to feel better.

"He talked to you—without anyone else around?" This was the juiciest gossip Deborah had heard all day.

This story is told as a midrash on the story of Isaac and Rebecca in Genesis 24, a connection that is made explicit by the fact that the two stories take place at the same well, the well of Jacob (or Isaac). In Genesis, Isaac is the son of Abraham and the child of promise. Since it is necessary that Isaac marry and have children so that the promise to Abraham's progeny would be fulfilled, a servant is sent to find a wife from Abraham's people. The servant, with the help of God, devises a test. When he comes to a well, he asks God to send the woman whom God has chosen for Isaac to the well. The servant will ask her for a drink, and if she gives him a drink and offers to water his camels, he will know this is the one. It happens just as he prayed it might, and in this way Rebecca is identified as the woman whom God chose to bear the seed of promise from whom all nations would be blessed.

"Yes, dear. I thought it was pretty presumptuous, too. Humph. Like I don't have trouble enough with the one I've got. Well, as I was saying, this Jewish man. . . ."

"Jewish?"

"Did I stutter?"

Sarah was aghast. She had missed this part of the story. "A Jewish man talked to you? Jewish—as in a Jerusalem worshiper?"

"Yes! That's what I'm trying to tell you! Not only a man, but a foreigner, too, walked right up to the well!"

"How presumptuous!"

When the narrator points out that "Jews do not share drinking vessels with Samaritans" he is referring to a tradition that Samaritans were considered ritually impure and would impart that ritual impurity to any eating or drinking vessels they touched. There was even a more specific tradition that stated that all Samaritan women were ritually impure because, according to popular Jewish belief, they were menstruants from their cradle. Thus the mere touch of a Samaritan woman would render a Jew ritually impure. (Brown, *The Gospel According to John* 1.170)

"This is not their territory!"

"Cheeky!"

The women were enjoying this.

"He probably came to be sure you were doing it right," Sarah noted.

"Or to see what other little jobs they could think up for us to do," Deborah added.

"So, what did he want?"

Elizabeth motioned them closer. "Well, first he asked for a drink of water."

"I told you so!" Deborah announced with a flourish. "That's men for you—always wanting us to do something for them that they could do themselves!"

"Humph! A come on; that's what it was! I'll wager he wanted more than a drink of water!" Sarah said under her breath.

"No," Elizabeth answered thoughtfully. "Actually, that's when it got a little strange. He said he wanted to give me some water."

"From the well?" Deborah asked.

"No, he called it living water."

Deborah frowned. "Water with living things—in it?"

Her reverie broken, Elizabeth turned to her friend. "Honestly, Deborah, sometimes you're worse than a child! He was being serious."

"Okay," she conceded. "So, what's living water?"

"I think he was talking about God."

Sarah interrupted her. "Why would a Jewish man talk to a Samaritan woman about God? It doesn't make any sense. My own husband won't even talk to me about something so . . . deep, so important."

"That's just it! Why not? Isn't our God the God of all of us? This man was different from any man I've ever met. I believe he might have been sent to us by God. I believe he is the Messiah."

"The Messiah! Here?" For once in her life, Sarah found herself speechless.

"I just don't buy it, Elizabeth," she said, shaking her head. "Even if, by some miracle, this man *were* the Messiah, *why* would he talk to a woman? And if he *were* to talk to a woman, I can't imagine why—no offense, Elizabeth, but. . . ."

"Why would he talk to me?"

"Nothing against you personally, Elizabeth; you're my friend, but, well, you haven't exactly led a . . . spiritual life, if you know what I mean. If he really wanted to start including women in theological discussion, wouldn't the Messiah have spent some time in selecting the woman to whom he was going to speak?"

Elizabeth flushed and answered softly, remembering the gentle stranger's pointed remarks. "I think he knew exactly what I was like." She struggled for the right words, gaining momentum and strength as the reality of her insight grew clearer. "I think that may even be why he chose me. Maybe the household of God is not about how much we know, or what kind of status or worthiness we may or may not seem to have, or what race or sex we happened to be born—not even what choices we may have made in the past. Maybe that's his point—to get past those differences. Maybe that's *how* we can begin to worship God in spirit and truth the way he said."

"Okay, *okay!*" said Deborah. "You win! Calm down! It sounds like you were really convinced by this Messiah."

"Is that what you told the men?" asked Sarah.

"Yes," said Elizabeth, "but they didn't really take me seriously—not until they met him themselves. Then they too came to believe he was the Messiah."

"So," said Sarah, "if they decided he was the Messiah—and he taught that God accepts us all equally—I guess that means things are really going to change for us around here."

"Not a chance," Elizabeth said drily. "Not until they get it into their heads *and* hearts. But it will happen. It will happen some day." *(Phyllis Williams Kumorowski)*

# Sapphira

*Sapphira conspires with her husband to defraud the church and is pun-ished by God.*

## The Story

But a man called Ananias sold a property, and with the connivance of his wife Sapphira kept back some of the proceeds, and brought part only to lay at the apostles' feet. Peter said, 'Ananias, how was it that Satan so possessed your mind that you lied to the Holy Spirit by keeping back part of the price of the land? While it remained unsold, did it not remain yours? Even after it was turned into money, was it not still at your own dis-posal? What made you think of doing this? You have lied not to men but to God.' When Ananias heard these words he dropped dead; and all who heard were awestruck. The young men rose and covered his body, then car-ried him out and buried him.

About three hours passed, and his wife came in, unaware of what had happened. Peter asked her, 'Tell me, were you paid such and such a price for the land?' 'Yes,' she replied, 'that was the price.' Peter said, 'Why did the two of you conspire to put the Spirit of the Lord to the test? Those who buried your husband are there at the door, and they will carry you away.' At once she dropped dead at this feet. When the young men came in, they found her dead; and they car-ried her out and buried her beside her husband.

Great awe fell on the whole church and on all who heard of this.

## Comments on the Story

This story of Sapphira, together with several others that follow in this com-mentary, shifts our literary focus. The move is from the Gospel stories to the Acts of the Apostles, a narrative that extends the Lukan story beyond the death and resurrection of Jesus into the expansion of the reign-of-God movement beyond Jerusalem and Palestine into Asia Minor and finally to Rome. The five women from Acts whom we shall consider are all named in a way that is in contrast to the women of the Gospel stories, most of whom are not named.

The story of Sapphira and her husband Ananias is located in the opening chapters of Acts (5:1-11) in the context of the establishment and expansion of the Jerusalem community. Twice in these chapters, with the second instance immediately preceding the story of Sapphira and Ananias, the ideal model for this community is articulated—radical redistribution of resources toward the establishment of a new household or fictive kinship, a Christian *koinonia* (2:44-45; 4:32-37). In the two verses immediately preceding this text, Barnabas is presented as the ideal type or representative of this redistribution, selling a field and bringing the money to lay at the apostles' feet (4:36-37).

If Barnabas is type then Sapphira and Ananias are antitype and their story could be considered a text of terror in which excessive violence is authorized and legitimized in the name of God. The rhetorical effect desired by the Lukan writer in this instance may have been what is presented as outcome in the concluding verse—a fear that would lead the "whole church" to undertake the ethic being proposed. There is a danger in such a text, however, in that it gives power over the life of another into the hands of those who have assumed or been given leadership in the community and that this power is narrated as having divine legitimation. It is difficult for us to imagine what is narrated as a historical incident in the life of the expanding reign-of-God movement. We must examine it, therefore, in its rhetorical effect, and examine it critically.

It seems that the Lukan writer intends that Ananias and Sapphira be read as a negative example of male/female pairs just as others are established as positive examples (Simeon and Anna—Luke 2:25-38; Aeneas and Tabitha—Acts 9:32-43; and many others throughout Luke–Acts). The implication of both is established by the repetition in verses 1 and 2 of phrases that connect the act of Ananias with Sapphira—he sells the property "with the consent of his wife" and keeps back some of the proceeds "with his wife's knowledge" (NRSV; the REB has only "with the connivance of his wife"). This seems to recognize her authority over the household resources together with Ananias and is not surprising to the Lukan reader who has the image of the women who followed Jesus ministering out of their resources, freely distributing them without it being necessary to say with their husband's consent or knowledge. The statements in Acts 5:1-2, however, seem to implicate Sapphira with Ananias in the deception in order that both the women and men of the Lukan community would be challenged by the story rather than to validate or even recognize women's authority over resources.

A careful reading of this story from the point of view of Sapphira raises significant questions. Although the narrative seems to establish Sapphira with Ananias as equally responsible, a knowledge of household structures in the Greco-Roman world would lead to a questioning of the level of Sapphira's involvement. The male *kyrios* or householder was head of the household and had authority over the women, children, and property of his household. One could speculate whether the property in question here belonged to Sapphira's dowry, but the text does not indicate this in any way. The reader is simply led to see Sapphira implicated in Ananias's action. Given the generally pervasive household ethos and ethic, the struggle for early Christian communities to move to another model, and the Lukan tendency to symbolically undermine women's assumption of more authority and power in certain households within emerging Christianity, the critical reader might question the level of Sapphira's involvement. The statements "with her consent" and "with her knowledge" in a situation of unequal power seems to recognize little of the power dynamics that may well have operated in such a situation. The subsequent striking of Sapphira dead would seem in such a context more capricious an act than even a surface reading might suggest. Female readers in the Lukan community who would have known well the power that functioned in households may likewise have recognized the more grave injustice to Sapphira.

The reader notes also the singular lack of compassion on the part of Peter who, instead of informing Sapphira of the death of her husband, greets her with a question about the distribution, implicates her in what is named as a testing of God's Spirit, and only then tells of her husband's death but in the context of the threat of her own imminent death. In the light of the Gospel that precedes Acts and in which it is clear that response to Jesus and to God can be invited but cannot be forced (Luke 5:1-11; 8:37; 10:25-37; 18:18-23), the position represented by Peter in relation to Sapphira (and Ananias) seems to be an assumption of authority greater than that of Jesus. The deception is equated with a putting of the Spirit of God to the test or earlier lying to God (11:4) or to the Holy Spirit (11:3) and may have been intended to be linked to the blaspheming against the Holy Spirit of Luke 12:10.

The rhetorical effect of this story is that it legitimates the authority over the life of Ananias and Sapphira that is given into the hands of Peter and the violence that results from such authority. By way of pairing, there is also an obscuring of the power imbalance between Ananias and Sapphira and hence the more capricious nature of the action in her regard. Sapphira emerges as a negative character type in relation to the ideal of redistribution of resources with Ananias. She is a reminder to the community of women's involvement not only in the establishment of the early Christian community but also actions that could undermine it. Her characterization raises questions for readers, however, in relation to power and where it really resides, thus not allowing us to rest with a surface equality or an equality of appearance. Her story cries out against the use and abuse of women's struggle toward equality and liberation, which characterized and characterizes the first century as well as our own. The small gains by women are used against them to counteract their gains or, in a more sinister fashion, to bring about their destruction as in the case of Sapphira. Her story is truly a text of terror!

### Retelling the Story

'You have lied not to men but to God.'. . . At once she dropped dead at his feet. (Acts 5:4*b*, 10*a*)

The dark eyes of the young Jewish mother looked, searchingly, into those of the harried Nazi soldier at the desk. "Are you sure our things will be safe here?" she asked. "I don't know what lies ahead for us. . . ."

"Yes, of course," the woman responded as she had so often before. "I will see to them myself." Sophie smoothed her uniform skirt as she replied, "Everything will be just fine. Bavaria should be beautiful this time of year. You'll be safe there until all this turmoil dies down. While you're away, your belongings will be kept safely here as long as they are properly tagged, I assure you. Please move on now."

She watched as the Jewish woman and her children, part of a long line of Jewish families, reluctantly placed their bags in the appointed area and went to wait for the train. Sophie did not particularly enjoy her work, but did feel good about how it supported "the Cause."

She and her husband both worked at the station, receiving, tagging, and storing the belongings of the Jewish families before they were loaded on the train for Dachau. After the train had departed, they would move quickly to sort through the luggage, saving and filing what would help the Cause, discarding the unusable memorabilia, and making room for the belongings of the next group to be relocated.

When she stopped to think about it in the still of an early morning, it gave her some discomfort to be involved in that particular job. She felt as if she were living a lie. It wasn't a bad lie, though. It made things easier for everyone. It was more polite, more civilized, and it was, ultimately, for the good of the Cause.

She believed in the Cause. She and her fiery husband had been among the first in their village to enlist in its service. Their work would help the Fatherland, and, as her husband had said that first day in Relocations, "If we play our cards right, it won't hurt us either." "This is war," he had said, confidently. "The Cause is great, but we've got to look out for ourselves, too." Heinrich had seemed so sure of himself.

She had felt a little guilty the first time she pocketed some jewelry. No one had found out, though; at least no one had said anything.

"They're probably all doing the same thing, too," she thought each time she

Why should Sapphira be responsible for her husband's transaction of the sale of the land? The story seems to presuppose an aspect of the Jewish law of property rights in marriage. The category of *kethuba* applied to the share of the husband's property that was to be transferred to the wife if the marriage was dissolved. Thus if property was sold, the wife had to agree to the sale in order to ensure that she was relinquishing her rights to her portion of the property, namely her *kethuba*. Contracts for the sale of property from this period that have been found among the papyri from Egypt show that wives were often listed as co-sellers. (Richter Reimer, 4-5)

'skimmed a little off the top' for herself. Besides, what kind of wife would she be if she went against the wishes of her husband? If he thought it was best for them, he must be right; her mother had instilled that within her long ago. None of this whole thing was her fault anyway. So she continued to tell her soothing story, then sort and skim.

Today had been a bad day, though. She was eager to get this last group through. Absentmindedly, she reached for one of the confiscated lunches. "They don't like for you to bring food aboard," she had told the elderly woman. "They have plenty for you already."

She stared at the bits of dried meat peering from between two huge slices of homemade rye bread. Her superiors frowned on her eating the confiscated food, especially while the Jews were still on the property. It spoiled the illusion they were trying to create in order to make the process go more quickly and smoothly.

"So what?" she thought. "I work hard. I deserve it."

As she raised it to her lips she happened to look beyond—into the eyes of a rabbi standing at the station window. At first she hesitated. Did he know where she had gotten it? What would he think? What would he do?

"Get a hold of yourself," she said out loud. Who cared what he or anyone else thought? She'd been playing the good little girl all her life. It was time she did something for her. She would eat it, all right, in front of him. Let him figure it out; he would soon enough anyway. She would eat every bit of it in spite of him.

His eyes met hers. He knew. He'd probably seen it all.

"Fine. You want to watch me eat? Go right ahead. See if I care," she told the passive face behind the glass. Let him watch her enjoy stuffing herself. With a defiant toss of her head she squared her shoulders and took a huge, lusty bite— too big of a bite.

Trying to chew the oversized morsel, a piece of meat lodged in her airway. As she gasped for breath, it seemed to wedge in her throat even more tightly. She clutched at her throat, trying to call for help, but no sound came forth. She gagged, she struggled, she fell to the floor, and still found no relief. Why was this happening to her?

"It's not my fault," she was thinking as the dizzying world around her turned dark and she faded from the life she found so unfair. *(Phyllis Williams Kumorowski)*

The rather gruesome death of Sapphira, following that of her husband Ananias, seems shocking to modern audiences, as accustomed to violence as we are. But such stories were staples of ancient storytelling as seen in the popular novels of the day, which are full of stories of gruesome tortures, beheadings, lashings, rape, and other acts of violence, all of which appealed to the readers of the day. (from Pervo, 48-49)

# Tabitha

*Tabitha, renowned in the church for her exemplary discipleship, is brought back to life by Peter.*

### The Story

IN Joppa there was a disciple named Tabitha (in Greek, Dorcas, meaning 'Gazelle'), who filled her days with acts of kindness and charity. At that time she fell ill and died; and they washed her body and laid it in a room upstairs. As Lydda was near Joppa, the disciples, who had heard that Peter was there, sent two men to him with the urgent request, 'Please come over to us without delay.' At once Peter went off with them. When he arrived he was taken up to the room, and all the widows came and stood round him in tears, showing him the shirts and coats that Dorcas used to make while she was with them. Peter sent them all outside, and knelt down and prayed; then, turning towards the body, he said, 'Tabitha, get up.' She opened her eyes, saw Peter, and sat up. He gave her his hand and helped her to her feet. Then he called together the members of the church and the widows and showed her to them alive. News of it spread all over Joppa, and many came to believe in the Lord.

### Comments on the Story

The Lukan use of paired male/female stories seems to function at the close of chapter 9 of Acts of the Apostles. At Lydda, Peter heals Aeneas who has been bedridden for eight years, thus causing many to turn to belief in Jesus (9:35). He is then called to nearby Joppa where a disciple, Tabitha, has just died and he restores her to life, with many coming to believe as a result of this restoration (9:42). The story of Tabitha's resuscitation, however, is a more spectacular story than that of Aeneas's healing, with more characterization and description.

Tabitha is introduced as a "disciple," the only time that a woman is specifically named as a disciple and the only time, therefore, that the female form of this very familiar word is found in the Christian Testament. Tabitha is not introduced as embedded in a patriarchal family structure and as the story later indicates, may well have been a widow or a householder, a woman of resources who used these for a group of widows in Joppa. This would be at least one explanation for their profound grief at her death. Without her good works (REB: "acts of kindness") and acts of charity, they may have been left destitute.

137

It is difficult to reconstruct the nature of the "good works" and "acts of charity" to which Tabitha is said to be devoted (the REB translation "acts of kindness and charity" tends to collapse them). Since she is named "disciple," it would be reasonable to assume that she, like other disciples, was engaged in the establishment and spread of the reign of God or kingdom. We have already noted that the ideal for this emerging community was a right distribution of resources so that no one was in need in keeping with the prophetic preaching of Jesus. Tabitha's acts of charity or compassionate deeds ensured that the widows of Joppa were not in need. Her "good works," which are distinguished in the narrative from her "acts of charity" may have extended to providing a household in which the community at Joppa might gather and she, as leader of the house, may have provided for and lead the community in its communal meal in remembrance of Jesus. There is no other use of these two phrases that describes Tabitha elsewhere in Acts. It is difficult, therefore, to establish her role with certainty. It is, however, clearly one that means that her death causes great grief not just to the widows but to the whole community in Joppa.

At the death of Tabitha, it emerges that there are a number of people called disciples in the Joppa community and one could assume that there were women in the group as well as men. It is this group that sends messengers to find Peter. On Peter's arrival at the house in which Tabitha is laid—presumably her own house—the reader meets the widows who show Peter the garments she has made. It would seem that this was the activity that provided them with the necessary resources for survival and they may well have been engaged with Tabitha in their production. This text also creates an impression in readers that "the widows" is a clearly marked group and this group is linked to another designation "the saints" in 9:41 in the NRSV.

A recognition of an established group of widows in Tabitha's story reminds readers of an earlier reference to widows as a group (Acts 6:1-4). That story, likewise, narrates the care of widows, by way of "daily distribution." There is a remarkable discrepancy, however, in the terminology that the Lukan author uses in relation to male and female care of the widows. We have already noted that Tabitha was characterized by "acts of kindness and charity" while the service of the twelve males is designated *diakonia*. In Acts 6, male *diakonia* of the table and the word are distinguished with the Twelve continuing the *diakonia* of the word and appointing seven men to the *diakonia* of the table, the distribution to the widows. This was the developing language of ministry in the early church and it seems that the Lukan writer, especially in Acts, reserves it for the men who are engaged in the establishment and spread of the reign of God. Women's *diakonia,* as already seen in Luke 8:3, is modeled on that and yet they are denied *diakonia* in the narrative of the emerging church.

We have already noted that Tabitha may well have been engaged in the very same activities as the group called the Twelve. The Lukan terminology alerts us, therefore, to the tendency in Acts to contain women's active engagement in the work of spreading the gospel. Tabitha's ministry is described as contained within the household and we meet her in death and not in life until she is presented alive at the end of the story. Her story and her being named as a "disciple" may, however, have originated and developed in women's circles, perhaps by women engaged in the *diakonia* ministry in a similar way to Tabitha. They may have named her ministry and their own as *diakonia* just as they may have claimed the title of disciple for themselves. They may also have provided more details of Tabitha's engagement in the spreading of the reign of God either as leader of the Joppa house-church or as early missionary with other disciples or both.

Death could not confine Tabitha or her story. She is shown to us, the readers of her story, as alive and this glimpse of her life leads us to want to know more: How did she and her sisters survive? What did she contribute to the church of Joppa beyond her daily distribution to the widows among whom she lived? How many more of her sisters were considered disciples? What stories did they tell of this discipleship? We seek to see through the veil of the Lukan androcentric narrative to discover the woman disciple, Tabitha, and her Joppan sisters.

## Retelling the Story

In Joppa there was a disciple named Tabitha who filled her days with acts of kindness and charity. (Acts 9:36)

"How can I make you understand?" The Joppan widow searched for the right words. This was Peter; if he couldn't help them, no one could. How could she make him see that he had to do something—something *now*. Tabitha could not die! God could not want for this to happen. Not now. Not to her. As they walked together back toward Joppa, she tried to explain.

"This year," she began, "has been like no other. There were times when I knew I could not make it—did not want to make it."

The apostle remained silent.

Where could she start? Perhaps at the end of her life. "My husband, Joel, died of the fever last year. What remained of my family and my life died with him," she said. "I had no idea of what would become of me, and I didn't really care."

Peter stopped and laid a gentle hand on her shoulder. He knew. He did not know Joppa, but he knew that there were very few places in which a woman alone had any hopeful options open to her. Without a man, without family, she would have no home, no resources. Unless she were fairly well-to-do or a freedwoman with a trade, her options would amount to little more than prosti-

> The rabbis interpreted the Elijah and Elisha stories as follows: "The woman of Zarephath because she maintained Elijah was rewarded by having her son brought back to life. The Shunammite because she gave food to Elisha was rewarded by having her son brought back to life" (*Midrash Song of Songs* 2.5 [98a]). This suggests that a similar interpretation would have been readily at hand for the listeners of the Tabitha story. (Richter Reimer, 53)

tution or starvation. He looked, reassuringly, at this earnest middle-aged Jewish Christian, and squeezed her shoulder in understanding.

"And then she came into my life." The widow's look of hopelessness had been replaced by a light the apostle had not seen before. He brought his wandering mind back to the present conversation.

"Who came into your life?" he asked.

"Tabitha," she responded. "That day when the disciple of our Lord came to my home, my life began again.

Peter was confused. "I'm sorry. I thought you were going to tell me more about this Tabitha woman you want me to see. Did she accompany a disciple to your house that day?"

Diana had not thought she would have to explain to Peter, of all people. "Don't you understand? Tabitha is a disciple of our Lord—the disciple who changed my life."

Peter was somewhat taken aback by the emphatic response of this sincere convert, but decided to withhold his opinion until he heard more.

"Like I was saying," she went on, "she changed my life. I am not being overly dramatic to say that she gave me purpose and she gave me hope at a time when I questioned whether I would even have life. She brought me into her own home; she, too, was a widow and understood the pain I felt. I found I was not the first woman she had brought in, either. There were other women there already, and she treated each of us as close sisters. She is a wonderful craftswoman, and taught us what she knew about the making and selling of clothes—I'll show you some of her work when we get there. We were all originally quite unfamiliar with this aspect of the marketplace, but she was a patient and encouraging teacher. Together we discovered we were able to support ourselves. More important, though, we also learned how to reach out in support of others.

"So," the apostle concluded, "she was your teacher."

"Yes, our teacher," the woman replied, "but so much more. Her house was not only our home but our place of worship. She was the one who saw to it that the clothes we sewed not only went to the market for a fair price, but were also provided for those around us who were in genuine need. She not only taught us about Christ, she taught us how to be Christ's hands."

They had arrived at the house. The apostle turned to the woman. "Thank you, Diana. Today I came to teach and heal but it was I who learned and received healing in my heart. For a long time have I followed the words of my Lord. Today I have heard his words anew. My vision was narrowed before and I did not see. Today I find our Lord's vision was not as limited in whom he called. I'll do what I can to bring her back to you. I believe that the light of the Lord is within her, and this community needs that light to beckon it forward."

She touched his arm. "Just go in to her, now. Touch her in God's name. Bring her back to us."

"I will try," said Peter. "I will pray for her, and I will also pray that my life will grow to be as Christlike as hers." *(Phyllis Williams Kumorowski)*

This story would probably have reminded the listeners of two famous Old Testament healings by Elijah (1 Kings 17:8-24) and Elisha (2 Kings 4:8-37). Just as Tabitha was known for her good works, so also the women whose dead sons are restored to life by Elijah and Elisha first came to the attention of the prophets when they offered hospitality to them and thus showed their righteousness. In all three stories, the healer is summoned by messengers after the death of the one to be healed. He then enters the room of the dead person by himself, shuts the door behind him, and accomplishes the healing by prayer. Additional acts of healing include breathing on the child (Elijah), lying upon the child and breathing upon him (Elisha), or commanding the person to rise up (Peter). Similar motifs are found in other New Testament healing stories (e.g., Luke 7:11-17; 8:41-56; John 11:1-44) as well as in contemporary pagan healing stories (e.g., Lucian, *Philopseudes* 11; Philostratus, *Apollonius* 4.10). (Theissen, 49-50, 65)

# ACTS 12:1-17

# Rhoda

*The maidservant Rhoda leaves Peter standing at the door in her excitement over his miraculous prison escape.*

## The Story

It was about this time that King Herod launched an attack on certain members of the church. He beheaded James, the brother of John, and, when he saw that the Jews approved, proceeded to arrest Peter also. This happened during the festival of Unleavened Bread. Having secured him, he put him in prison under a military guard, four squads of four men each, meaning to produce him in public after Passover. So, while Peter was held in prison, the church kept praying fervently to God for him.

On the very night before Herod had planned to produce him, Peter was asleep between two soldiers, secured by two chains, while outside the doors sentries kept guard over the prison. All at once an angel of the Lord stood there, and the cell was ablaze with light. He tapped Peter on the shoulder to wake him. 'Quick! Get up!' he said, and the chains fell away from Peter's wrists. The angel said, 'Do up your belt and put on your sandals.' He did so. 'Now wrap your cloak round you and follow me.' Peter followed him out, with no idea that the angel's intervention was real: he thought it was just a vision. They passed the first guard-post, then the second, and

reached the iron gate leading out into the city. This opened for them of its own accord; they came out and had walked the length of one street when suddenly the angel left him.

Then Peter came to himself. 'Now I know it is true,' he said: 'the Lord has sent his angel and rescued me from Herod's clutches and from all that the Jewish people were expecting.' Once he had realized this, he made for the house of Mary, the mother of John Mark, where a large company was at prayer. He knocked at the outer door and a maidservant called Rhoda came to answer it. She recognized Peter's voice and was so overjoyed that instead of opening the door she ran in and announced that Peter was standing outside. 'You are crazy,' they told her; but she insisted that it was so. Then they said, 'It must be his angel.'

Peter went on knocking, and when they opened the door and saw him, they were astounded. He motioned to them with his hand to keep quiet, and described to them how the Lord had brought him out of prison. 'Tell James and the members of the church,' he said. Then he left the house and went off elsewhere.

## Comments on the Story

The Lukan Acts of the Apostles is predominantly concerned with telling the story of the establishment, growth, and geographical expansion of the reign of

God or Jesus movement as the work of Peter and Paul. The glimpses we catch in the Lukan narrative of women's involvement in what must have been an exciting, life-challenging as well as life-threatening and spirit-filled time of the birth of the Christian church are brief and fleeting. They are also at the service of the Lukan agenda not only to glorify Peter and Paul but, it would seem, to obscure and therefore undermine women's contributions. The story of Rhoda (and Mary) in Acts 12:12-17, together with the stories of their sisters that precede and follow, demonstrate this tendency. Their story serves to close Peter's mission in order that the reader can be lead into the Pauline mission at the beginning of the next chapter. Close attention to the story of Rhoda and Mary will, however, contribute to the task of reconstructing women's lives and ministry in the emerging church.

The literary context for this story is Peter's miraculous release from a Herodian prison in Jerusalem (Acts 12:1-11). His first place of call for refuge is the house of Mary. Mary is introduced as the mother of John whose other name was Mark, one who will accompany Paul and Barnabas on their first missionary journey (12:25). This mode of introduction seems, however, to be a way of distinguishing Mary from others of the same common name, as it is Mary who is the householder and it is in her house that many had gathered and were praying. That Peter goes there directly suggests that this was a well-established house-church rather than a casual gathering. Mary is, therefore, a leader of a house-church in Jerusalem but we are told nothing of her activity as such a leader. She simply serves the story of Peter.

In verse 13 of this story, the reader meets Rhoda who is described as "a maid" (NRSV) or a female slave. Her slave status may well have been underscored not only in the descriptive word that accompanies her introduction—the female diminutive form of one word for "servant"/*pais*—but also her very name itself. It too is in the diminutive form and may mean either "little rose"/"rosebud" or female one from the island of Rhodes. Her name indicates her Hellenistic origin but we find her in a house in Jerusalem. It should be noted, however, that there is no indication in the text that she is maid in the house of Mary. Rather, she stands alone in the narrative apart from her brief description as maid and she may well represent the early church's openness to slaves or freed women and men participating in the house-churches in their own right. In the narrative this is certainly so in that she, unlike Mary the householder, is narrated as speaking and acting.

Rhoda's introduction as maid and her recognition of Peter reminds the reader of another encounter between Peter and a maid who was keeper of the door or the gate, namely the one who recognized him as a disciple of Jesus during the trial of Jesus (Luke 18:17). While this earlier unnamed woman faded from the story, Rhoda, upon recognizing Peter, is overjoyed and runs to announce to the gathering that Peter is at the gate.

The reader does not hear Rhoda's voice. It is the narrator who alerts us to it announcing Peter's release. She is like the women who returned from the tomb and similarly announced to the assembled eleven and all the others that Jesus had been released from the tomb, that he had been raised (Luke 24:9). The response of the assembled group, in both instances probably women and men, although the Gospel narrative moves confusingly between terms like "the eleven and all the others" and "the apostles" (Luke 24:9, 10), is disbelief. The Gospel states simply that "the story appeared to them to be nonsense, and they would not believe them." In Rhoda's case, however, the assembled group say: "You are crazy." When she insists, they provide a counterexplanation. While her story parallels that of Mary Magdalene, Joanna, and Mary the mother of James and the other women of the Lukan Gospel, one wonders whether the articulated disbelief and its repetition are not indicative of the layers of marginalization of Rhoda even though it seems that she is a member of the assembled household. She is not only a woman whose testimony is by definition, virtually suspect; but she is also slave woman.

Rhoda's participation in a Jerusalem house-church and her active role even in this one instance of the development of the early church point to the alternative vision and praxis that these house communities sought. The responses to Rhoda's engagement indicate, however, how difficult such shifts are and how deeply cultural values and norms shape consciousness. The retelling of Rhoda's story today will seek to recapture the vitality not only of this woman as full participant in the expansion of the early church, but also her powerful voice raised in announcement of Peter's release. Her words may echo through the centuries as she challenges her community and ours today to look continually at the layers of discrimination that characterize our attitudes and responses even when we have changed our social structures. Her voice will also enable us to hear the story of the early Christian church not only in a male register but also inclusive of active and engaged women.

## Retelling the Story

> She [Rhoda] recognized Peter's voice and was so overjoyed that instead of opening the door she ran in and announced that Peter was standing outside. (Acts 12:14)

There was some slippage from time to time in the links between Rhoda's mouth and her mind. Don't get me wrong. She was plenty smart. Her thoughts and insights just came so fast, her tongue sometimes outdid itself trying to say what was in her head. Rhoda was also pretty. Amend that: She was cute, irreparably cute—like a Raphael cherub. When Rhoda first took up with the Christians in Jerusalem, her coworkers down at the Merry Maids House Cleaning Agency called her a "debutante for Christ." They were implying, of course, that she had nothing but air between her cross-shaped earrings. They couldn't have been more mistaken.

When the new converts first began meeting at Mary's home, Rhoda was working there three days a week as her housekeeper. Not only did she clean Mary's spacious dwelling, she also organized Mary's busy life. Had it not

Roman comedy used stock characters to play stereotyped roles. One such stock character was the maid, who often appeared in the plays of Plautus, for example, for comic effect. Luke, as a master storyteller, uses the Rhoda story in a similar way. (Duckworth, 254)

been for Rhoda's skills, Mary would never have kept track of all her appointments or managed to get through her mountains of correspondence. And Rhoda loved nothing more than greeting callers at the door.

Rhoda stayed late one day to jot a few notes on Mary's calendar. People began to arrive for Mary's "evening social." Mary was clever to call it that, because the government officials were suspicious about anti-Roman activity groups, particularly gatherings of the followers of that radical Jew called Jesus. Even though Jesus had been executed, these so-called Jesus-Christians continued to organize and meet and plot against Herod. That was Herod's interpretation and his obsession.

When Peter arrived at Mary's house that evening, Rhoda was quite smitten with him. Sure, he was twice her age. But he was so muscular, and hairy, and bronzed by the sun, nobody could ignore his physical attributes. She asked Mary his name. "Simon Peter," said Mary, "and he's married."

"I should've guessed. The good ones are always married. Why didn't I meet him ten years ago?"

"Because," chuckled Mary, "you were seven and he was twenty-two. Besides, he wouldn't have noticed you then, either. He was too busy trying to be the world's greatest fisherman. We used to call him Captain Ahab behind his back. And talk? Oh mercy, that man can talk. Everybody loves to listen to him. Such a sense of humor! But he's as likely to put his foot in his mouth as he is to wax eloquent. Rhoda, why don't you stay this evening and listen to him? He's a hoot, really. And he's a lot smarter than many folks give him credit for."

"A Christian with a sense of humor?" mused Rhoda. "This I've gotta see. Maybe this preacher Peter can help me figure out why you and your neighbors are so sold on this new religion."

Mary asked her son John Mark to do the introductions. "Peter, I'd like you to meet someone. This is my mother's social secretary, Rhoda Pappadopolis. And Rhoda, this is Simon Peter. He's a disciple, one of the *the* Twelve."

Rhoda's grin spread all over her face. "How do you do, Peter? I've heard stories about you before. I'm honored to meet so famous an evangelist. Now, don't deny it, you are famous. Get it? Deny. Oops, sorry, that just slipped out." Rhoda's cheeks turned pinker than usual. So did Peter's.

"It's all right, Rhoda, I get it. And I'm delighted to meet you, too. Mary has told me about you. She says she couldn't manage without you. But I wish I had my toolbox with me. I'd check to see if you really are about a half bubble off plumb."

Rhoda understood the game. "Only *half* a bubble? Oh, I've worked so hard at being a full bubble off. Well, may I get you a beverage and a napkin? I just noticed the footprints around your lips. You sometimes have a little trouble getting your foot in there on the first try?"

Peter could hardly contain his laughter. "I see that your lamps are lit, but you're not home."

"Of course!" countered Rhoda. "And your stairway doesn't go all the way to the upper room."

"You're a couple of matzos shy of a dozen!"

"And you don't have both oars in the water!"

Rhoda and Peter both burst into laughter and barely managed to get themselves under control when the evening worship began.

That was the beginning of Rhoda's relationship with Mary's house-church. She was welcomed by the group and quickly became their ambassador of good cheer. She visited the sick and delivered care packages to the prison. She took charge of the eat-and-greet portion of the worship meetings. She was forever running back and forth from the table to the door. She organized support groups and committees. She could talk anybody into anything. Peter said Rhoda was like a honeycomb. She was always showing up for the meetings at Mary's house with somebody new stuck to her.

Of course, Rhoda wasn't good at everything—such as being quiet, for instance. And focusing on one task at a time wasn't Rhoda's style. Sometimes she tried to juggle too many balls at once. She'd go running into the courtyard and then stop and ask, "Why did I come out here?" Rhoda was what Mary called "hyperactive." She got excited about everything. She made jokes while others made prophecies. But Rhoda found friends and a place for her talents in this new community. And in Simon Peter she found someone who understood that humor isn't heretical.

When Peter was arrested and put into prison, Rhoda became a fireball of nervous energy. The others shared her misery in different ways. The day following his arrest, a prayer meeting was called. Rhoda was the first to arrive at Mary's house. She arranged the room for the meeting, practiced the poem she had composed for Peter, and trimmed and filled the lamps. When the members began to assemble, she greeted them at the door and chatted about news from the other disciples as she showed them into the meeting room. The worship time began and everyone settled into meditation and prayer—everyone except Rhoda. She kept scurrying about, looking for things to send Peter.

Knock-knock.

Rhoda heard something. No one else did. "What was that?" she asked.

"Sit down, Rhoda," begged Mary. "If you must talk, talk to God. Pray for Peter with us." Rhoda tried, but she wasn't very good at quiet piety.

Knock-knock.

It was louder this time. Everyone heard it. "I'll get that," shouted Rhoda, jumping to her feet again.

"Yes, Rhoda dear, I knew you would," Mary answered.

Rhoda hurried to the door. "Now who could be arriving this late? Probably Julius. He never watches the time. No, wait, Julius is here. He was over there in the corner, next to Martha." Suddenly it occurred to Rhoda that Herod's goon squad might be lurking outside the door. So, she dropped to her knees and cautiously lifted the small door that Phido, Mary's dog, used for coming and going. She peeked out and, there on the porch, she saw two feet, with hairy toes, in familiar sandals.

And then a voice spoke from somewhere in the darkness above the two feet. "Hello, Rhoda! You wanna know how many Pharisees it takes to screw in a lamp wick?"

When one knocked at the door (or gate) of a modest or well-to-do household in the ancient world, who would one expect to answer it? Certainly not the matron of the house. In fact, in a highly organized household, one slave might be specifically designated the "doorkeeper" (as in Mark 13:34; see also John 10:3). In some parts of the classical world it would be considered unseemly for a respectable woman to answer the door; she was supposed to stay out of sight of the public in the interior of the house.

It was him! "*Peter!* It's Peter!" Rhoda dropped the dog door and ran back into the meeting room, screeching at the top of her lungs. "Peeeeter! It's Peeeeter! He's here! Hey, everybody, Peter is here!"

"You're kidding," said Julius.

"No, I'm not kidding." Rhoda's words were bubbling out of her lips. "Peter is really here! I saw him with my own two eyes—sort of. And I heard his voice. It's Peter, all right!"

"You're crazy, Rhoda. Peter is in prison," grumbled Trophimus.

"Rhoda, sit down, dear. You're red as a beet. You may have a fever." Mary was concerned.

"Mother." It was John Mark. "Could she have eaten some bad grape leaves for dinner? Perhaps she's hallucinating."

"Or maybe she saw Peter's ghost. Maybe they've already killed Peter!" cried Sophie.

Everyone began to talk at once. "Could it be Peter's guardian angel bringing us a message? Be careful, it may be a Roman soldier in disguise."

"No!" shouted Rhoda. "It's Peter himself! I'd know his voice anywhere. Besides ghosts don't wear sandals and angels don't tell jokes. Our very own Peter is standing outside the door."

Knock-knockity-knock-knock.

Rhoda ran to the door and rapped back: Knock-knock.

"Shave-and-a-haircut," she sang through the door.

"Two-bits!" Peter sang back.

Rhoda flung open the door. "Peter, I knew it was you! Come in!" Everyone fell upon Peter and hugged him.

When the rejoicing had ended and everyone began to depart, Rhoda stood in front of Peter, her hands on her hips, fingers pointed backward, her elbows wide. She was grinning from ear to ear. "So, Peter, tell me. How many Pharisees does it take to screw in a lamp wick? And by the way, you wanna know why the rabbi crossed the road?" *(Barbara McBride-Smith)*

# ACTS 16:11-15, 40

# Lydia

*Lydia, a businesswoman, becomes the first convert in Macedonia and a leader of the church in Phillipi.*

## The Story

We sailed from Troas and made a straight run to Samothrace, the next day to Neapolis, and from there to Philippi, a leading city in that district of Macedonia and a Roman colony. Here we stayed for some days, and on the sabbath we went outside the city gate by the riverside, where we thought there would be a place of prayer; we sat down and talked to the women who had gathered there. One of those listening was called Lydia, a dealer in purple fabric, who came from the city of Thyatira; she was a worshipper of God, and the Lord opened her heart to respond to what Paul said. She was baptized, and her household with her, and then she urged us, 'Now that you have accepted me as a believer in the Lord, come and stay at my house.' And she insisted on our going.

. . . . . . . . . . . . . . . . . . . . . . . . . . .

On leaving the prison, they went to Lydia's house, where they met their fellow-Christians and spoke words of encouragement to them, and then they took their departure.

## Comments on the Story

The opening verses of Acts 16:11-15 embed the story of Lydia, the householder and first conversion within the European expansion of the early Christian proclamation of the gospel, within the developing Pauline mission. In this, her story parallels that of Rhoda and Mary, Tabitha and Sapphira, whose stories were likewise embedded within the Petrine mission. Its location is in the Macedonian city of Philippi, which was a significant Roman colony.

The reader follows the movements of Paul and his companions to a place outside the city, a place of prayer by the river and there encounters a group of women gathered on the sabbath. Given the designation of the place as a place of prayer and the time as the sabbath, it can be presumed that they are Jewish women who have gathered to pray. Inscriptional evidence attests to women's participation in synagogal aspects of Jewish life in the Diaspora, even to their leadership of certain synagogues. In the light of such evidence, there seems little reason to doubt that this women's gathering is a reference to a synagogue assembly. This suggests that Jewish women and women converts to Judaism may have, in some circumstances, actively participated in their religious tradi-

149

tion in the Greco-Roman world just as other women participated in various other religious traditions, independent of their husbands. One wonders whether the leader of this synagogue was a woman and hence its attraction to other women.

The narrative focus turns from women at prayer to one particular woman from among the group, Lydia. She is identified as a "worshipper of God" or a God-fearer, a phrase around which there is a certain degree of obscurity. It could be, however, that she was one of the many Roman or Greek women who had chosen to become adherents of Judaism. She too is singled out first and foremost as listening to Paul, seeking to retain the reader's focus on Paul as the center of the story. Lydia, however, and the memory of her in the early church, distracts from the Pauline focus.

There are at least two possible reconstructions of Lydia's background on the basis of the hints in the narrative and sociohistorical data available. The first is that she was a former slave or freedwoman of the imperial household engaged in the imperial dye trade that produced purple-dyed products from the murex shell for the wealthy. If not a freed slave of the imperial trade, she may have been a former slave in a less prestigious and less lucrative branch of the trade. Her name, with its geographical association, may be a further indicator of her former slave status. The skills thus gained would have enabled her to continue her trade when she acquired her freedom and thereby to gain the resources to become an independent householder.

On the other hand, there is inscriptional evidence for the name Lydia among the citizen class of the Greco-Roman world. That she is named a householder with the suggestion that there are a number of members of her household and that she is identified by her business, as a "dealer in purple fabric," suggest, perhaps more realistically, that she is a free woman of Hellenistic or Roman origin. She may be widowed or never have married. She is a businesswoman and householder and has made a seemingly independent choice to join Jewish women in worship. This same independence is evident in her openness to the divine in the words of Paul and her response by way of the reception of baptism. Her authority is evident when she not only invites but urges Paul and his companions to stay in her home and they accept on the basis of her insistence (16:15).

Depending on the reconstruction of Lydia's context, this story presents two ways of hearing her story. On the one hand, readers or listeners may have heard the story of a freedwoman who had proven her economic independence then demonstrated her religiously independent quest that took her to Judaism among a group of women worshipers and then to Christianity in which her household became a base for itinerant missionaries. She would thus have symbolized possibilities for women of slave and freed status. Some readers, on the other hand, would have constructed Lydia as an independent householder of considerable status who, like other women with resources, offered her key resource, namely her house, for the Christian mission. As a leading woman of the community, her conversion would have provided an individual story that represented the many conversions of such leading women referred to in summary in Acts 17:4. It may also have been representative of the many women who were added to the number of believers (5:14) or who were baptized (8:12). That she and all her household were baptized provides the reader with a parallel in the Pauline mission to the conversion and baptism of Cornelius and all his gathered relatives and close friends in the Petrine mission (10:24, 48).

Like Mary's home, Lydia's home was a place of refuge for the missionaries, this time on their release from prison, rather than their escape from prison (16:40). As a householder, she provided this resource but she was given no active leadership role within the expansion of the church into Macedonia. This was reserved for Paul and his male companions in the Lukan narrative. Lydia's independence and authority in the social and economic realm was curtailed in the Christian realm. Even what seems like women's religious independence within the Philippi synagogue outside the gate of the city was harnessed to the service of male missionaries in Christianity. Lydia's story could have provided a model for some first-century women of different ethnic and social status choosing to join Christianity. It may also have sounded a warning to other women who had taken hold of the independence and authority that Lydia symbolized and who found it being severely circumscribed by the Lukan storytelling. She reminds women and men today that possibilities for liberation and for oppression lie very close at hand in the circumstances of the daily response to life. It is important to be ever vigilant.

## Retelling the Story

She was baptized, and her household with her, and then she urged us, 'Now that you have accepted me as a believer in the Lord, come and stay at my house.' And she insisted on our going. (Acts 16:15)

There wasn't a dry eye in Phillipi the day Miss Lydia died. She was the proprietor and pastor of Lydia's Lavender Lounge—a home away from home for pickers and singers, preachers and peddlers, bikers and truckers, anybody who needed a place to sit a spell and feel welcome. You might eventually find applause and glitter in Phillipi, the music Mecca of Macedonia, but before you did, it could be the loneliest place in the world. Miss Lydia was den mother to many a lonely and road-weary wanna-be.

Miss Lydia was born poor, dirt poor. She was the oldest of twelve children. Her mama died giving birth to the last one. Her daddy split soon after. At age fourteen, Miss Lydia was left to raise all her brothers and sisters. She took a

Weaving was considered the quintessential woman's work in ancient times, as noted by Homer: "By how much men are expert of propelling a swift ship on the sea, by this much are women skilled at the loom" (*Odyssey* 7.108-11). A tomb inscription in Rome honored a certain Claudia in this way: "Stranger, what I have to say is short. Stop and read it through. This is the unlovely tomb of a lovely woman. Her parents named her Claudia. She loved her husband with her whole heart. She bore two sons, one of whom she leaves on earth; the other she has placed beneath the earth. She was charming in conversation, yet her conduct was appropriate. She kept house, she made wool." (*CIL* 1.2.1211; from Pomeroy, 199)

job at Levi's Lounge, working sixteen hours a day waiting tables. The pay was lousy, but the tips were really good. The reason, of course, was that she was the best waitress in the joint, or anywhere in town for that matter. She greeted every customer at the door. She gave them just the perfect table. She got everybody's order exactly right, even the substitutions that weren't on the menu. Just give her a nod, and she was there to fill an empty glass. But, most important, she remembered everybody's name and made them feel special. No customers ever felt hurried at Miss Lydia's tables, and when they did decide it was time to hit the road, Miss Lydia always said, "Y'all come back real soon now. We'll keep the light on for you!"

When that band who called themselves "The Apostles" showed up at the lounge for the first time, Miss Lydia could see that they needed comfort and encouragement. They seemed like talented and dedicated fellas. The music scene in Phillipi was hard to break into, but those guys had charisma—especially the band leader, Tall Paul. That's what everybody called him, but it was a joke. Paul was short, bowlegged, and had a nose the size of a melon. Paul said if he and the other fellas had that stuff called charisma, they got it all from their mentor, J. C. This J. C. they talked about so much was no longer a traveling companion. Seems as how he had wound up in trouble with the law in Jerusalem and gotten himself killed. The band missed him a bunch and were trying to pull themselves together and get on with playing their music—his music.

Over the next couple of years, Miss Lydia was mighty good to that group of boys. She was their counselor, financier, and booking agent. Many a time, Miss Lydia gave them a small loan for their next road trip, a place to sleep on the back porch of her house, or a good word to her boss about having the band play a gig at the lounge on a slow night.

Miss Lydia's boss, Levi Lowenstein, had always appreciated her hard work and her hospitable nature, too. He finally asked her to marry him. After a

ACTS 16:11-15, 40

dozen years as his number-one waitress, she became his number-one-and-only wife. They had a few good years together, during which time Miss Lydia continued to be the friend and hostess of every customer who crossed Levi's threshold. And then Levi got sick and Miss Lydia nursed him till he took his last breath. That was when Miss Lydia inherited the lounge. Many women wouldn't have wanted it, and, by law, couldn't have owned it anyway. But Levi deeded it to Miss Lydia in his will, so the authorities decided to let her keep it. She redecorated it all in lavender, her favorite color, and she put a new neon sign out front that flashed LYDIA'S LAVENDER LOUNGE. She wore dresses of various shades of purple every day of the week. Miss Lydia was fond of telling folks, "I've been poor

Lydia, of course, was more than a matron weaver; she was a businesswoman of her day who traded in textiles and ran her own household. She would be classified as a merchant of her day, not necessarily wealthy, but sufficiently well-off to travel and run a household and business. Thyatira was a region known for its textile industry. Inscriptions from the general period of Acts mention a variety of guilds of workers in Thyatira, including leather workers and shoemakers, linen weavers, wool spinners, tailors, and dyers. (Richter Reimer, 98-109, esp. 99)

and I've been rich. Rich is better." But, really, things didn't change much for Miss Lydia. She continued to provide cold drinks and a warm atmosphere for every traveler who walked through her door.

It was a real pleasure one day when The Apostles came through town and stopped in to see Miss Lydia. They had finally gotten their act together and recorded some of J. C.'s songs. "It's brilliant material," Tall Paul told her.

"Yep, a brand new sound that the whole world needs to hear." Tiny Tim assured her. "And wait till you hear my mandolin solos." Miss Lydia listened to it herself, and discovered that the boys were right. J. C.'s melodies and lyrics touched her down deep in her soul. She bought a copy of everything they had.

Miss Lydia put that music on her jukebox, next to hits like "Your Cheatin' Heart" and "I Fall to Pieces," thereby giving it the best chance she could for getting played. And it did get played. The folks who paid attention, who really listened to the lyrics, got the message, and wanted more music by J. C. and The Apostles. They'd spend every quarter they had. Soaking in that music was better than a Saturday night bath. Pretty soon you couldn't go into Miss Lydia's Lavender Lounge or any place else in Phillipi without hearing the sweet sounds of J. C., the star who burned out too soon.

Everywhere the band played, Tall Paul told folks, "It was Miss Lydia over in Phillipi who made the difference for us. She was the closest thing to a business

153

manager we ever had. She's got a big heart. Wish we had more friends like her."

Everybody wished for more friends like Miss Lydia. When she died, in her eighties, they laid her out in a lavender casket and surrounded her with violets and orchids. They played her favorite song, "Meet Me at the Pearly Gates" by J. C. and The Apostles. Tall Paul preached her funeral. It was his finest moment of rhetoric. Too bad nobody thought to record it. Luke, an up-and-coming young writer, wrote her obituary for the *Macedonia Times*. It appeared along with a color photo of Miss Lydia—wearing her best purple dress and a string of pearls—on page one. There wasn't a dry eye in Phillipi the day Miss Lydia died. *(Barbara McBride-Smith)*

# Priscilla

*Priscilla, along with her husband Aquila, becomes an important
coworker of Paul, often hosting the church in their home.*

## The Story

After this he left Athens and went to Corinth. There he met a Jew named Aquila, a native of Pontus, and his wife Priscilla; they had recently arrived from Italy because Claudius had issued an edict that all Jews should leave Rome. Paul approached them and, because he was of the same trade, he made his home with them; they were tentmakers and Paul worked them. He also held discussions in the synagogue Sabbath by Sabbath, trying to convince both Jews and Gentiles.

. . . . . . . . . . . . . . . . . . . . . . . .

Paul stayed on at Corinth for some time, and then took leave of the congregation. Accompanied by Priscilla and Aquila, he sailed for Syria, having had his hair cut off at Cenchreae in fulfilment of a vow. They put in at Ephesus, where he parted from his companions; he himself went into the synagogue and held a discussion with the Jews. He was asked to stay longer, but he declined and set sail from Ephesus, promising, as he took leave of them, 'I shall come back to you if it is God's will.' On landing at Caesarea, he went up and greeted the church; and then went down to Antioch. After some time there he set out again on a journey through the Galatian country and then through Phrygia, bringing new strength to all the disciples.

There arrive at Ephesus a Jew names Apollos, an Alexandrian by birth, an eloquent man, powerful in his use of the scriptures. He had been instructed in the way of the Lord and was full of spiritual fervour; and in his discourses he taught accurately the facts about Jesus, though the only baptism he knew was John's. He now began to speak boldly in the synagogue, where Priscilla and Aquila heard him; they took him in hand and expounded the way to him in greater detail. Finding that he wanted to go across to Achaia, the congregation gave him their support, and wrote to the disciples there to make him welcome. From the time of his arrival, he was very helpful to those who had by God's grace become believers, for he strenuously confuted the Jews, demonstrating publicly from the scriptures that the Messiah is Jesus.

. . . . . . . . . . . . . . . . . . . . . . . .

Give my greetings to Prisca and Aquila, my fellow-workers in Christ Jesus. They risked their necks to save my life, and not I alone but all the gentile churches are grateful to them. Greet also the church that meets at their house.

. . . . . . . . . . . . . . . . . . . . . . . .

Greetings from the churches of Asia. Many greetings in the Lord from

Aquila and Prisca and the church that
meets in their house.

Greetings to Prisca and Aquila, and
the household of Onesiphorus.

. . . . . . . . . . . . . . . . . . . . . . . . . .

## Comments on the Story

When the reader of Acts meets Priscilla and her husband Aquila, both of
whom are clearly early Christian missionaries and teachers, the Lukan tendency
of subordination of all others to Paul becomes most apparent. The reader must,
therefore, read against the grain of this Lukan tendency as well as listen to the
traditions about Priscilla and Aquila in other documents of the Christian Testament in order that their contribution to the spread of early Christianity might
emerge in its own right.

Priscilla does not stand alone in the narrative. She is constantly linked with
Aquila but she is not subordinated to him. Together, therefore, they represent a
male/female missionary couple who are engaged in the spreading of the
gospel. This is clear in the Pauline trajectory in which they are constantly
named as a couple and there is reference to the "church in their house" (Rom.
16:3-5; 1 Cor. 16:19). From this perspective, we can then turn back to the
Lukan narrative.

In the light of the tendency within the tradition to name Priscilla before
Aquila (Acts 18:18, 26; Rom. 16:3; and 2 Tim. 4:19), the awkward Lukan
introduction of the pair renders Luke's attempts to obscure the significant leadership and contribution of women to the early Christian mission more than
transparent. Aquila is introduced first as Jewish; then according to his place of
origin, Pontus; and finally, as a refugee from Italy because of an edict of
Claudius who expelled members of a Roman synagogue from the city.
Between the reference to Aquila's recent move from Italy and the explanation
of its cause, the Lukan writer inserts the phrase "and Priscilla his wife." The
REB rescues Priscilla from this grammatical morass and makes it clear that
Paul meets Priscilla with Aquila. She, however, is not named as Jewish
although her involvement in the synagogue later in the narrative would certainly suggest this; nor is the reader given her place of origin. Also the Lukan tradition names her by the diminutive form "Priscilla" rather than "Prisca" as
found in the Pauline tradition. This can function rhetorically to diminish
Priscilla's significance.

Such an introduction could well obscure for many readers Priscilla's
engagement with Aquila not only in Christian mission but also in their trade of
tentmaking. Historical and archaeological evidence make it clear that this is
not an impossibility and the repetition of the third-person plural pronoun
through 18:2b and 3 renders this a more than plausible reading. Priscilla, therefore, is in many ways like Lydia. Both were either freed slaves or free women

who worked in demanding trades learned in slavery or engaged in for economic livelihood or both. Lydia stands alone in such a context while Priscilla belongs to a male/female couple representing two trajectories of women's life contexts in the Greco-Roman world and in which their Christian involvement was grounded.

As the narrative of Acts develops, two quite extraordinary aspects of Priscilla's story emerge and even though they are not significantly developed, for those reading against the grain of the centrality of the Pauline mission, they are of import. First, Priscilla is not confined to a household ministry as were Mary and Lydia but is said to accompany Paul and Aquila on a missionary journey by way of Cenchreae to Ephesus where Paul leaves Priscilla and Aquila, presumably to carry on the work of the gospel, until his return. This is the only glimpse in Acts of a woman who accompanies Paul and also the only woman who is engaged in the Christian mission in the public arena outside the household. While this reference is minute, it gives, together with the actual Pauline traditions of women coworkers, a richer and more inclusive insight into the spread of the early church.

But Priscilla is not only a partner with Aquila in itinerant missionary work but also in teaching. Their authority in Ephesus is clear when they take on the role of "[expounding] the way . . . in greater detail" to Apollos (Acts 18:26). He is described as "an eloquent man, powerful in his use of the scriptures" (18:24). Priscilla's knowledge and competence as a teacher, together with that of her husband Aquila, is made clear from this description of Apollos. She is able to engage with such an orator and open up to him knowledge of the Way that he did not have. She is indeed a skillful early Christian teacher and a teacher of men engaged in a work similar to hers—the spreading of the gospel. In both the itinerant mission and the role of teaching, Priscilla is mentioned prior to Aquila.

The leadership role of Priscilla and Aquila that is clear in Acts despite the Lukan tendency to silence women's active and public ministry is further authenticated in the Pauline traditions. The house of Prisca and Aquila, whether in Corinth or Ephesus or Rome (many scholars suspect that the greeting in the final chapter of Romans may have been misplaced from Ephesian correspondence), is clearly a significant house-church, one that is well known to many other Christian communities.

Priscilla emerges, therefore, even from the Lukan text, as itinerant missionary, householder, and teacher in the establishment and spread of the early Christian mission in Asia Minor and Greece. She may stand with and be representative of many other women who shared in similar activities but whose stories have been silenced and forgotten as the Lukan tendency to obscure their role continued into the subsequent centuries and down to our own. She helps to place the Pauline mission in perspective and enables readers to construct the early Christian mission not as the work of Peter and Paul but as the shared task of many men and women working together and working alone. Her story continues to challenge any exclusive focus on male leadership as the heart of the Christian story today, which obscures the leadership, the authority, and the teaching power of women. Stories of women like Priscilla must be told in the public arena in which she taught and carried out her missionary activities in order to redress this imbalance of centuries, which remains with us today.

## Retelling the Story

Because he was of the same trade, he made his home with them; they were tentmakers and Paul worked with them. (Acts 18:3)

When most folks look at me, one word comes to mind: tentmaker! Am I right? I look like a tentmaker, don't I? Nobody would ever mistake me for a ballet dancer or a gymnast. Not with this 6'4" physique and these size thirteen sandals. I could be captain of the basketball team—if we had a basketball team here in Corinth. But tentmaking takes a strong body, and I qualified early.

I was born big, you know what I mean? My mama was sure I was a boy the whole time she was carrying me. And then when I came into the world at a whopping fifteen pounds, I surprised everybody by being another daughter. My folks already had nine daughters, and I—being the last one—was supposed to have been their long-awaited son. I guess that's why my daddy taught me all the things he would have taught a son. Of course, my mama also insisted that I learn women's work. I'm still pretty good at all of it, if I do say so myself. I can cook up a meal fit for a king, or I can handle an ax or an awl with as much finesse as any fella you'll ever meet.

When my folks retired, I was the only one of all the daughters who cared one whit about the family tent business. So they passed it on to me. I was still a teenager, but I learned every detail about running this business. Not only can I make tents, I can sell 'em, too. I've just got a gift for gab, you know what I mean? I also keep the books, but I've never been as much of a tightwad as my daddy. I'm willing to spend a little more for quality materials. And during the busy season, my policy is to hire extra hands and pay decent wages.

That's how I met my husband Aquila. It was back in Rome where my business used to be located. This big guy came in one day looking for work, and it was love at first sight for both of us. My sisters said it was a match made in heaven because Aquila was the only boyfriend I'd ever had who could beat me at arm wrestling five times out of ten. Ah, but the attraction was more than muscle. We knew right from the get-go that we were soul mates. My folks gave their blessing and, after a proper courtship, Aquila and I were married.

Aquila was the one who gave me the nickname Priscilla. His "little Prisca."

We both laugh about it but, comparatively speaking, it's true. Have you seen my Aquila? He makes me look positively petite! A giant of a man he is, but a gentle giant. He'll take in stray kittens and nurse injured birds back to health, but he can haul an extra large family-size tent on one shoulder without breaking a sweat. Aquila was a tentmaker when I met him, all right, but his skills needed refining. I taught him things about style and longevity that he'd never heard about before. He still insists that I do the intricate design work, but he's the expert at sewing those tiny little backstitches that hold the seams tight and make them waterproof. I swear that man can get ten stitches to an inch. He could have been a champion quilter.

You ought to take a tour of our shop when you've got time. This one is even bigger than the one we had in Rome. I've told you the story about how the government kicked us out, haven't I? When we set up the new shop here, I changed the sign out front from "Prisca's Tents" to "Priscilla & Aquila: Tents R Us." Nowadays some tentmakers are diversifying into leatherwork and canopies for weddings and bar mitzvahs and such. But me and Aquila, we're specialists. Yep, we're the champion tent builders of Corinth. Well, the truth is, and forgive me for bragging, but you're face-to-face with the best tentmaker in Greece. Sure, our tents cost a little more, but they're worth it. We make 'em to last. Every tent carries a six-month warranty and a twenty-five year guarantee. That's what comes from paying for the best.

Our tents are a bit more stylish than some you'll see, because we keep up with the latest trends. Of course, we never sacrifice quality for fashion. Our most economical tents come in basic black, woven from the finest goat hair available. Or we can give you a more expensive two-tone with designs, using natural fibers in various shades of beige and gray. I recommend the two-tone. It's easier to see the contrast at night. There's nothing more disconcerting than having some wild thing bump into your tent in the middle of the night because it didn't see you parked in the dark. We also can make you a tent in a lovely ivory color, using albino goat hair, but they're not practical if you plan to be

What a tentmaker did is a matter of some debate today. Most scholars identify it as a leather-working craft that involved not only tents but also other leather articles. Some, however, identify it as the manufacture of tent coverings or awnings from a linen fabric. In any case, we may assume that women worked alongside men in the workshop of Priscilla and Aquila. An artisan's workshop often became a place of serious conversation where artisan-philosophers like Simon the Cynic were known to teach. As a coworker in the workshop, Priscilla was also ideally placed to be a coteacher as well. (Richter Reimer, 199-205; Hock, 31-42)

159

setting up in muddy locations. They require a lot more dry cleaning. Most folks who order one are usually just trying to look uppity. They want the best tent on the block. You know the temptation. But if you really want an ivory tent, we'll make it.

We can sell you a standard one-room tent or a deluxe two-room with a privacy curtain down the middle. We can even add on a mother-in-law wing. It's a special order, and takes a few extra days, but you'll be happier in the long run giving your mother-in-law her own quarters.

As for the door flaps, you can order a front flap or a back flap or both. The flaps all come with ventilator holes and your choice of design. We can give you stars—five points or six—of course. Or we can give you crosses. We're ecumenical when it comes to ventilators. Most people these days are going for the moon-shaped crescents, and they do make a nice gentle reflection on your inside wall. But it's entirely up to you. Take your time and think it over. We never rush our customers into snap decisions on ventilator holes, because once we cut 'em, they're cut.

Priscilla and Aquila were a husband and wife team who shared with Paul the occupation of "tentmaker." It was their shared occupation, as well as their shared ethnicity, that gave them their initial connection. Travelers in the ancient world relied on such connections to provide them with places to stay; inns were unreliable.

Now as to the construction, we can make you a tent that's preshrunk or we can cut it a skosh roomy and you can shrink it yourself using the natural rain method. If it were me, I'd pay extra for the preshrunk version and rest secure that it's going to fit those poles when you get out there in the wilderness.

All the workers here in our shop are certified and experienced. One of our best part-timers is Paul. You remember him, the one they call the Apostle. He shows up and stays with us awhile when he needs some traveling money. He's the most experienced cutter we've got. He can cut the straightest edges, and do it faster than any tentmaker I know. He's worth his weight in gold with a pair of scissors. Besides that, he's good company. He can't arm wrestle worth squat, but he's the only person I know who can outtalk me. What a preacher! His sermons are what you'd call cutting edge.

Lately Paul has been trying to persuade me and Aquila to get shed of this mortgage and join up with him on his mission trips. He says we don't need a shop, that we can be tentmakers anywhere. He says we'd be real good evangelists. Well, I'm a talker all right, but Aquila's a little shy when it comes to speaking up in a crowd. I told Aquila I can do the preaching and he can do the baptizing. Lord knows, he's big enough to dunk 'em two or three at a time. But shucks, I was just settling in here. Pulling up roots again is mighty hard to think about. Aquila says he's happy as long as we're together. He says it's my business, my decision.

I've always believed I did the right thing going into the tent business. I never dreamed that I might have hitched my cart to the wrong star—that I should have studied homiletics or mission development. Paul says tentmaking was just the first step in my career. He says I can bloom wherever I'm transplanted. He's got an idea for a new kind of tent and a new kind of church meeting— calls it a tent revival. He wants me and Aquila to design it, build it, advertise it, and do the soul saving in it. Paul thinks it's time for me and Aquila to diversify,

> It was not uncommon in the ancient world for women of means to welcome foreign cults into their homes, though moralists of the day, like the satirist Juvenal, might take a dim view of it: "And watch out for a woman who's a religious fanatic: in the summer she will fill the house with a coven of worshippers of strange oriental deities" (*Satires* 6.511f [early-second century c.e.]). (from Schüssler Fiorenza, *In Memory of Her,* 177).

and we could get in on the ground floor of this new venue for preaching. Imagine! Hundreds of people in one tent that I built, listening to words that I preach. Gives me goose bumps just thinking about it. I've been praying that God won't let my ego make my decision, but it's hard to be humble when you're this good.

Well, here I am flapping my jaw while there's work to be done. If you hear of anybody looking to buy some choice real estate, tell 'em to come see me. And you let me know when you decide on which kind of them ventilator holes you want cut. Shalom! *(Barbara McBride-Smith)*

# Phoebe

*Phoebe is greeted by Paul as a deacon and patron of the church at Cenchreae.*

## The Story

I COMMEND to you Phoebe, a fellow-Christian who is a minister in the church at Cenchreae. Give her, in the fellowship of the Lord, a welcome worthy of God's people, and support her in any business in which she may need your help, for she has herself been a good friend to many, including myself.

## Comments on the Story

Paul's commendation of Phoebe to the church in Rome (or Ephesus if one holds to the suggestion of a misplaced conclusion to the Letter to the Romans), heads a long list of greetings to members of that church. At least one third of those thus greeted are women and all are engaged in the work of the church in a variety of capacities. The language used to describe their involvement is that employed repeatedly throughout the Pauline correspondence. This literature differs, therefore, from the narrative construction of either the Gospels or Acts of the Apostles. Despite a Pauline rhetorical purpose, it tends to be more directly descriptive and hence, more foundational for historical reconstruction. The brevity of these references are, however, both frustrating and tantalizing because of the little that they tell us of the lives of these women in early Christianity.

Of all the women referents in Romans 16:1-15, Phoebe is described in most detail. First, the commendation of Phoebe to the recipients of the letter suggests that she is to be the bearer of the letter and hence that she is a traveling missionary. Only a woman of significance in that mission would have been given such a task. This possible construction of Phoebe's position is further demonstrated by the designation of "our sister" (REB: "fellow-Christian"), which places her at the heart of the Christian community or household.

Second, Phoebe is called a minister or deacon/*diakonos* of the church of Cenchreae, a city on the Corinthian isthmus opposite Corinth. This second designation of Phoebe places her among other Christian ministers or deacons in the early Greek churches. Paul calls himself and Apollos "God's agents" or ministers, deacons to the Corinthian church in 1 Corinthians 3:5-9; he names Jesus, as the Christ, a servant or *diakonos* of the Jewish people (Rom. 15:8);

and he specifies bishops and deacons in his opening greeting to the church at Philippi (Phil. 1:1). Phoebe is, therefore, clearly in a leadership role in the church of Cenchreae although the exact nature of that leadership cannot be specified. The title may have carried over into early Christianity some of its usage in the wider society in relation to cult officials. Hence Phoebe may have had a liturgical role as well as that of teacher and missionary as the broad use of the term for early Christian leaders suggests. In subsequent centuries, a woman's diaconal role was limited and the female form of the noun—translated deaconess—was used to designate their ministry and distinguish it from the male role, which was integrated into the emerging hierarchical model. Inscriptional material, however, from fourth-century Jerusalem refers to a certain Sophia as deacon and second Phoebe. Perhaps the model of Phoebe of Cenchreae continued to inspire women's leadership roles in the face of a church seeking to contain and control them.

The third designation of Phoebe—*prostatis* or patron, benefactor, leader—has proved most problematic to both translators and interpreters of this text. Romans 16:2 has the only occurrence of this noun in the Christian Testament although its corresponding verb is used in a number of instances in the Pauline literature—Romans 12:8; 1 Thessalonians 5:12; 1 Timothy 3:4, 5, 12. It designates authority or household management and resourcing of the church's mission. The common root gives rise to two noun forms in other literature and inscriptional material of the first century, which refer respectively to a patron or to his or her patronage or benefaction of persons as clients or of cities and public projects. Indeed, a mid-first century inscription honors a Corinthian woman, Junia Theodora for her patronage and her numerous benefits bestowed on large numbers of citizens.

It should not be surprising, therefore, that Phoebe, who belongs to the same time and geographic location, would receive the same title. Therefore, she must be considered not merely as a "good friend" to many including Paul (REB translation), but as a patron, a woman of considerable resources who provided perhaps a household and other resources for the Pauline mission generally and for the church of Cenchraea in particular. The authority that such women had in other associations within the Greco-Roman world, both religious and secular, also gives foundation to the interpretation of Phoebe as leader of the church of Cenchraea.

While Phoebe clearly emerges as an example of women's possible authority, power, and leadership in the early church, there are gaps and silences in her brief appearance in the literature. We seek glimpses of the style of leadership she exercised, the type of house-church that she led. Moreover, we raise questions regarding her teaching, her theology. Was she developing a theology that was an alternative to that of Paul in the same way that later gospel communities would develop different theologies? While there is clearly indications of

163

some shared vision with Paul, did she question and even resist aspects of the Pauline gospel in the church of Cenchraea, developing early Christian insights that have been lost to us? And what is the mission on which she is being sent, for which she may require the help of the recipients of the letter? Answers to these questions would enable us to gain much greater insight to the role of women in the early Christian churches that is merely hinted at in this almost passing reference to Phoebe. She enables us to realize, however, that the centrality given to Paul, not only in Acts, but also in the consciousness and worldview of early Christianity generally, has obliterated the extraordinary contribution of others and particularly of women from our Christian histories and memories. To tell Phoebe's story in greater detail from the fragments left to us will be one further step in the reconstructing of Christian genealogies, which will provide a new memory and new imagination for contemporary women and men.

## Retelling the Story

I COMMEND to you Phoebe, a fellow-Christian who is a minister in the church at Cenchreae. (Rom. 16:1)

She wouldn't want me to use her real name, so I'll just call her Phoebe. When she won the lottery a few years back, she didn't want any publicity, but the paparazzi wouldn't leave her alone. They put her picture in every newspaper and on every TV show in the country. She was exactly the kind of person you'd hope would win a fifty-million-dollar jackpot: a real deserving human being who had never before in her life won anything.

Phoebe grew up in a blue-collar family. Her mama took in sewing and her daddy worked in a grain mill. Phoebe was bright enough to get a scholarship to college, where she earned a degree in English and her certification to teach high school. She married Wilson the day after graduation, and by the end of the summer she had her first teaching job. Wilson was a bricklayer who had always wanted to go to college. Phoebe and Wilson saved every penny they could spare, and three years after they married, Wilson started taking classes at the university.

Before he finished the fall semester, Wilson was diagnosed with lung cancer. He died shortly after Easter. What he never knew was that Phoebe was pregnant with their child. Willie was born the following summer. He was a beautiful baby, bright-eyed and alert. He was the joy of Phoebe's life. It was hard to leave him every morning when she went back to her teaching job that fall. But her mama promised to be the best granny a little boy could have. Every evening she delighted Phoebe with all the details of Willie's day. Willie grew like a weed, and before long he was into everything around his granny's house. But something wasn't quite right. Willie didn't respond when his name was called. He seemed oblivious to loud noises. Just before his second birthday, Phoebe took him in for tests at the university medical center. They discovered that Willie was deaf.

Phoebe and Willie began taking sign language classes together at the YMCA. After a year, they could sign faster than most people can talk. And, on their own, they learned to lip-read. They had each other. What else mattered?

When Willie turned three, Phoebe tried putting him in a nursery school for half days, but he was confused and frustrated, so he went back to his granny's. Phoebe continued to search for a nursery school or daycare center where someone could communicate in sign language, but there wasn't one. During her inquiries, however, she found a church that had a class for deaf persons of any age. It was taught by a deaf man named Tom who had been born hearing, but because of rubella was deafened at the age of twelve. Tom invited Phoebe to visit the class and assured her that Willie was welcome, no matter how rambunctious he was. That class turned out to be a godsend for both Phoebe and Willie. They found others like themselves. It wasn't just a Sunday school class. It was their support group, their family.

They could hardly wait for Sundays to come. They arrived at church early and stayed late. Hands flew as people shared their lives and their faith. Phoebe asked Tom if he might consider holding a midweek evening class. It was such a long time between Sundays for all the class members. Tom said he wished he could, but he had to work the late shift every weeknight. He wasn't being paid by the church, you see, even though he spent countless hours every day helping the deaf community learn day-to-day living skills. He spent almost as many hours studying so that he could be a knowledgeable teacher of the Bible. He wanted to start a deaf worship service—some-

Phoebe is identified as a *prostatis,* a term that can be translated in various ways (REB: "good friend"). It represents a position of leadership in a group or organization. When Philo refers to such a person in the Jewish community in Alexandria, we tend to translate it as "president" or presider at the assembly. In a Hellenistic religious society, however, such an officer would be one who served as patron of the community, that is, one who provided support—financial and otherwise—and who represented and defended the interests of the group in the larger community. Such a role is quite similar to that of the "mother" or "father" of the synagogue that is often mentioned in Jewish inscriptions. A third-century Jewish inscription from Aphrodisias identifies a certain "Jael," which could be either the name of a man or woman, as *prostates* or "president" of the Jewish community. (Reynolds and Tannenbaum, 41)

thing more effective than the interpreted hearing service that never quite met the spiritual needs of the deaf. But Tom hadn't been to seminary and didn't feel competent to preach. His dream was to be an ordained minister for the deaf. But his job at the newspaper company, his own family, and his volunteer work with his flock left no time to spare. And, of course, seminary cost money, and he was as short on cash as he was on time.

Phoebe began to attend board meetings at the church. She asked the board members to consider paying Tom for his work with the deaf in their community. "It's just not possible, Ms. Phoebe. We all volunteer our time in the work of this church." She urged the church leaders to establish a scholarship for Tom to attend seminary, but they had already committed their funds to a new landscaping and fountain project for the front of the church building.

Meanwhile, Willie continued to grow and learn under Tom's tutelage. When it came time to start kindergarten, Willie was ready. Phoebe wasn't. Leaving him that morning was the hardest thing she had ever done. But Willie had learned from his role model, Tom, how to survive—in fact, how to excel—in a hearing world.

That fall, Phoebe began to petition the church board to buy education materials especially designed for deaf persons. Sorry, they said, the budget was already stretched thin. In the spring, she asked if the deaf class could borrow the bus that belonged to the youth program to take field trips, to go places that deaf folks might be too shy or too inexperienced to manage on their own. Oh no, said the board, insurance and gas were very expensive, not to mention paying a driver. Out of the question.

There were a lot of other things Phoebe asked for. A larger classroom, for example. Because of Tom's wonderful work, their class size had doubled. She thought the church ought to provide a coffeepot and a lemonade thermos for their classroom. She would bring the beverages and snacks herself, she said. She also wanted an overhead projector so that transparencies of biblical texts could be shown on the wall where everyone could see them as they watched Tom's teaching hands. She would make the transparencies herself, she said. She wanted to organize a bowling league for the deaf and asked the church to buy shirts and pay the fees. She wanted books and videos and board games for the deaf children. Phoebe was relentless in her requests.

The church board was polite. They even took some of her requests under consideration. Finally they bought a coffeepot and a five-gallon thermos, presented them to the deaf class with much pomp and ceremony and felt content in their generosity toward marginalized persons.

That summer Phoebe won the state lottery. It was the biggest jackpot ever awarded, and Phoebe won it. All fifty million dollars of it.

Her personal life didn't change much at first, except for the publicity. She continued teaching English at the high school. The kids started calling her Ms. Moneybags, but she could afford to laugh with them. She and Willie did move out of the apartment. She bought a cozy house in a neighborhood with lots of kids. Willie got a deluxe swing set and a dog. After that, Phoebe became a "patron." It was a word she had learned from Tom in Sunday school. He had taught them about early Christians who were patrons—folks with money who supported the apostles in their work to spread the gospel. Phoebe used her considerable resources to provide for the needs of the deaf community.

She set up and funded a scholarship so that Tom could attend seminary. The endowment she established would make it possible for many "physically challenged" persons to acquire an education in the years to come. When Tom graduated with his Master of Divinity degree, she provided the funds to pay his salary as a full-time member of the church staff. He began a worship service for the deaf and it grew by leaps and bounds.

Phoebe bought a brand-new bus for the deaf ministry program and scheduled field trips all over the city and even to the mountains in the winter and to the beach in the summer. She paid for the insurance, the gas, and the driver. She and Willie were the tour guides on every trip. On Saturday nights, the bus took the deaf teams to the bowling alley. They had the classiest shirts in the league, their very own bowling balls and shoes, and more self-confidence than you could shake a stick at.

Phoebe's money built a new wing onto the church—the Deaf Education Wing. At the street entrance, right next to the fountain, she had a sculptor design a huge bronze hand posed in the familiar sign that means "I love you." She organized sign language classes, stocked a resource center, and provided counselors who were available at any hour for anybody who needed assistance in coping with a world that couldn't communicate with them.

The deaf ministry at the church flourished. The whole church flourished. And the church board was not at all reluctant to take the credit. They saw, at last, the wisdom of this woman named Phoebe and appointed her to the board. She continued to make waves and raise hackles, but now she was too valuable a person not be taken seriously.

Phoebe, whose real name shall remain undisclosed, was a hero even before she had money. But the money gave her clout. It made a difference. And she made a difference. *(Barbara McBride-Smith)*

The good works of a woman deacon are exemplified in this epitaph from Cappadocia (sixth century C.E.): "Here lies Maria the deacon, of pious and blessed memory, who in accordance with the statement of the apostle reared children, practiced hospitality, washed the feet of the saints, distributed her bread to the afflicted. Remember her, Lord, when you come in your kingdom." (Kraemer, *Maenads, Martyrs, Matrons, Monastics*, no. 100)

167

# Junia

---

*Junia is identified by Paul as a famous apostle.*

---

### The Story

Greet Andronicus and Junia, my fellow-countrymen and comrades in captivity, who are eminent among the apostles and were Christians before I was.

### Comments on the Story

Romans 16:7 has had a vexed and vexing history, especially in relation to the genderization of the second in the missionary pair who are to be given greetings from Paul. Andronicus is clearly a masculine name but there have been periods in the history of transmission of the text, especially its more recent history, in which the name "Junia" has been rendered as "Junias" and the Greek work accented in such a way as to suggest a masculine noun. Recent attention to women's ministry in the early church, has, however, brought further light to bear on this issue.

It seems that prior to the thirteenth century there is no manuscript evidence that we know of for the masculine name Junias in Romans 16:7. Early church writers such as Origen, Ambrose, and Jerome considered the word feminine and John Chrysostom wrote of Junia: "Oh! How great is the devotion of this woman, that she should be counted worthy of the appellation of the apostle!" (*Epistle to the Romans, Homily* 31). Today we might question his apparent surprise that a woman should be granted this appellation but his words are evidence that there was no question as to the gender of the second person named in this missionary pair. There is also no known attestation for the masculine name "Junias" whereas the feminine forms, "Junia" and "Julia" were very common in the first century. The evidence is clear, therefore, that Paul greets a male/female pair, Andronicus and Junia.

One of the circuitous arguments that has been proffered in recent discussions of Junia's name relates to the second half of the verse, which places Andronicus and Junia as eminent among the apostles. It was argued that women were not numbered among the apostles and hence the pair must be a male pair. The evidence of Chrysostom and other early church sources indicates that those closest to the Pauline mission and ministry did not have the same problem. Hence, it is clear that we have in Romans 16:7 a female apostle. In order to understand her role, however, it is necessary to inquire what the term meant in the Pauline literature. First, Paul sees himself as an apostle and names himself thus at the beginning of most of his letters (Rom. 1:1; 1 Cor. 1:1; Gal. 1:1; Eph. 1:1 and Col. 1:1). Paul is teacher and preacher; he is theologian who interprets the message of the gospel for the variety of situations he meets; and he is missionary who takes the message to different corners of the Empire. One aspect that Paul makes clear about his own apostleship is that it has been received as a gift through Jesus Christ and has been authorized by a resurrection appearance (Rom. 1:5; 1 Cor. 15:8-9). That there are others who share this apostleship beyond the Twelve is clear from his listing of resurrection appearances, the Twelve following upon Cephas and James and "all the apostles" listed subsequent to the five hundred "brothers" (1 Cor. 15:5-7). Given the androcentric language usage that was typical of the first century and hence all Christian Testament writings, there may have been women included among the "brothers" and the "apostles." Paul's reference to Andronicus and Junia being apostles who were "Christians before I was" may well mean, therefore, that he included them among the apostles who experienced a resurrection appearance before he did.

Junia and Andronicus are a male/female pair, perhaps husband and wife as were Priscilla and Aquila, or companions in the mission (1 Cor. 9:5). One can assume that they, together with many others, shared in the gift of apostleship, like Paul, being preachers and teachers, theologians and traveling missionaries. They share, therefore, in one of the key ministry functions in the early church as emphasized by Paul in 1 Corinthians 12:28 and Ephesians 4:11. Here Paul seems to distinguish ministries such as teaching, prophecy, and evangelization from apostleship in a way that we do not see in relation to his own ministry. Since Paul's accomplishments tend to overshadow those of other apostles, persons today who wish to study the accomplishments of Andronicus and especially Junia, need to ask about the functions that they, as well as Paul, performed.

This seems to be particularly relevant in relation to Andronicus and Junia because Paul indicates that they were "fellow-countrymen" with him (Rom. 16:7), perhaps indicative of their coming to belief in Jesus very early in the preaching of the gospel as it spread north beyond Galilee into Syria. He also indicates that they shared his captivity, a sign that theirs was an apostleship like that of both Peter and Paul, which brought them into conflict with both Jewish and Gentile officials. Junia is, indeed, the only woman missionary who is specifically mentioned as being imprisoned in the course of the establishment and expansion of the early church within the Christian Testament. Interestingly, however, Paul himself imprisoned both women and men in his persecution of the followers of the Way prior to his conversion (Acts 22:4). She may, therefore, provide a glimpse into the experience of her other sisters who shared the itinerant mission.

Junia is a woman of courage, unafraid in the face of the threats and dangers that she faced in her role as apostle, preaching the gospel of Jesus in the early days of the Christian mission, teaching and interpreting the message with Andronicus in a way similar, perhaps, to Priscilla's teaching of Apollos with Aquila. The brief greeting Paul sends to her becomes a window slightly ajar on the world of the early Christian mission, which confirms our suspicion that the language was androcentric and that the roles that have been presumed to be filled only by men are now seen to have been undertaken by women also. In deference to Chrysostom we might say today: How great is the courage and the commitment of this woman (and her many sisters) who were faithful to their call, authenticated by their experience of a resurrection appearance, to be apostles, deacons, teachers, preachers, prophets, and healers!

## Retelling the Story

> Greet Andronicus and Junia, my fellow-countrymen and comrades in captivity, who are eminent among the apostles and were Christians before I was. (Rom. 16:7)

I can't tell you how much fun it was for all of us who grew up with her when Jenny June, our "J. J.," got elected to the U.S. Senate. We always knew she had it in her genes.

Her mother, Johanna, was elected the first female mayor of our town nearly twenty years ago. She beat out an incumbent who was for prayer in the schools and against pay raises for teachers.

J. J.'s grandmother, Julia, worked long and hard for women's suffrage back at the beginning of this century. Up until Julia was thirty-five years old, the law said everybody in the state could vote, except "idiots, imbeciles, aliens, the insane, and women." Things have improved somewhat since then, thanks to a lot of modern suffragettes.

And, of course, as J. J. has reminded us time and time again, her great-great-great- (heaven only knows how many greats) grandmother was Junia, an apostle of Jesus Christ in the first century. Even Paul recognized her as an apostle, calling her by name in his letter to the Romans. It's in the Bible. Look it up!

How in the world J. J. ever traced her family tree back to Junia is a mystery to all of us. She was dogged about it. Her research took her all the way to Rome and beyond. She said the genealogical records on the men in her family were a lot easier to come by. But she finally put together a matriarchal time line, and she's convinced that the apostle Junia was her ancestral grandma.

She says Junia was married to a fellow named Andronicus, who was a shopkeeper when they first met. After they married, Junia worked in the shop, too. Then one day she heard an evangelist who came through town preaching about

Christianity. She was really impressed by what he said, it seems, because she was the first in town to be converted. She convinced her husband and a good number of other folks in town to join the Christian movement. She turned the back of the shop into a meeting room for their new little church. And she didn't just sweep the floor and serve the cake. No, ma'am. She did the preaching!

Junia eventually talked her husband, Andro, into letting his brother, Amos, run the shop so that he could accompany her when she went on mission trips. She must have been quite a public speaker, because she was in demand everywhere. She did more traveling than any other woman from her part of the world had done before. She met with Paul himself on several occasions to plan strategies. Paul respected her opinions and took her advice seriously.

In the early centuries of the church, women served in many high offices. A sixth-century mosaic in a Roman basilica in honor of two women saints, Prudentiana and Praxedis, portrays four female figures: the two saints, Mary, and a fourth woman identified as Bishop Theodora (Theodora Episcopa), wife of Emperor Justinian and named coruler with him. At some point, the last letter of her name was effaced, evidently by someone who was trying to erase the fact that her name was feminine, Theodora, rather than masculine, Theodorus. Such leadership roles for women were soon to be suppressed by the church. (from Torjesen, 9-10)

Some ancient prison records prove that Junia was even arrested and held for a few weeks on trumped-up charges. The officials never could make their accusations of "scheming to overthrow the government" stick, however, because Junia was a model citizen. If women could have held office, she would have run for a government position herself. She had the influence and the intelligence. She just happened to be the wrong gender for her time.

That didn't keep Paul from appointing her an apostle. A FEMALE apostle—the first of her kind! There were others later, but Junia was the one who broke the gender barrier. Paul wasn't exactly lavish in his praise of women and he rarely recommended them as preachers, but he wrote to several churches telling them they should invite Junia to run a revival. She was a mover and a shaker. Even crusty old Paul had to admit that.

Andronicus was a wonderful, supportive husband and Junia's number one fan. He knew he didn't have the political abilities she had, but he could lay the groundwork for her and hold the purse strings for their travel campaigns. He was an honest but shrewd businessman. Paul felt obligated to give him the title of apostle, too, and Andro graciously accepted, but he knew that as a preacher and a teacher, he just wasn't in Junia's league.

In the second-century gnostic gospel, the Gospel of Mary, Mary Magdalene is called "Apostle to the Apostles," indicating that calling women apostles was not unheard of. A woman could also be a priest or presbyter, as indicated by a burial epitaph from the third or fourth century found on the Greek island of Thera in which a woman named Epiktas is called a *presbytis* (presbyter). (from Torjesen, 10)

Junia and Andro traveled as missionaries well into their eighties. They had half a dozen kids of their own, but they were also "Mom and Dad" to thousands of folks who learned the gospel from them. When they finally had to retire from the circuit, Junia settled into a late career as a writer. She couldn't get published under her own name. Female authors got no respect back then. So sometimes she used "Junius" as her byline. Editors assumed she was a guy! Other times, she just signed her work with "Anonymous." She produced some of the best treatises on Christian doctrine, not to mention some terrific travel guides, that came out of the first century. J. J. located copies of some of them in her research, and that's how she knows so much about her great-grandma Junia.

Well, when J. J. decided to run for the U.S. Senate, her husband Ambrose said he'd take time off from his automobile dealership and help her with the campaign. He said if ole Andro could do it for Junia, he sure could do it for J. J. The campaign trail was rigorous, but J. J. took to it like a duck to water. She outtalked and outsmarted her opponent, a former preacher turned politician. He tried to convince the voters that J. J. had no business representing our state at the national level. She might make a sweet little ole small-town mayor like her mama, he claimed, but she'd probably do the most good running the PTO. It was a high-stakes election, and the going got mighty rough before it was over.

J. J. won with 52 percent of the vote. That night there were parties all over the state, most of them hosted by women like me who had raised big money in small chunks to keep J. J. in the running. Perhaps because women show their emotions a skosh more easily than men, the intensity factor in the celebrations that night was formidable. Especially in our town, where Senator Jenny June grew up.

When J. J. made her acceptance speech, it was clear she had inherited a thing or two from Johanna and Julia and Junia—and all the others in between. Jenny June Jones is a competent, straight-shooting, hard-working, really nice woman. Who knows? One of these days, she just might get elected president. The times they are a'changing, and I can't begin to tell you how much fun it is to be part of it. *(Barbara McBride-Smith)*

# Tryphaena, Tryphosa, Euodia, Syntyche

*Four women church leaders are commended by Paul, but two are also counseled to stop quarreling.*

## The Story

Greet Tryphaena and Tryphosa, who work hard in the Lord's service, and dear Persis who has worked hard in his service for so long.

. . . . . . . . . . . . . . . . . . . . . . . .

Euodia and Syntyche, I appeal to you both: agree together in the Lord. Yes, and you too, my loyal comrade, I ask you to help these women, who shared my struggles in the cause of the gospel, with Clement and my other fellow-workers, who are enrolled in the book of life.

## Comments on the Story

Continuing the references to women in Romans 16, Paul sends greetings to Tryphaena and Tryphosa as well as Persis who are said to have "worked hard" in the service of the gospel. Earlier in the letter (16:6), Mary was greeted in a similar way. The exact nature of their work is not made explicit, but Paul uses the verb to describe not only his own labor (1 Cor. 15:10; Gal. 4:11; Phil. 2:16), which is his Christian missionary activity, likewise described as apostleship or diaconal service, but also the labor of others who work in the mission (1 Thess. 5:12). While we cannot make any more explicit claims for the work of Persis, Tryphaena, and Tryphosa, we do at least have their names, and their presence makes clear yet again that women are to be continually included in references to early Christian missionary activity in its various aspects unless they are explicitly excluded.

A closely related term that is used for Prisca and her partner, Aquila, in Romans 16:3, is that of "co-worker" or "fellow-worker." Indeed, the two terms are used together to describe the roles of Titus in 2 Corinthians 8:23 and "co-worker" describes a number of other male missionaries such as Apollos (1 Cor. 3:9); Timothy (1 Thess. 3:9); and Philemon (Philem. 1) to name but a few. The scope of this term seems to have been broad and one among many that did not specifically distinguish an aspect of the early mission but pointed to general participation in it together with Paul. It stands to reason that there had to be many involved in the establishment and spread of the early reign of God or Jesus movement beyond the death of Jesus. The only slight glimpses that both Paul and the Lukan author afford us of that involvement is by way of passing references in works whose focus is the centrality of Paul.

In the church of Philippi, one of the earliest converts was Lydia (16:11-15). She is not named a coworker by the Lukan writer whose tendency was to obscure women's active ministry, but a reconstruction of her leadership of a house-church suggested this. Paul, however, specifically names two women in the church of Philippi, Euodia and Syntyche, as "fellow-workers" in the gospel with himself and with Clement (Phil. 4:2-3).

It seems that Euodia and Syntyche are specifically addressed by Paul in the context of a letter to the entire community because there is a lack of agreement between them, which is having an effect on that community. One of the key concerns in this letter is that the community be of one mind or think alike (2:2, 5; 3:15) and this disagreement must have been one of the causes of the lack of unity that Paul addresses because he urges the two women to also be of one mind or "agree together" (4:2). One important thing to take account of in considering the disagreement between Euodia and Syntyche is that it is not trivialized as so often happens with aspects of women's lives. Indeed, its importance to the Philippian community may have been equivalent to the disagreement between Paul and Peter at Antioch to the expanding early Christian mission (Gal. 2:11-14).

When we seek to reconstruct the possible causes of such a deep disagreement from the point of view of the women of Philippi and especially of two of its women leaders, Euodia and Syntyche, the context is important. Recent studies of women in Philippi have pointed to the rock carvings and inscriptions that indicate that the worship of two female deities, Diana and Isis, was particularly attractive to women. Women such as Euodia and Syntyche whose names indicate a Hellenistic background, and other women like them, may well have come to Christianity from these religious traditions. We know little of the religious experience of women within these religions or of the cultic or leadership positions available to them. It may have been, however, that there were differences between the house-churches lead by Euodia and Syntyche in relation to women's leadership, authority, and liturgical roles. Some women may have been prepared to surrender to Pauline authority and leadership within the Christian tradition and to surrender female deities or images of the deity for the male god and male savior central to Christianity. Others may have resisted. Euodia and Syntyche may have represented these or other struggles associated with women and their entry into the Christian tradition. As such, the disagreement symbolized in Euodia and Syntyche would have been a significant threat to the unity of the Philippian church.

The exact nature of Euodia and Syntyche's quarrel will never be known to us. The above reconstruction does not, however, trivialize it. Rather, it indicates that women's involvement in the teaching, leadership, and missionary roles in the early Christian community must have had profound theological implications as they interpreted the gospel from their experience and their backgrounds within Judaism or other Hellenistic religious traditions. Like their ministries, their theologies are all but hidden from us and we can only guess at them through the fissures in the text, which reference to such as the disagreement between Euodia and Syntyche opens up. They are significant foresisters for women and men today who struggle to be faithful to women's experience and women's theological insights even when this means that communities may not be able to "agree together" (Phil. 4:2) as leaders such as Paul would wish.

### Retelling the Story

Greet Tryphaena and Tryphosa, who work hard in the Lord's service, . . .
Euodia and Syntyche, I appeal to you both: agree together in the Lord.
(Rom. 16:12; Phil. 4:2)

Euodia and Syntyche had been friends forever, it seemed. They had grown up in the same neighborhood, played together as children, and learned the feminine arts of cooking and sewing with equal skill. They had both married young, as dictated by culture and parental preplanning. For Euodia, marriage meant motherhood, and she was eager to nurture. Her husband, an older man, considered himself a unique and special individual. He wanted a woman who agreed with his self-assessment. Euodia understood his needs and provided them. Syntyche married a man who admired her for her independent and assertive nature. Theirs was a competitive but mostly comfortable partnership.

When Euodia began birthing babies, Syntyche remained childless. Syntyche placed no blame and felt no shame for

Philippi, the city of Euodia and Syntyche, is a community where the religious leadership of women is indicated by archaeological data. On the city's acropolis is found a series of 187 rock-cut reliefs of various pagan deities (ca. first to third centuries c.e.). Along with depictions of the goddess Diana are found depictions of women who worshiped her. In a location near the theater, other goddesses are pictured along with various women cult officials. (Hendrix, 5.316)

her barrenness. Euodia's pregnancies were always difficult, and each labor was more prolonged and painful than the last. Syntyche was there with her every time, squeezing her hand, serving as her coach and comforter. Euodia would always say afterward, "Syntyche, I wouldn't have survived this one without you. Promise you'll always be here for me."

Syntyche would respond, "I promise, Euodia, but don't you think eight (or whatever the latest number was) kids are enough. You've proven to everyone that you're Supermom!" But Euodia possessed a deep inner-imperative to pro-

The goddess Diana, or Artemis, was prominently worshiped at Phillipi. She was best known as the virgin huntress. One famous story tells of Actaeon, a hunter who came upon Diana/Artemis while she was bathing and thus gazed upon her nude body. In punishment, she turned him into a stag so that he was then set upon by his own dogs and killed. Diana/Artemis was especially invoked by women in periods of passage to puberty, marriage, and motherhood. (Kraemer, *Her Share of the Blessings*, 22-23)

create and nurture. Her fulfillment and joy were centered in her family.

Syntyche sought success outside of her role as wife and homemaker. She was one of the youngest women in her worship community when she became a leader in the Diana Temple. The other women knew that she was a born leader, confident as any man they'd known, and they respected her authority. Syntyche gave their worship new definition—a sharing of sisterhood in sacrifice and praise to their goddess, Diana the huntress. In a few short years, Syntyche was appointed to the priesthood.

Meanwhile, Euodia continued to mother her husband and children—until they no longer needed her. Her children grew up and left home. Her husband died in a chariot accident. Suddenly, Euodia's world came crashing down around her. First she raged, and then she grieved. In despair, she began to visit the Temple of Isis. The goddess Isis was, in Euodia's view, the ideal woman. She was a model of constancy and fidelity, always putting her husband and children ahead of herself. Isis, after all, rescued her own husband Osiris from the claws of death. During her visits to the Isis Temple, Euodia found solace and hope. The women and men who worshiped there assured her that her life could still be meaningful and productive. But when she was asked to take a position of leadership in the rituals, she declined. Surely a man with experience in public service was a more appropriate choice. For years she resisted the call to serve. Finally after more than a decade of devoted work, Euodia accepted an official position as a priest of Isis. When Syntyche heard the news, she ran to embrace her dear friend and declared, "It's your turn, beloved earth-mother. It's your turn to find authority in the strength you've always possessed."

Once again, as in their youth, Euodia and Syntyche had time and a need to enjoy their friendship. They learned from each other and shared in the rituals to each other's goddess. As time passed and their hair grayed, the reputation of Euodia and Syntyche as wise elders became known throughout Macedonia.

When Christianity arrived in the city of Phillipi, Euodia and Syntyche were naturally curious about its teachings. At the invitation of neighbors, they attended a worship meeting at the home of two sisters recently arrived from Rome, Tryphaena and Tryphosa. A dynamic young man named Paul spoke of a new kingdom where all, regardless of earthly status, were welcome and equal. Euodia and Syntyche began to worship with these new Christians. They were busier now than they had ever been. Their temple sisters still depended on their guidance and leadership, and their Christian friends wanted their support and validation.

When Paul moved on to establish new Christian communities, he instructed the Phillipian church to elect leaders from their membership. It was obvious to Syntyche that she and Euodia were the best candidates. Their experience exceeded that of anyone else. Euodia never doubted their competence, but felt that perhaps it was time to turn the reins of authority over to the younger women who showed leadership abilities. Syntyche worried that Euodia was

The goddess Isis was also prominent at Philippi. She was known as the wife of the god Osiris. When Osiris was killed by the rival god Seth, his body was dismembered and scattered abroad. Isis went in search of it and eventually was able to restore the corpse. She also had a child by Osiris, Horus (or Harpocrates), who avenged his father's death. Isis was seen as the model for the ideal wife and mother and as the protector of marital fidelity. (Kraemer, *Her Share of the Blessings,* 74-79)

abdicating her power, falling back into old habits—putting "family" before self.

Syntyche tried to reason with her friend. "Tryphaena and Tryphosa are strong young women, Euodia, but their authority will be questioned. You and I have seen it all and done it all before. We must continue to direct the spiritual journey of our congregants. These young women will have their turns, but they are not ready for the uncharted path ahead."

Euodia disagreed. "These young women have dreams that you and I, because of our upbringing, never dared to dream. The teachings of Christianity will give them fertile ground in which to grow. We have shown them how to lead. Now we must allow them to do so. We are the midwives and they are the mothers who must give birth to a new religion for a new world. Oh, we still have many good years left in us, my dear Syntyche, but let's be honest, we are the crones. It is time for the matrons among us to take their rightful place."

Syntyche chuckled through her clenched teeth. "I see, old girl, that you and I, as always, shall continue to agree to disagree. Nevertheless, Euodia, I love you as a sister."

"And I love you the same, my sweet Syntyche. Let us promise, that whatever happens, we'll always be here for each other." *(Barbara McBride-Smith)*

# Chloe

*Chloe emerges as a coworker in Paul's mission by informing him of problems in the church at Corinth.*

## The Story

I APPEAL to you, my friends, in the name of our Lord Jesus Christ: agree among yourselves, and avoid divisions; let there be complete unity of mind and thought. My friends, it has been brought to my notice by Chloe's people that there are quarrels among you. What I mean is this: each of you is saying, 'I am for Paul,' or 'I am for Apollos'; 'I am for Cephas,' or 'I am for Christ.' Surely Christ has not been divided! Was it Paul who was crucified for you? Was it is Paul's name that you were baptized? Thank God, I never baptized any of you, except Crispus and Gaius; no one can say you were baptized in my name. I did of course baptize the household of Stephanas; I cannot think of anyone else. Christ did not send me to baptize, but to proclaim the gospel; and to do it without recourse to the skills of rhetoric, lest the cross of Christ be robbed of its effect.

## Comments on the Story

Chloe appears but once in the early Christian literature, in the opening verses of Paul's first letter to the Corinthians (1:11). Of all the Pauline letters, the First Letter to the Corinthians is the one that reflects most the issues of the community that Paul addresses. Its opening and the immediacy with which Paul moves into addressing the issue of divisions in the community, is indicative of this.

Chloe and her household are cited by Paul in his appeal to the community regarding the divisions among them, which have been brought to his notice. Indeed, Paul begins 1 Corinthians 1:10-17 with a powerful rhetorical appeal. The actual appeal to avoid divisions or schisms in the center of verse 10 is surrounded by a much more positive entreaty, to "agree among yourselves" and to let there be "complete unity of mind and thought." The focus is, therefore, unity within the Corinthian Christian community, which presumably consisted of a number of different households or house-churches that were claiming different origins, perhaps in support of different theological positions—"I belong to Paul," "I belong to Apollos," or "I belong to Cephas." Some scholars suggest that the final claim to belong to Christ is Paul's parody on the rhetoric of the various households in order that he might then construct his theology of unity in Christ crucified.

Within this context, Paul cites "Chloe's people" (1 Cor. 1:11) as the source of his information regarding the quarrels in Corinth. From this meager information, we can begin to reconstruct some of the possibilities for Chloe's position in Corinth. First, since it is Chloe's name that is used to identity Paul's messengers, it seems reasonable to imagine that she is a person of known authority in the church of Corinth. Also naming her as having a group so identified with her suggests that she is a householder. As such, she takes her place with other women householders already encountered—Lydia (Acts 16:15); Mary (Acts 12:12); and Martha (Luke 10:38)—as well as ones such as Nympha who lead a house-church in Laodicea (Col. 4:15).

Second, the concern of Chloe and her household regarding the divisions in Corinth, suggests that this household, with Chloe as its leader, has known a time when such divisions did not exist. This allows us to imagine, therefore, that her household is one of the earliest groups or houses that provided a nucleus from which the Corinthian community has grown. As such it places Chloe and her household as foundational to the church of Corinth as Lydia was in Philippi. The picture emerging, therefore, is not of Peter and Paul as lone founders of the church. Indeed, they, together with other women and men, were significant early itinerant messengers of the gospel. Its message was only able to take root and grow, however, as a result of those early believers who provided not only their houses as a gathering space but also their skills of leadership and authority that helped to shape a community and nurture its new beliefs. Chloe and a number of women like her were of this group and made such a contribution and must be remembered, therefore, as foundational members of our community of faith.

No doubt a variety of theologies developed in these house-churches between the visits of Paul or receipt of his letters. Unfortunately, we have no access to the theology of Chloe's household—whether she was in agreement with Paul or whether her household was more resistant to what seemed like Pauline claims to authority in order to harness the charismatic gifts developing among some community members in Corinth (see 1 Cor. 1214).

Chloe's story and her theology have been subordinated to Paul and his theology. She is not remembered as a foundational member of the Christian church and she is not celebrated as one of its saints as are so many of the male participants in its foundational mission. One reason for this, which deserves our attention, especially in the two verses of 1 Corinthians 1:10-11, is the androcentric nature of the language and culture of the first-century Mediterranean world that permeates the Christian Testament and has shaped Christian consciousness until today.

The opening phrases of both verses 10 and 11 are followed by the third-person masculine plural noun, *adelphoi*, for Paul's addressees. This has been literally translated as "brothers" until most recently (REB: "friends"; NRSV:

"brothers and sisters"). Within this context, there is a passing reference to Chloe, whom we have seen above may have been a significant authority and leadership figure in the Corinthian church. She and all her sisters are subsumed under the masculine terminology with the effect that they and their participation in and contribution to the Corinthian church are obscured and hidden. The long-term effect down through history of this androcentric language is that Chloe and her sisters have been forgotten and the world of early Christianity has been reconstructed in the same androcentric fashion, a world of men that has subsumed and silenced women.

Today, therefore, there is a need to use the language of "brothers" and "sisters" even more so than the more general "friends" to remind readers of the women of Corinth who, like Chloe, led households or house-churches, constructed theologies, and struggled with the divisions and problems that confronted an emerging Christian church. Such issues confront churches today also so that Chloe and her story provides a prototype for the importance of facing the struggles in order that the gospel vision might survive and be carried into the future for those sisters and brothers who will come after us.

## Retelling the Story

My friends, it has been brought to my notice by Chloe's people that there are quarrels among you. (1 Cor. 1:11)

Chloe just wanted everybody to get along. She believed in life, liberty, and the pursuit of happiness for all persons. That wasn't the same as "separate but equal," she told her congregants. They, in turn, accused Chloe of reckless hospitality and unbridled tolerance.

It all started when Chloe initiated a Love Feast, a free evening meal, for the poor and hungry of inner-city Corinth. The church officials agreed that she could serve the meal in the church basement. Some of the members volunteered to help and felt righteous about their good works. Then Chloe saw a

Although religious leaders were usually assumed to be men, it was not uncommon for women to be leaders in various religious settings in the ancient world. Jewish inscriptions mention several women who held positions of leadership in the Jewish community. For example, a certain Rufina is identified as "head of the synagogue" in a second-century inscription from Smyrna. This means she apparently functioned as presider at worship, among other things. Other women received the title of "mother of the synagogue" indicating that they were probably financial benefactors as well as administrative functionaries of some kind. (Brooten, 5-33, 57-72)

need to provide a warm and safe place for the homeless to sleep. She donated the cots and blankets and asked the church elders to allow overnight use of the building. That's when the difference of opinion became noticeable. "Let those people sleep in our holy place? What's wrong with the city park or the YMCA? Don't they have relatives somewhere who can take them in? The vote was close at the board meeting, but Chloe's influence carried the day.

As Chloe came to know the people who sought the shelter of the church, she began to understand that they needed more than food or a roof over their heads. They also needed to hear the good news and to share in the community of faith. She invited them to worship, and they came.

The congregation was in shock. "What are these people doing here? That's MY pew! They aren't wearing appropriate clothes and their feet are dirty. They don't even know the right words to the hymns. They're liturgically impaired! Who are these riffraff anyway? You mean to tell us you've opened up our church doors to sinners and republicans, gypsies, tramps, and thieves, rednecks and wetbacks, ex-cons and addicts, the diseased and the unclean, the uneducated and the uncouth, even eunuchs and other persons of uncertain and immoral sexual orientation? And you expect us to share communion with them? We don't know where their hands have been! Drink from the same cup? What if we catch something? We've got our health to think about, not to mention our reputation."

The church board met to discuss the situation. Chloe reminded them that Paul had preached to them about unity—unity of their diversities. "We are one in Christ. Remember? All are welcome at the table."

"Oh, Chloe, don't be so literal. He didn't mean we have to drink from the same wineglass or worship in the same building. But if you insist on turning over this church to these misfits, then some of us are going to be forced to start our own congregations. This one is getting too big and inclusive anyway. It's time to downsize. How about if we make a list of the criteria we feel strongly about, and then we can split up accordingly. Anybody who wants to stick with Chloe and her open-door/open-mind policy can be the Saint Paul Congregation. We can have a Saint Apollos Congregation, and a Saint Cephas Congregation, and those who just aren't sure yet can be the Saint Thomas Congregation. Each congregation can determine its own membership requirements. We'll all still be part of The Christ Church, of course. One body, with many parts. All in favor, say 'Aye.' "

Chloe couldn't believe her ears. These good church folks were generosity challenged and theologically dysfunctional. She called her servants (to whom she paid fair wages and an excellent benefit package) and said to them, "Please go find Paul and tell him that this church is going haywire. Tell him to send help and to make it snappy. I'll try to stall the congregational vote until we hear from him." *(Barbara McBride-Smith)*

The earliest Christian communities met in houses. The householder, or head of the house, would act as the host for the church meeting. Such householders would have to be persons of sufficient means to have a house big enough to accommodate the Christian group. Both men and women, as well as couples, are named in the New Testament as being individuals who hosted the church in their homes. Especially interesting are the women who hosted the church, such as Lydia, Priscilla (with Aquila), and Phoebe. Chloe, as a householder with a coterie of servants, who was close to Paul, may have been such a woman.

# 1 CORINTHIANS 11:2-16; 14:33*b*-36

# Corinthian Women Prophets

*Women who prophesy at the worship services in Corinth worry Paul because they do not wear veils.*

### The Story

I COMMEND you for always keeping me in mind, and maintaining the tradition I handed on to you. But I wish you to understand that, while every man has Christ for his head, a woman's head is man, as Christ's head is God. A man who keeps his head covered when he prays or prophesies brings shame on his head; but a woman brings shame on her head if she prays or prophesies bareheaded; it is as bad as if her head were shaved. If a woman does not cover her head she might as well have her hair cut off; but if it is a disgrace for her to be cropped and shaved, then she should cover her head. A man must not cover his head, because man is the image of God, and the mirror of his glory, whereas a woman reflects the glory of man. For man did not originally spring from woman, but woman was made out of man; and man was not created for woman's sake, but woman for the sake of man; and therefore a woman must have the sign of her authority on her head, out of regard for the angels. Yet in the Lord's fellowship woman is as essential to man as man to woman. If woman was made out of man, it is through woman that man now comes to be; and God is the source of all.

Judge for yourselves; is it fitting for a woman to pray to God bareheaded? Does not nature herself teach you that while long hair disgraces a man, it is a woman's glory? For her hair was given as a covering.

And if anyone still insists on arguing, there is no such custom among us, or in any of the congregations of God's people.

. . . . . . . . . . . . . . . . . . . . . . . . . . .

As in all congregations of God's people, women should keep silent at the meeting. They have no permission to talk, but should keep their place as the law directs. If there is something they want to know, they can ask their husbands at home. It is shocking thing for a woman to talk at the meeting.

Did the word of God originate with you? Or are you the only people to whom it came?

### Comments on the Story

The women encountered between the lines of 1 Corinthians 11:2-16 and 1 Corinthians 14:33-36 are not veiled and submissive women. Indeed they are quite the opposite. Readers of these two texts must recognize that they are dealing with prescriptive texts, texts in which the male theologian, Paul, argues for women to be veiled when they pray and prophesy and then to be silent in the churches. They offer a male perspective on and vision for women's activities in the church of Corinth, not women's actual experience. In order to discover the latter, we must read between the lines of these Pauline prescriptions.

First, these two prescriptive texts relating to women are contained within the latter half of Paul's Letter to the Corinthians, which is concerned with order in the worshiping assembly and order in relation to the spiritual or charismatic gifts that seem to have been strong among the Corinthian Christians. That Paul moves easily from what seem to be general prescriptions about both contexts to those related specifically to women allows readers to assume women are full participants in both the worship and the exercise of the spiritual gifts in the community. Indeed, it is clear from 1 Corinthians 11:5 that women are praying and prophesying and in 1 Corinthians 14:34 that they are members of the worshiping assembly, giving prophesies and their interpretations as well as speaking in tongues (14:26-32).

These insights, which allow readers to encounter the Corinthian women prophets and worshipers in their imaginative reconstruction of Paul's audience, enable them also to reconstruct a second aspect of women's experience in Corinth. Women's prophetic gifts must have given them confidence in their own authority to theologize on their experience in relation to Scripture and the preaching of the gospel that they had encountered. From the Pauline arguments in 1 Corinthians 11:2-16, it seems that Paul is presenting a countertheology and since we have only his theology, we must once again read between the lines to try to hear the theology of the Corinthian women prophets.

At the heart of Paul's elaborate arguments and definitions put forward in relation to women covering their heads in worship is a claim for women's graded subjugation to men. It appears, therefore, that women were claiming parity with men in the worshiping assembly and the sign or expression of this was to pray and prophesy with their heads uncovered. One basis for their claim may well have been the Pauline preaching of oneness in Christ expressed in the baptismal formula of Galatians 3:27-28. Interestingly, when Paul uses this formula in 1 Corinthians 12:13, he omits the male/female pair, perhaps because of his attempts to quash both the theology and praxis of the Corinthian women. The women, on the other hand, have clearly drawn what may well have been the formula of their baptism into the heart of their theology as well as seeking to give full actual expression to it in their context of worship.

It seems, too, that these women prophets have developed more fully the theological basis of the baptismal formula, namely Genesis 1:27, claiming that women are in the image of divinity as men are said to be. It is this theology that draws forth the Pauline argument of 1 Corinthians 11:7 that only man is the reflection of God while woman is the reflection of man. This is then supplemented by Paul's claim on Genesis 2, that woman was made for man, not man for woman (1 Cor. 11:9). His circuitous recognition of reciprocity (11:11-

12), which may also have been part of the Corinthian women's theology, in no way counters his argument for subordination because it returns to God as the source of all and this same God has been established at the head or source of a graded system of subjugations in the opening verses of this section (11:3).

The freedom women were claiming in Christ, which found expression in their worshiping without head covering and their prophesying in the Christian assembly in a way that gave instructions to men as well as women is argued by Paul to be contrary to nature (11:14), contrary to the culture of women's shame which was to be preserved in the public arena by their compliance with the gender codes of the society, contrary to the law, and contrary to the custom of all the churches. As Paul piles up these arguments, he becomes more confident in moving from merely restricting women to having them veiled for worship to silencing their voices. The necessity to lay up arguments from such a variety of perspectives suggests that Paul did not expect his prescriptions to be demurely received by the women of Corinth (or perhaps some of the men of the community as well). Rather, from the Pauline rhetoric, we catch another glimpse of resistance to Paul and his authority. This resistance is based on sound theological arguments that interpreted Scripture and received teachings in a way that led to Christian praxis of which Paul disapproved. Tragically, we do not hear these theological voices or their responses to Paul. Paul's voice drowns them out and it is the Pauline voice alone, the Pauline perspective that has provided the foundation for a continued praxis in Christian churches of male hierarchical domination of women.

At this point in history, however, women's prophetic and theological voices are being heard in theological halls and in Christian assemblies. Some would still seek Pauline authority to silence these voices, but now the voices of the Corinthian women prophets are being raised together with those of their twentieth- and twenty-first-century sisters. They are being raised in resistance to a theology of graded subjugations divinely sanctioned and to a praxis of order and peace that silences women and renders them submissive. The Corinthian women's inspirited resistance to what they experienced as abusive authority inspires women's resistance today to any Christian theology or prescriptions that mar the foundational vision of women and men as the image and glory of God, not only metaphorically but actually in the structures and praxis of the churches.

## Retelling the Story

> A woman brings shame on her head if she prays of prophesies bareheaded; it is as bad as if her head were shaved. (1 Cor. 11:5)

It was bound to happen, sooner or later. The Daddy Warbucks of our community, Brother Billy Bob Neanderthal, showed up at church last Sunday just in time to hear me preach at the 11 o'clock service. He didn't exactly oppose my appointment to this congregation. Even he had to admit that I do know my stuff when it comes to homiletics. But he did make it clear from the day I arrived that "wimmen in the pulpit" have to work extra hard at "lookin' right." He warned me more than once about being careful lest I become an "occasion of sin" for the men of my flock. I promised not to wear short shorts, halter tops, or even a Wonderbra while preaching. He didn't know I was being facetious. I don't even own any of the aforementioned items.

Well, last Sunday I put on my new outfit, the one I ordered from the businesswomen's section of the mail-order catalog. It was a conservative gray suit with a mid-calf-length skirt, a loosely fitted jacket, a simple ivory blouse, and a tie. Yes, a tie! Ties are very fashionable in the "businesswomen's world" these days. Anyway, that's what the mail-order catalog said. Looking in the mirror, I felt quite professional. Once I put on my clerical robe, however, I might just as well have been wearing short shorts, a halter top, and a Wonderbra. The only thing that really showed, peeking out the top of my robe, was the tie. It was a standard-issue tie, nothing fancy. No flamingos or bold geometric designs. Not fuchsia or puce or even scarlet. Just a tiny paisley pattern on a dark blue background. How could I offend? I felt worthy enough as I stepped into the pulpit that morning. I also felt uncomfortable. Around the neck. I decided that men get to wear ties to make up for the fact that they don't ever have to be pregnant.

Brother Billy Bob confronted me immediately after the service. "Why are you wearing a tie?"

"Why not?" I responded. I felt like a rabbi, answering a question with a question.

"Ties are for men, " said Brother Billy Bob.

"Where in the Bible or the U.S. Constitution does it say that women can't wear ties?" My voice went up a notch. Now I was really feeling discomfort around my neck—and everywhere else.

The "maenads" or crazed women worshipers of the Greek god of wine, Dionysus, were celebrated in Euripides' fifth-century drama, *The Bacchae.* He told of women brought to a state of crazed ecstasy by Dionysus—women who would leave their homes and wander through the mountains killing wild beasts with their bare hands and eating them raw. How much of what he said was myth and how much represented actual practice are matters of debate. Maenads were widely represented in Dionysiac scenes on vase paintings as women dancing in various stages of ecstasy. Some have argued that it was fear of a maenadlike ecstasy among Christian women that partially accounted for Paul's hesitations about proprieties for women prophets in 1 Corinthians.

"My dear young lady, you really have gone too far. WE gave you ladies the right to vote. WE even gave you the right to preach in public! But WE did not give you the right to wear a tie! Why do you insist on making a mockery of your femininity? A woman's proper neckwear is a ruffle or a lace collar or even a string of pearls. Perhaps rubies, but certainly not a tie! If you don't understand my logic, go home and ask your husband." Brother Billy Bob's eyeballs were starting to bug out.

"But sir," I reminded him, "I don't have a husband."

"You're right about that," retorted Brother Billy Bob, his face turning red. "That man you are living with is not your husband!"

"No, he's not," I confessed. "He's my sixteen-year-old son. He doesn't own a tie, and he hasn't engaged in logic since he turned twelve. But he does have an earring—in his nose. His hair is long and green and he wears his T-shirts wrong-side-out. I don't think a discussion about clothing etiquette with him would be fruitful."

Brother Billy Bob was gasping for breath. I thought the veins in his neck were going to pop. "Brother Neanderthal, sir, I can see that you are as uncomfortable as I am. Let's both loosen our ties and try to calm down. We're both being a little silly."

"Silly? My dear young woman, God does not condone silliness in his house!"

Women prophets later came to be associated especially with Montanism, a Christian movement that began in Phrygia in the late-second century c.e. led by a man named Montanus. He emphasized the outpouring of the Holy Spirit on himself and his female coleaders, the prophetesses Prisca and Maximilla. Montanism continued for several centuries, and attracted many women worshipers to its ecstatic form of Christianity. The church father Tertullian was sympathetic to the movement and described a woman prophet in this manner: "We have now amongst us a sister whose lot it has been to be favored with gifts of revelation, which she experiences in the Spirit by ecstatic vision amidst the sacred rites of the Lord's Day in the church; she converses with angels, and sometimes even with the Lord; she both sees and hears mysterious communications; some men's hearts she discerns, and she obtains directions for healing for such as need them" (*On the Soul* 9 [second to third century c.e.]). Other church leaders condemned Montanism, however, and among other reasons criticized them for "magnifying these wretched women above the Apostles" (Hippolytus, *Refutation of All Heresies* 8.12). Montanism was eventually judged by the larger church to be a heresy. (Kraemer, *Maenad, Martyrs, Matrons, Monastics,* nos. 101 and 102)

My mistake. I had forgotten: Holiness and humor don't mix. "I'll tell you what," I said. "I'm taking this tie off right now, and I'm never wearing it again. I promise."

"At last you've come to your senses. I knew you'd see it my way. I've got to be getting back to the golf course now. But allow me to compliment you on your hairdo. Long hair is a woman's glory."

I wondered if leg hair was worth as many glory points as head hair. Probably not. I also wondered if long male head hair was as glorious as long female head hair. Probably not. I had noticed as Brother Billy Bob departed that the back of his head was bald. Good thing he hadn't seen my sixteen-year-old son lately.

After some serious study and some quiet reflection on this incident, I came to the conclusion that women do have the right to wear a tie anytime and anywhere—even in the pulpit. But I, a woman, have chosen (of my OWN FREE WILL) not to wear one. Neckties are detrimental to one's health, regardless of gender. I've discovered that men who wear neckties all the time tend to be high-strung and nervous and irrational. Perhaps it's because they've got a piece of cloth tied very tightly around their necks. I propose that ties, not cholesterol, cause heart attacks and strokes. It is also very likely that wearing a tie eventually leads to baldness. The tie, you see, hinders the circulation of blood to the scalp, and that's why a man's hair falls out. It's a mystery to me why the apostle Paul failed to mention that in one of his letters.

Me wear a tie? In the pulpit? Heaven forbid! I might go bald and lose my glory. *(Barbara McBride-Smith)*

# The Woman Robed with the Sun

*The woman robed with the sun bears a male child and is protected by the earth from the fury of the dragon.*

## The Story

AFTER that there appeared a great sign in heaven: a woman robed with the sun, beneath her feet the moon, and on her head a crown of twelve stars. She was about to bear a child, and in the anguish of her labour she cried out to be delivered. Then a second sign appeared in heaven: a great, fiery red dragon with seven head and ten horns. On his heads were seven diadems, and with his tail he swept down a third of the stars in the sky and hurled them to the earth. The dragon stood in front of the woman who was about to give birth, so that when her child was born he might devour it. But when she gave birth to a male child, who is destined to rule all nations with a rod of iron, the child was snatched up to God and to his throne. The woman herself fled into the wilderness, where she was to be looked after for twelve hundred and sixty days in a place prepared for her by God.

Then war broke out in heaven; Michael and his angels fought against the dragon. The dragon with his angels fought back, but he was too weak, and they lost their place in heaven. The great dragon was thrown down, that ancient serpent who led the whole world astray, whose name is the Devil, or Satan; he was thrown down to the earth, and his angels with him.

I heard a loud voice in heaven proclaim: 'This is the time of victory for our God, the time of his power and sovereignty, when his Christ comes to his rightful rule! For the accuser of our brothers, he who day and night accused them before our God, is overthrown. By the sacrifice of the Lamb and by the witness they bore, they have conquered him; faced with death they did not cling to life. Therefore rejoice, you heavens and you that dwell in them! But woe to you, earth and sea, for the Devil has come down to you in great fury, knowing that his time is short!'

When the dragon saw that he had been thrown down to the earth, he went in pursuit of the woman who had given birth to the male child. But she was given the wings of a mighty eagle, so that she could fly to her place in the wilderness where she was to be looked after for three and a half years, out of reach of the serpent. From his mouth the serpent spewed a flood of water after the woman to sweep her away with its spate. But the earth came to her rescue: it opened its mouth and drank up the river which the dragon spewed from his mouth. Furious with the woman, the dragon went off to wage war on the rest of her offspring, those who keep God's commandments and maintain their witness to Jesus.

189

## Comments on the Story

A woman clothed with the sun, confronting the dragon, being carried off into the wilderness on two wings of a great eagle—these and many other images in Revelation 12:1-17 are archetypal images found in many legends of the Ancient Near East. There are parallels in stories of Artemis of Ephesus, Atargatis of Syria, Isis of Egypt and Asia Minor, Leto's giving birth to Apollo and many more. They represent the great cosmic struggle between good and evil with which apocalyptic literature is concerned and the two images of women in this story and the last one dealt with in this volume have come to represent the two great stereotypes of women—the virgin/mother and the whore.

It is challenging to have to deal with these two images at the conclusion to this volume because they are indeed metaphoric and seemingly divorced from the lives of the women encountered in the reconstruction of early Christianity undertaken to this point, which has placed women at the center of the reign of God or gospel movement. On the other hand, it is crucial to confront both images as they functioned for women and men in the first century and as they function today to maintain hierarchical dualisms that are central to patriarchy. This tension is a reminder of the necessity of a multivalent approach to the elimination of patriarchy, which is itself a many-layered form of oppression. It is imperative to change not just sociopolitical structures and practices but foundational images as well if liberation is to be effective.

Apocalyptic literature emerged from contexts of oppression and held out hope for a victory over such forces of evil. It was, therefore, potentially social and political as well as metaphorical or imagistic. The book of Revelation and its traditions developed in Asia Minor in the last decades of the first century and it used images to depict the chaos being experienced and to give hope for enduring through the chaos. Its images are highly genderized. They may have functioned at the end of the first century to order women's lives as a generally accepted way of ordering society. Today's readers need to be attentive to the way in which such imaging continues to function both in literature like that of Revelation and in the plethora of images that confront today's peoples in a multimedia society. Patriarchy is maintained by the power of the images that can be generated toward its maintenance.

The reader/listener who encounters the woman clothed with the sun and her battle with the dragon is aware of the force of dualistic oppositions in this text. The woman has no name and yet the cosmic imagery that surrounds her (Rev. 12:1) represents her as a woman of power. She is voiceless except for the narrative reference to her crying out in birth pangs (12:2); but there is a loud voice that comes forth from the heavens (12:10-12). She is the mother who gives birth even to the favored or expected son and yet the subsequent stereotypical role of nurturing the child is snatched away from her and the child is taken up to God (12:5). Divine power replaces female power and female roles. The woman is powerless before the dragon but is given the powerful wings of the great eagle. The dragon is not able to overcome or subdue her and therefore goes off from this encounter to wage war on others of her offspring. The text is finally inconclusive in that either the future safety or potentiality, or both, of the woman is left open-ended.

Contemporary readers need to be very aware of the imaginative power of these images to lock them into dualisms around gender and all other forms of oppressions. The images open up the potential of female power but as patriarchy is wont to do, restrict this power by stereotypical association with birthing and with nature. The power of the serpent or great dragon, an image often associated in mythology with female generative and untamed power, is set over against that of the woman. The images of Revelation had a social and political function for first-century women and men to subdue women's power, the power that had been claimed to support and sustain women's leadership and authority, women's praying and prophesying, women's teaching and theologizing, in the face of social, cultural, and religious forces that worked continually against such female power.

Today, the struggle to free female power from the ravages of patriarchal oppression in its various guises of the feminization of poverty, violence against women and their children, barriers to women's full participation in all political and social arenas, as well as all the structures of their oppression within the world's religious traditions is of cosmic proportions. Reading the account of the woman clothed with the sun in Revelation against the grain of the androcentric text may empower contemporary women and men to face and claim the power of the dragon or ancient serpent in the movement through and then beyond the dualisms of the text and its social context. Not only can women's power of birthing be affirmed but all the power of female sexuality as expressive of both desire and pleasure can be imaged as life-giving. Women then may not be driven out into the wilderness away from the center of male power and culture nor linked only with nature as distinct from culture. The power of the woman clothed with the sun and the dragon need not be set up in an oppositional struggle that is death-threatening to one, but the struggle of difference, however it be manifest, might lead to life rather than to death.

A different reading of the images of Revelation 12:1-17 may lead to alternative reimaging of divine-human relationships as cooperative rather than conflictual and able to be imaged in multiple-gendered and nongendered ways. The woman clothed with the sun may not simply image Israel, the church, Jerusalem, or Mary, as she has done in the history of interpretation, but may offer a female representation of divinity that breaks the bounds of the struggle between good and evil. The serpent or dragon can point metaphorically not

191

only to the force of evil to which the face of the Other is so often attached but also to what seem to be the dark powers in women and men which, when encountered with courage rather than fear, can be embraced for their liberating potential. The woman clothed with the sun points beyond patriarchy not to an idealized future but to the changes in political and social structures as well as religious imagination necessary to realize a future known only in its being brought to birth by women and men of courage and vision.

## Retelling the Story

After that there appeared a great sign in heaven: a woman robed with the sun, beneath her feet the moon, and on her head a crown of twelve stars. (Rev. 12:1)

Every ancient listener to this story would note its parallels to the well-known stories of Greek and Roman goddesses who had given birth under similar perilous circumstances. One of the most famous such stories is that of Leto, who was seduced by Zeus, the king of the gods, and became pregnant. When jealous Hera, the wife of Zeus, heard about this, she sent the monster serpent Python in pursuit of Leto. He pursued her all over the world, but she escaped to the island of Ortygia where she bore the first of her twins, the goddess Artemis. Then Artemis helped her mother with the birth of her twin brother, the god Apollo, who was born on the nearby island of Delos. Delos became a famous tourist attraction in the ancient world as the birthplace of Apollo and the story of the circumstances of his birth was spread far and wide.

According to Shinto mythology, the birth of Amaterasu, the sun goddess, was a dazzling, golden moment in time. Her parents, Izanami and Izanagi, the Mother and Father of all, said, "This girl-child is the most brilliant of all our many children. She is too wondrous for us to keep on the earth. She must live in the sky where everyone can see her and bask in her warmth."

Her parents gave her a necklace of five hundred kidney-shaped jewels—jade and amber and crystal. Amaterasu put on the beautiful necklace and said good-bye to her parents. She climbed the Floating Bridge that arched between earth and sky. Her journey was short, for earth and sky were not far apart in that long-ago time. The sky became Amaterasu's kingdom.

As the days passed, she grew into a woman. She shone down on all the people of the earth, and they called her Heaven Shining Great Woman—the Sun. The people learned how to grow crops, and everyone prospered in her light.

Meanwhile, Amaterasu's mother died

giving birth to another child, the fire god. Izanami went to the land of the dead, a hideous place called Yomi. Her husband followed her and shamed her by seeing her rotting and swarming with maggots. Izanagi purified himself by washing his body. As he cleaned his nose, he produced a son, Susa no Wo, the storm god. This strong and impetuous boy began to bellow the moment he came into the world. Unable to control his boisterous son, the father sent Susa no Wo to live in the sea. But Susa no Wo was not happy as ruler of the sea, and so he began to rage across the earth. He tore down trees, flooded the land, destroyed crops, and killed a great many people.

Izanagi called out to Susa no Wo, "What is wrong with you? Your anger is destroying the earth!"

The boy answered, "I weep and wail because I want to see my mother."

"Then go to her," replied his father. "If you wish to see her, go down to Yomi, the place of the dead. You are banished from the earth. Be gone, and good riddance!"

A parallel to the story of Leto was the story of the goddess Isis whose brother/husband, the god Osiris, was murdered by the monster Typhon and his remains set adrift in a casket. Isis searched far and wide for the casket and when she found it, she copulated with her husband's corpse and conceived a child. Like the story of Leto being pursued by Python, Isis was pursued by Typhon until the child Horus was born. Horus eventually avenged his father's death by killing Typhon. During the formative years of Christianity, the cult of Isis was one of the most popular in the ancient world, and the popular image of Isis suckling her child, known as an infant by the name Harpocrates, became the model for the Christian iconography of Mary suckling the infant Jesus.

As Susa no Wo left the earth and began his journey to the land of the dead, he thought of his older sister, Amaterasu, the sun goddess. When he came to the Floating Bridge that arched between earth and sky, he decided to climb it. His sister heard him stomping a long way off, and she became worried. "Why is my brother Susa no Wo coming here? Is he coming to steal my kingdom? Does he wish to take my place as ruler of the sky?"

Quickly Amaterasu tied up her dress into trousers. She twisted and braided her long black hair on top of her head. She tied her necklace of five hundred jewels around her head and arms. She picked up her bow and quiver full of arrows, and went out to meet her brother.

"Why have you come here?" she demanded. "I have seen the destruction your temper caused on the earth. I will not allow you to destroy the sky."

Susa no Wo looked at Amaterasu, all decked out for battle. He took a step backward, bowed low, and said, "Dear sister, your highness, I have not come to fight you. I only came to say good-bye. I am going on a long journey to see our mother in the land of the dead. I wish to bring her news of you."

Amaterasu still did not trust her brother. She stood tall over him, brandishing her bow and arrow. "How do I know that you are telling the truth, Susa no Wo? Prove to me that your intentions are not evil."

Susa no Wo began to plead with his sister. "I do not wish to harm you or take away your realm in the sky. Let us make a promise of trust and love to each other. Let us bear children together, as our pledge of peace."

Amaterasu was moved by her brother's words. She lowered her weapon, and spoke gently to him, "Give me your sword." Susa no Wo held out his sword, and Amaterasu took it, broke it into three pieces, tossed the pieces into her mouth, chewed and swallowed them. And then suddenly out of her mouth came three strong and beautiful goddesses.

Susa no Wo said to his sister, "Give me your necklace of five hundred jewels." Amaterasu unwrapped the jewels from her body and handed the necklace to her brother. He tossed the necklace into his mouth, chewed and swallowed it. Then he opened his lips and out of his mouth came five strong and handsome gods.

Amaterasu looked at their offspring and smiled. "Our children, our pledge of peace."

"Ho, ho," shouted Susa no Wo with glee. "My children, these females, made from my sword, are better than your sons. But you may keep the whole lot of them!" And Susa no Wo laughed and began to run headlong across the sky smashing everything in his path. He wrestled with the storm clouds and threw them down onto the planted fields on the earth. He destroyed the crops and defiled the earth with his garbage. He laughed at the misfortune of the earth people.

Amaterasu tolerated Susa no Wo's wild destruction for a while. He was, after all, her brother and the father of their children. But one day, as Amaterasu sat weaving in the most sacred place of her kingdom, Susa no Wo tore open the roof and polluted her temple. Amaterasu was so startled, she pricked herself with the weaving shuttle.

Amaterasu cried out in pain and anger, "I will not be violated again! I will leave this place forever. I will go where my brother cannot find me." The Sun Goddess fled from the sky. She ran down, down into a dark cave. She rolled a stone over the opening of the cave, and there she hid herself.

Now the sun was gone from the sky. The earth was dark. The people called out to Amaterasu, "Please, come back. We need your light!" But Amaterasu did not answer them.

Amaterasu's children, the eight young goddesses and gods, gathered along the starry sky path we call the Milky Way. They discussed how to persuade their mother to return to the sky. Together they made a plan. Two of them traveled to a faraway forest and dug up the five hundred-branched sakaki tree. They brought it back to the cave where Amaterasu had hidden herself, and they planted the tree just outside the cave. Then they designed a new necklace of five hundred kidney-shaped jewels—jade and amber and crystal. They hung the necklace on the branches of the sakaki tree. They hung pieces of bright cloth around the trunk of the tree. In the crux of the branches they placed the eight-sided bronze Yata mirror, which had been made by the metalsmith god. They brought roosters and placed them around the cave entrance.

As the roosters began to crow, the gods and goddesses formed a circle and started to dance. They were led by the rosy-cheeked goddess of mirth, Ame no Uzume. She leaped onto an overturned tub and performed a jig that made the other goddesses and gods shake with uproarious laughter. The sound of the laughter and the crowing of the roosters rocked the earth and the sky.

Amaterasu, still hiding herself in the cave, heard the merriment, and she called out, "Why is everyone happy? It's dark out there—isn't it?"

"Oh no," Ame no Uzume called back. "There's a goddess out here who is brighter than you."

Amaterasu was curious, so curious that she rolled the stone away from the door of the cave and peered out. She saw her own resplendent face reflected in the Yata mirror. Confused and dazzled, she stepped out of the cave. One young god-son took her hand and drew her into their circle. Two of her children moved behind her and stretched a plaited rope, made of rice straw, across the cave entrance. "We beg of you, Mother, don't ever go back into the cave. Please do not leave us in darkness again."

Amaterasu smiled on her children and the light returned to the sky and to the earth. Everyone shouted for joy.

Then they summoned Susa no Wo, their tumultuous father, before their divine council. Once again he was banished from earth and sky. But this time, everyone watched to make sure that he went down into the murky depths of the sea and stayed there.

Amaterasu returned to her place in the sky, and her golden radiance brought peace and harmony to heaven and earth. *(Barbara McBride-Smith)*

# The Woman Clothed in Purple and Scarlet

*The atrocities are detailed and the imminent end foretold of the woman imaged as a great whore who personifies the evil empire that makes war on the people of God.*

## The Story

ONE of the seven angels who held the seven bowls came and spoke to me; 'Come,' he said, 'I will show you the verdict on the great whore, she who is enthroned over many waters. The kings of the earth have committed fornication with her, and people the world over have made themselves drunk on the wine of her fornication.' He carried me in spirit into the wilderness, and I saw a woman mounted on a scarlet beast which was covered which blasphemous names and had seven heads and ten horns. The woman was clothed in purple and scarlet, and decked out with gold and precious stones and pearls. In her hand she held a gold cup full of obscenities and the foulness of her fornication. Written on her forehead was a name with a secret meaning: 'Babylon the great, the mother of whores and of every obscenity on earth.' I saw that the woman was drunk with the blood of God's people, and with the blood of those who had borne their testimony to Jesus.

At the sight of her I was greatly astonished. But the angel said to me, 'Why are you astonished? I will tell you the secret of the woman and of the beast she rides, with the seven heads and the ten horns. The beast you saw was once alive, and is alive no longer, but has yet to ascend out of the abyss before going to be destroyed. All the inhabitants of the earth whose names have not been written in the book of life since the foundation of the world will be astonished to see the beast, which once was alive, and is alive no longer, and has still to appear.

'This calls for a mind with insight. The seven heads are seven hills on which the woman sits enthroned. They also represent seven kings: five have already fallen, one is now reigning, and the other has yet to come. When he does come, he is to last for only a little while. As for the beast that once was alive and is alive no longer, he is an eighth—and yet he is one of the seven, and he is going to destruction. The ten horns you saw are ten kings who have not yet begun to reign, but who for a brief hour will share royal authority with the beast. They have a single purpose and will confer their power and authority on the beast. They will wage war on the Lamb, but the Lamb will conquer them, for he Lord of lords and King of kings, and those who are with him are called and chosen and faithful.'

He continued: 'The waters you saw, where the great whore sat enthroned, represent nations, populations, races, and languages. As for the ten horns you saw, and the beast, they will come to hate the whore. They will

strip her naked and leave her destitute; they will devour her flesh and
burn her up. For God has put it into
their minds to carry out his purpose,
by making common cause and confer-
ring their sovereignty on the beast
until God's words are fulfilled. The
woman you saw is the great city that
holds sway over the kings of the
earth.'

## Comments on the Story

Starkness of imagery is at times the only thing that can confront the human community, which so readily settles into the numbness created by everyday-ness, to face the enormousness of what is not only life-enhancing but also death-dealing in its midst. By the end of the first century, early Christianity had become more at home in the Empire, taking on its household imagery and praxis, accommodating to its administrative structures and yet, at the same time, experiencing the lash of its oppressive powers. The danger of compromise or acquiescence in such a situation was overwhelming.

In Revelation 17:1-18, the apocalyptic seer, in the tradition of the earlier prophets of Israel, castigates those forces that work against the establishment, maintenance, or development of the Christian tradition within the Roman Empire, in vivid, sexual, and highly genderized imagery. It is that of the great whore who is clothed in purple and scarlet (Rev. 17:1, 4). She is parodied as enthroned on what is described as a scarlet beast, her clothing is imperial scarlet and purple and she is adorned as a queen in gold, jewels, and pearls with a golden cup in her hand. Like the woman of Hosea, however, she is to be stripped naked and rendered destitute (Rev. 17:16; cf. Hos. 2:10-13), her flesh will be devoured and she will be burned with fire.

The rhetorical effect of such imagery in the lives of women and men of Asia Minor at the end of the first century must have been profoundly different. For the male reader, the image of the highly seductive female figure who rides the scarlet beast is intended to be erotic and compelling. Female sexual imagery draws such a reader into the realm of desire; but with incredible irony the journey of desire is rapidly parodied as a journey of death when the woman is identified with a city, Babylon, "drunk with the blood of God's people, and with the blood of those who had borne their testimony to Jesus" (Rev. 17:6). Most interpreters understand this imagery to be representative of Rome and hence the Empire. The reader is, therefore, tossed between highly charged sexual imagery and sociopolitical memories and experiences. The strong emotions evoked by the memories and the realities of imperial oppression stimulated in this text are intimately linked with female imagery. The rhetorical tool employed to bring about a catharsis of such memories in order to stimulate hope for the future is the imagery of violence and destruction directed against the woman. It is difficult to know whether or not such imagery arose in a misogynistic imagination desirous of curtailing women's power as well as the power of the Empire that were seen as destructive of male Christian leaders' symbolic, religious, and political power. Its powerful effect in creating and sustaining such a violently misogynist worldview is readily demonstrated in the history of Christianity in which women have been burned as witches, stripped naked for interrogation, or stripped of their powers of participation in the churches. Women's flesh has been devoured by laws of sexual morality written on their bodies by men who have sought to control what they most feared, the power of women's sexuality imaged as the devouring whore.

But what of the effect of such imagery on the lives of women like Chloe, Phoebe, Lydia, Nympha, and their sisters of Asia Minor and Greece? They would not have been drawn into the dynamic of desire and its cathartic destruction as were their brothers. Rather, one might imagine that the experience for some of these women included seeing the images that they associated with female aspects of divinity, which they sought to incorporate into their Christian theologizing, being violently parodied and destroyed. Female power, whether divine or human, was demonized, in contrast to its idealization in the women clothed with the sun as well as the bride of Revelation 21. The effect of establishing such polarities around female gender in the symbolic universe of Christian theology was to polarize the symbolic universe of women with profoundly detrimental effects. Unless women identified with the virgin/mother or the whore, there was no symbolic space for them in the constructed universe. When such polarization was combined with a curtailing of women's actual power, authority, and leadership in the functioning of the Christian community—as it was toward the end of the first century—then it had the effect of pitting women against one another as demonstrated in the story of Martha and Mary. It thus proved to be a weapon that could be used by male leaders to control women. Women could be threatened either with the ideal of the woman clothed with the sun whose power is ambiguous and ambivalent and not necessarily to be desired by actual women or with the demon of the whore of Babylon who is to be stripped naked, have flesh devoured, and be burned in the myriad of ways authorized by ecclesiastical powers.

History would indicate that the female imagery of Revelation has had its gendered effect within subsequent centuries. Today, however, women have been made aware of the power of such images. No longer will the idealized or demonized images of Revelation have the last word in the Christian Testament. Rather, women are reading the entire Testament with new eyes, retelling the stories of their foresisters from the many social locations in which they stand today. They are also drawing into their female genealogies the women who carried out priestly and diaconal ministry in the churches over the centuries, the women who preached and prophesied in those churches who would be named heretical as well as orthodox, the women whose lives are storied not only in canonical texts but in a wide variety of literature, in stone and in the memories inscribed in a sacred thread of tradition.

This is the continuous tradition of those women of Christianity who have preserved the stories of their foresisters as constitutive of the telling of the gospel. Their stories have been told and will be told in memory of her and in memory of them.

## Retelling the Story

> The woman was clothed in purple and scarlet, and decked out with gold and precious stones and pearls. In her hand she held a gold cup full of obscenities and the foulness of her fornication. (Rev. 17:4)

There was one thing everybody knew for sure about Ruby. She took her love to town. She also took her love to the woods, to the county fair, to the lake, and to the drive-in movie. When folks were being polite, they'd call Ruby "a young woman of ill repute." Some of the pious churchgoers called her a hussy. Grandma declared, "That gal's got more'n one dasher for her churn." The superintendent of schools came right out and called her a whore. There was no denying it. Nothing good would ever come of Ruby May Winesapp. She was a BAD GIRL.

Maybe it wasn't her fault. She was just born with P.P.P.—pitiful poor protoplasm. When a woman's got that stuff, she can just forget any hopes she might have of being a decent upright citizen. There's not a chance in the world she'll end up as somebody's idea of the perfect wife—a cross between Marilyn Monroe, Betty Crocker, and Mother Teresa.

Whoredom was a widely used metaphor in biblical literature for idolatry. The book of Hosea tells of the prophet Hosea acting out this metaphor by actually marrying a whore, thus illustrating to Israel how they had left the true God to take up with a foreign deity.

Now having P.P.P. doesn't mean a person is physically underenhanced. On the contrary, Ruby May Winesapp, for example, was one of the most perfectly constructed human beings ever born. She made the lovliest Dallas Cowboys cheerleader look like a bowling shoe. Ruby had more blond hair than Trigger. She had a perfect face, long legs, and a flat belly. She could stop the Indianapolis 500, a stampede of wild horses, or the U.S. mail. To say that her clothes were seductive is an understatement. Her favorite outfit was a tight-fitting red satin halter top, a purple leather micro-skirt, gold earrings the size of dinner plates, and a pair of boots. The boys at the high school could be heard moaning in the hallways, "She can walk all over me any day she wants to."

Ruby could sit down at a table in the truck stop and before she finished her Cherry Coke, she would have offers for a starring role in a soap opera, a condo on Galveston Island, a weekend in Kansas City, and several opportunities to go riding in an eighteen-wheeler.

Ruby's parents were a couple of hippies who met at Woodstock in August 1969. They parted company the same day they met, and Ruby May was born nine months later. Her mama later married an ex-marine, and he moved Ruby and her mother to his hometown in Texas. Ruby's stepdaddy worked at the tire factory on the midnight shift. Her mama had the 3:00 to 11:00 shift at the all-night doughnut shop. Ruby could come and go as she pleased. She was, as the song says, a hard dog to keep under the porch.

They lived in the Happy Hollow trailer park on the edge of town, the third double-wide on the right. By the time Ruby was fourteen, the front of her trailer resembled a taxi stand on most nights. Young callers queued up for a chance to take her on a long drive around the lake, or on a short ride over behind the Dairy Queen. Ruby May Winesapp spent her junior high school years teaching acne-faced boys about the "feminine mystery." But Ruby was a faceless figure in the dark of the backseat. She was an oft-sliced loaf, and the hometown boys eagerly partook.

When Ruby May was seventeen, her stepdaddy came home drunk one night and beat her up pretty badly. She went down to the truck stop and got a ride in the frontseat of a rig hauling longhorns. She ended up in Dallas, working as a dancer in a joint on Greenville Avenue called "The Babylon." Nobody had to explain to us what kind of a dancer she was. We knew. She danced without her clothes.

She'd start out with scarves—you guessed it, red and purple. Gradually she'd remove them. Her dancing music was always Simon and Garfunkel's "Bridge Over Troubled Water." She said it was a dance of metaphors, but nobody understood what she meant. Her boss suggested she get a tattoo across her flat belly. She did. It was a tongue of fire, dripping into her navel. Anyway, that's what we heard.

In between her dance numbers, she waited tables—topless. She was very popular and made good money. Told her customers she was working her way through seminary. They laughed. She didn't.

One hot summer night she took a guy

The image of the woman sitting enthroned on seven hills was an easy image for the first hearers of this story to interpret. It was widely known that Rome was built on seven hills. Furthermore, it was customary to have a goddess represent a city. For Rome, that goddess was Roma. Worship of Roma was most often combined with emperor worship, and temples in her honor were found throughout the Roman Empire.

home with her after work. Everybody told her he was crazy, but she didn't seem to care. That's how she got killed. Her landlady found her body. Her throat was cut. She was a headline in *The Dallas Morning News* on August 15, 1989—twenty years to the day after Woodstock—"Stripper Slain in Her Own Apartment."

All of us back in her hometown were shocked, but we weren't surprised. We had always said that nothing good would ever come of Ruby May Winesapp. We were right.

To this day, I think about her and wonder if things could have been different. Our treatment of her was shameful. What if just one of us had treated her like a human being instead of a self-fulfilling prophecy? *(Barbara McBride-Smith)*

# Selected Bibliography

References in the text are cited by author.

Anderson, Janice Capel, and Stephen D. Moore. *Mark and Method: New Approaches in Biblical Studies.* Minneapolis: Fortress, 1992.

Boring, M. Eugene, Klaus Berger, and Carsten Colpe, eds. *Hellenistic Commentary to the New Testament.* Nashville: Abingdon, 1995.

Brooten, Bernadette J. *Women Leaders in the Ancient Synagogue.* Brown Judaic Studies 36. Chico, Calif.: Scholars Press, 1982.

Brown, Raymond E. *The Birth of the Messiah.* New York: Doubleday, 1993.

———. *The Death of the Messiah.* 2 vols. New York: Doubleday, 1994.

———. *The Gospel According to John.* 2 vols. Anchor Bible 29 and 29A. Garden City, N.Y.: Doubleday, 1966–1970.

Corley, Kathleen E. *Private Women, Public Meals: Social Conflict in the Synoptic Tradition.* Peabody, Mass.: Hendrickson, 1993.

Davies, W. W. and Dale C. Allison. *The Gospel According to Saint Matthew.* The International Critical Commentary. 3 vols. Edinburgh: T. & T. Clark, 1988–1997.

Duckworth, George E. *The Nature of Roman Comedy: A Study in Popular Entertainment.* Princeton: Princeton University Press, 1952.

Fantham, Elaine, Helene Peet Foley, Natalie Boymel Kampen, Sarah B. Pomeroy, and H. Alan Shapiro. *Women in the Classical World.* New York: Oxford University Press, 1994.

Gillman, Florence M. *Women Who Knew Paul.* Zacchaeus Studies: New Testament. Collegeville, Minn.: Liturgical Press, 1992.

Haskins, Susan. *Mary Magdalene: Myth and Metaphor.* New York: Harcourt Brace, 1993.

Hendrix, Holland. "Philippi," Anchor Bible Dictionary. 6 vols. Garden City, N.Y.: Doubleday, 1992.

Hock, Ronald F. *The Social Context of Paul's Ministry: Tentmaking and Apostleship.* Philadelphia: Fortress, 1980.

Kinukawa, Hisako. *Women and Jesus in Mark: A Japanese Feminist Perspective.* The Bible and Liberation Series. Maryknoll, N.Y.: Orbis, 1994.

Kraemer, Ross Shepard. *Her Share of the Blessings: Women's Religions Among Pagans, Jews, and Christians in the Greco-Roman World.* New York: Oxford University Press, 1992.

———, ed. *Maenads, Martyrs, Matrons, Monastics: A Sourcebook on Women's Religions in the Greco-Roman World.* Philadelphia: Fortress, 1988.

Miller, Robert J., ed. *The Complete Gospels.* Sonoma, Calif.: Polebridge Press, 1992.

Newsom, Carol A., and Sharon H. Ringe, eds. *The Women's Bible Commentary.* Louisville: Westminster/John Knox, 1992.

Niditch, Susan. *Underdogs and Tricksters: A Prelude to Biblical Folklore.* San Francisco: Harper, 1987.

Pervo, Richard I. *Profit with Delight: The Literary Genre of the Acts of the Apostles.* Philadelphia: Fortress, 1987.

Pomeroy, Sarah B. *Goddesses, Whores, Wives, and Slaves: Women in Classical Antiquity.* New York: Schocken, 1975.

Reid, Barbara. *Choosing the Better Part? Women in the Gospel of Luke.* Collegeville, Minn.: Liturgical Press, 1996.

Reynolds, Joyce, and Robert Tannenbaum. *Jews and Godfearers at Aphrodisias.* Cambridge: Cambridge Philological Society, 1987.

Richter Reimer, Ivoni. *Women in the Acts of the Apostles: A Feminist Liberation Perspective.* Minneapolis: Fortress, 1995.

Schüssler Fiorenza, Elisabeth. *In Memory of Her: A Feminist Reconstruction of Christian Origins.* New York: Crossroad, 1983.

———, ed. *Searching the Scriptures-Volume 2: A Feminist Commentary.* New York: Crossroad, 1994.

Seim, Turid Karlsen. *The Double Message: Patterns of Gender in Luke and Acts.* Nashville: Abingdon, 1995.

Stählin, Gustav. "Chera," in *Theological Dictionary of the New Testament,* ed. Gerhard Friedrich, 9:440-65. Grand Rapids, Mich.: Eerdmans, 1974.

Theissen, Gerd. *The Miracle Stories of the Early Christian Tradition.* Philadelphia: Fortress, 1983.

Torjesen, Karen Jo. *When Women Were Priests: Women's Leadership in the Early Church and the Scandal of Their Subordination in the Rise of Christianity.* San Francisco: HarperSanFrancisco, 1993.

White, L. Michael. *The Social Origins of Christian Architecture.* 2 vols. Harvard Theological Studies 42. Valley Forge, Pa.: Trinity Press International, 1997.

# Index of Readings from
## *The Revised Common Lectionary*

# Index of Parallel Stories

## INSCRIPTIONS